"If you've never read Mark Spitzer's work, you're missing the most electric and original voice of the twenty-first century. *Monster Fishing* is his masterpiece, crackling with audacious life as it invites us on a dazzling adventure with the bravest, funniest, and most knowledgeable guy ever to cast a rod. If you love words, if you love fish, if you love the world—you'll want to read this addictive and ingenious book."

—NINA DE GRAMONT, *New York Times* bestselling author of *The Christie Affair*

"*Monster Fishing* is a culmination of Mark Spitzer's full-bodied and brilliant career. Always wild, and wildly prolific, he writes sentences that are alive, spilling over with energy, electricity, occasional ecstasy, and always, raw fun. You can read this book for the fishing alone and be inspired, as well as impressed by the description of the internal ethical wrestling match that is the work of a true essayist. But the art of *Monster Fishing* is also a metaphor for a certain kind of life, a vital and elemental life close to the currents of nature, a life beyond the merely human, a life that is no mere trudge from birth to death but an embrace of this joyous and wild world and all it offers."

—DAVID GESSNER, *Quiet Desperation, Savage Delight* and *All the Wild that Remains*

"Spitzer is a unique voice in angling literature."

—MATTHEW MILLER, author of *Fishing Through the Apocalypse*

"Spitzer is a walking encyclopedia on all things gar as well as a tireless champion of this 'very despised, hated fish'…a unique zoological relic that is worthy of our protection."

—JEREMY WADE, host of *River Monsters*

"I deeply respect where Spitzer is coming from about catching, harassing, and killing fish. He is one of the few enlightened anglers (former anglers?) who has the courage, decency, mind, and soul to take on this issue."

# MONSTER FISHING

# MONSTER FISHING

## CAUGHT IN THE ETHICS OF ANGLING

MARK SPITZER

TORREY HOUSE PRESS

Salt Lake City • Torrey

First Torrey House Press Edition, July 2023
Copyright © 2023 by Mark Spitzer

Published by Torrey House Press
Salt Lake City, Utah
www.torreyhouse.org

International Standard Book Number: 978-1-948814-77-5
E-book ISBN: 978-1-948814-78-2
Library of Congress Control Number: 2022939752

Cover design by Kathleen Metcalf
Interior design by Rachel Buck-Cockayne
Distributed to the trade by Consortium Book Sales and Distribution

Torrey House Press offices in Salt Lake City sit on the homelands of Ute, Goshute, Shoshone, and Paiute nations. Offices in Torrey are on the homelands of Southern Paiute, Ute, and Navajo nations.

# Table of Contents

# Preface

E VER SINCE I was a kid, I've been crazy for creatures. Whether they be toads or snakes or mutant locusts or squawking baby birds, I brought them home, put them in tanks, cages, boxes, jars, and I observed them for as long as I could. When it came to fish, I had aquariums filled with the wiggiest, wiggliest, most unusual species I could capture. We had a primordial, boneheaded bowfin with a rippling, eely fin; that fish treaded in place for years staring at its bored reflection. And there were always stripy pike and beat-up bullheads coming and going, spreading fungal diseases and occasionally eating each other, all for my wide-eyed amusement.

My parents saw that I was obsessed, and they encouraged this interest. They watched me make nets and bring home buckets filled with amphibious larvae and unidentified bottom feeders. When I caught a fish big enough to eat, my mother cooked it.

It was the seventies in South Minneapolis, a mile from where George Floyd would later be murdered by police. We were a white, middle-class family, and my younger sister and I went to the public schools, which had just begun to desegregate. My father was a sociologist who preferred to play the blues, and my mother was an art teacher involved with the community. In the summers, we'd make the cross-country drive to Washington State, and at rest stops along the way, I'd pluck whatever exoskeletons happened to be plastered to the grille of the '69 Chevelle station wagon and go running for the nearest body of water with my Zebco rod and reel.

Later, when I was a teenager, these trips became more just my father and me getting away on the weekends. He'd smoke his corncob pipe and drive the El Camino, and we'd get to a lake and launch the canoe. It was usually quiet, neither of us speaking much, with me watching the water, intent on hauling some monstrosity up, and him staring into the trees, playing the harmonica.

I was out there to catch something; examine it; ogle it; and record as many details as possible about its scales, slime, barbels, eyes. I was always amazed by how our waters contained living, breathing, reproducing mysteries we couldn't see beneath the surface that were amplified every time a gnashing, thrashing grotesque reared its bulging, bastardly head.

But for my father—with his dark, curly hair and pensive squint that lent a youthful expression that other mothers in the neighborhood found forbiddingly attractive—it was more about getting away from the circumstances he'd created for himself in his marriage, or job, or expectations as a father. But whenever a fish hit, everything changed. Suddenly, there'd be splashing, shouting, then something slapping around in the hull with flashing fangs and razor-tipped fins. At that point, we'd both be kids, wrestling something into submission.

That awe never went away. In college, I'd take friends fishing under the I-35 bridge that later collapsed into the Mississippi. I'd catch scores of murk-lurkers with great gashes across their noggins, deformed tails, and parasitic worms squiggling in their skin. And when I went away to graduate school, first in Colorado and later in Louisiana, the compulsion to meet the freakiest species I could catch didn't lessen one bit. If anything, it manifested into hard-core quests for carp, gar, catfish, whatever, and the butt-uglier, the better.

The older I got, the hotter the fever grew. I went through four programs in creative writing, and I always focused on fish: fish poems, fish fiction, fish nonfiction, even fish in translation.

It got to the point that I wasn't just "the fish guy" to family and friends (meaning fish socks for Christmas), but I also became "the fishing professor" (meaning fish ties instead).

My first two fish books were first-person narratives about gar, and especially alligator gar: all tubular with coats of armor, sometimes growing eight feet long. These supersized throwbacks to the Jurassic had survived ice ages and dinosaurs, and their ferocious reptilian heads always blew my mind to think that after one hundred million years, they were still swimming around in the South where I had transplanted myself.

Then my fixation became "monster fish," meaning any denizen that had scary, gross, dangerous, or weird aspects that caused people to turn away. But I ran straight toward those features as I always had, with my net and camera and continuous impulse to document the experience as a form of bearing witness to squillions of real-world, living nightmares right here, right now trying to survive along with us.

That research resulted in two more fish books founded on the concept of "the grotesque." In pursuit of getting to the core of what "fugly fish" and humans have in common, I traveled the world interviewing experts, hiring guides, and studying ecology, biology, and fishery science while employing the details of the hunt. For me, such phantasmagoric phenomena illustrated the sacred complexities we'd be fools to flush away.

In other words, those quests had been environmental, a perspective which is critical because you can't have problems without a planet to have problems on. I was also beginning to realize that after a half century of capturing, killing, cooking, and sometimes releasing what I was studying, I couldn't continue this modus operandi. Having quoted the hell out of Bill McKibben and Elizabeth Kolbert, the whole pantheon of eco-authorities, I was having trouble focusing on global warming, mass extinctions, habitat loss, sea level rise, invasive species, toxic pollution, and fishery problems, which I'd been doing half my life. Through my studies and publications of practical solutions for long-term sustainability and my emphasis on the urgency of taking responsibility, I might've influenced students and readers here and there; but, for the most part, writing in a vacuum that would soon allow for even less human interaction, it felt like no one was listening.

Hence, my primary quest became to reflect my adventures in "monster fishing" without any agenda for spreading awareness—something I had never done before. It was a vision that I wanted to approach like the Western writer Zane Grey did with his fish books. In his later years, he fished every day and wrote about catching slashing swordfish and back-breaking sharks. He might've moralized a bit about the ethics of using light tackle and the ecological toll of overfishing, but not in a didactic way. Grey told fish tales for the sake of telling fish tales, and everything else was secondary. That's what I wanted to do: tell fish stories for the love of fish and storytelling.

But that's not what happened in this collection of interlinking narratives, which started off with magazine pieces centered in Arkansas, then waxed ecological as I ventured further out into the world. Like all books and all humans, the chapters struggled to find their identity, becoming more and more existential as they evolved. After COVID reset the terms for travel and research in the new pandemic reality, I was essentially forced to fish in isolation while considering my role as a stressor to fish. The narrative then found its course and took me on a path I never expected, chronicling the trials of a time filled with uncertainty about how an unfamiliar, terrifying virus was spreading. This uncertainty created an era of extreme edginess, packed with mis- and disinformation skewed by partisan politics, and that's the way it still is.

I'll let what follows speak for itself; however, one thing I'd like to address is the lack of pictures in this book. Sure, I could've provided photographs, but this time I wanted the words to carry the work. I felt that if I had to rely on JPEGs to show the nature of the creatures I caught, then I wasn't describing the subject matter as vividly as possible.

Meanwhile, I'm glad for the discoveries which happened along the way, and I count myself lucky for the epic gar and explosive carp I was privileged to meet, and for the game-changing sharks and buffalofish which amazed me to the point that I changed my ways.

Still, there's a lot of hesitation to embrace such hideous, outlandish, mystifying fish and to understand their needs. This indifference exists mainly because such anomalies scare the hell out of us. And even if a fish's physical form doesn't curdle our collective plasma, there's the flawed thinking that, in focusing on something considered "abnormal," we're looking at something lacking value. As if lampreys and stingrays weren't created by the same chains of events that over the course of eons begat us and all we consider beautiful. As if the slimiest, slipperiest, most primeval fish rejected by the mainstream aren't legitimate enough for serious attention. As if the most maligned, misunderstood aquatic pariahs we can think of don't ignite the imagination.

In my book, these are all reasons enough to celebrate all the leper-fish we've historically stigmatized. Because, ultimately, these creatures are not so much different from us as they are gateways into our past, our future, and what we need to do to protect what we've got left.

Maybe I'm naïve for believing this, but that's fine with me. I've always been fascinated by how we create out-of-grace icons of wildness as scapegoats for our sins. Monsters have always been our response to what we can't directly address in our own natures, and in Nature as well. Just ask Freud, Jung, Stephen King, and the oldest texts we have on record, all of which have spelled out exactly what we're afraid of. From the Menominee myth of Mashenomak the man-eating sturgeon, to all the bibles, songs, stories, artwork, and architecture humankind has ever created to reflect our relationship with water, there's frequently an antagonistic underworld element bent on devouring us. And of all the animals on this planet that we have trouble connecting with, bizarro behemoths have always been the strangest familiar aliens we have ever known. From Jonah, to *Jaws*, to all the tales we've ever told of bloodthirsty, underwater demons, humans have a history of creating fantasy fusions of what we like to think we know. Thus, these Others have become part of us, yet a part we do not know.

But I say we can know them and that knowing them makes us stronger, smarter, better humans. That's what this book is about: preserving and propagating in the most humane way possible what popular culture has come to term "monster fish," which make this planet a wilder, more colorful, more action-packed place.

—Mark Spitzer,
    Mayflower, Arkansas,
    2021.

## CHAPTER 1

# THE GAR THAT WOULDN'T DIE

'VE CAUGHT FISH all over the world, and I always release them when I can. I've killed them for food as well as in the name of science, usually for data-gathering purposes with state and federal agencies. But the time I killed a gar for art...well, I'm still trying to make sense of that.

I'd met Bruce Koike, a professional fish-print artist, at an American Fisheries Society conference, and I was impressed by his rockfish and amberjack, which he rendered through a Japanese technique called gyotaku. I asked him if he'd ever done a gar. He said no, but that he'd always wanted to, so I told him I'd get him one.

My trotline on Lake Conway, which I live on in Arkansas, became an addiction. Sunset after sunset, I skewered live bait and checked for gar. Whatever drove me to fish as a kid was still driving me to paddle out twice a day, jonesing for a gar.

After weeks went by and two dozen sunfish had been sacrificed for bait, the float was finally bouncing. My wife Lea was in the bow with her slightly freckled complexion and winning smile that had caught wels catfish with me in Catalonia, eight-foot sturgeon in Idaho, piranha in the Amazon, and barracuda in the Caribbean. After a whirlwind romance that involved a lot of traveling and poetry, we were newlyweds living and working in separate states but enjoying what was left of the summer. This was a few years before everything would radically change in everyone's daily lives: the way we learned, the way we worked, how we gathered, how we shopped, and how we feared one another.

At that moment, though, I was in the stern, looking down, and what I saw was a spotted gar, shimmering coppery in the twilight. It had that alligator-looking head full of minnow-munching rows of teeth, and its leopard-patterned spots were mesmerizing from its gills down to its spatulated tail. It was two feet of elongated, prehistoric, living fossil fishiness treading on the surface, and it was the perfect size for a print.

"It's such a pretty fish," Lea advocated for the gar. "It wants to live…"

"Nope," I remained firm. "This is the one."

After I unhooked it, it seemed calm enough just lying there. So as the sun sank behind the cypress trees, we watched the yolky orange of the sky spread across the horizon, and we poured a couple of premixed gin and tonics. Until WHAM! The gar suddenly exploded, leaping three feet into the air and slapping all around. On its way up, it chomped me a good one on the shin, and on the way down, it whacked my drink out of my hand. It continued going berserk, knocking tackle all over the place and causing general chaos. By the time I finally pinned it down, I was bleeding from four spots on my leg, and my palms were cut up from its gill plates.

"See," Lea tried again, "it wants to live."

But since that gar was destined to be art, I did what I thought had to be done. Lea turned away, and as its eyes were pleading up at me, my gut questioned why I was violating the number one rule of fishing I'd grown up with: If you kill it, you eat it. Nevertheless, the blade found its mark, and the deed was done.

"Can you pour me another?" I asked Lea.

"Sure," she said in a voice lacking its usual luster.

Five minutes later, the same thing happened again: Eruption of gar! Tail smacking! Teeth flashing! Slime slinging! And again, my gin and tonic in the bottom of the boat.

"Awww man," I said and opened up my knife again. I repeated what I'd just done, not seeing how the second time was going to make any difference. Then we headed in.

Following the directions I'd been given, I used multiple layers of tinfoil and at least three garbage bags to wrap the gar. Bruce had told me to protect the fins, so the fish was strapped to a board with duct tape. And even though it was technically dead, the gar sometimes flexed within.

*Vestigial impulses,* I tried to convince myself. *Leftover electrical signals…*

After boxing it all inside a three-foot-long cardboard casket, I wound it like a mummy in packing tape. Then I had to fit it in the freezer, which meant taking out all the food and shelves in there. When I finally shut the door, I couldn't be sure that gar wasn't thrashing inside its Freon tomb.

In the morning, I was too busy to take it to the post office, so I asked Lea if she could ship it for me. She gave me a look like I was asking her to be a criminal accomplice, but she agreed. Turns out the postal clerk who told me they could ship it overnight was wrong, so Lea ended up driving around all afternoon trying to find a delivery service that could get it there before it thawed. No such luck. She brought it back. And though we laughed at the notion that the gar was still doing all it could to thwart my designs, this laughter wasn't genuine.

The next day was a Friday, and I got it to a shipping place and spent more money than expected. They said they'd get it to Oregon on Saturday.

But by Sunday, it hadn't been delivered yet. I called the 1-800 number and frantically explained that if they didn't get it there pronto, the Hounds of Hell would go postal. They said they tried to deliver it, but the school was closed.

"A school?" I yowled. "I sent it to a house!"

They told me it would be in the shipping warehouse for the weekend. To that I replied it would stink up the entire state if they didn't deliver it ASAP.

Ten phone calls later, they finally got the gar delivered. Bruce unwrapped it the next day, but it didn't leap up and go ballistic. Instead, it just reeked. The gills had gone putrid, but the rest of the fish was still in good shape.

The print arrived six months later, the gar's curving image perfectly preserved. So I framed it and put it on the wall, where I thought it would just hang there looking pretty. But this fish isn't through reminding me that I could've let it go. In fact, every time I walk past its half-open grin, it asks me if killing it for art was worth the price.

And I'm not talking the price of shipping; I'm talking the price it ultimately paid so that I could consider what I took from it every time I saw its imprint: a consideration which has nothing to do with guilt or karma; if anything, it's a nagging, gut-wrenching sense that I did a fellow creature wrong, and I could've kept it from suffering.

But I didn't. I chose my desire to display its image of being alive and being free on my wall over its actual freedom to be alive and be free, slinking through the lily pads. And unlike the Osage, the Caddo, and the Quapaw, who fished these waters to feed their people centuries ago, I never ate an inch of that fish.

Meanwhile, the spirit of that gar lives on, rendered on rice paper. And as ridiculous as it sounds to start second-guessing what I've been doing for fifty years, I knew in the pit of my stomach that this was something I had to account for. But at that point, harvesting a gar for art, I had to look away.

## CHAPTER 2

# SECRETS FOR RESPONSIBLE
# GATOR GAR FISHING

THANKS TO A disturbing realization I recently had regarding gar, it occurred to me that I could do more to lessen the pressures I personally create. Also, since I know a lot about angling for this species, and since I wasn't sharing this information, it hit me that I might be complicit in contributing to conditions which negatively affect fish. Therefore, I decided it was my duty to advocate for responsible gar-fishing tactics, especially when it comes to the most threatened member of the *Lepisosteidae* family, the alligator gar.

Due to the recovery efforts of the US Fish and Wildlife Service (USFWS) and other agencies, along with a few years of heavy flooding, gator gar populations are now more stable in Arkansas than they've been in the last sixty years. The big rivers are thick with three- and four-year-olds, and the fishery has improved to the point that I can now share some of our most effective angling strategies for this granddaddy of the gar family, which is definitely worthy of its new classification as a "sport fish" in Arkansas. With their heavy dentine armor, even the little ones can weigh forty pounds. There are few rushes on this planet comparable to hauling in a snapping, lashing, dragon-headed leviathan.

In Arkansas, the first thing to know is that you need a special permit, which is free on the Arkansas Game and Fish Commission (AGFC) website at agfc.com. The second thing to know is that alligator gar are off limits during their official spawning season in May and June, and there's a harvest limit of one fish per year under thirty-six inches. All gator gar over three feet must be released immediately unless you have a special trophy permit awarded through a lottery system. If you catch an alligator gar, you're obliged to report it within twenty-four hours, which helps in tracking movements and collecting data to aid in fish conservation. Most importantly, these fish are extremely vulnerable in the reproductive department, so help an ecosystem out by treating gator gar compassionately and letting them go as soon as possible so they can grow nine feet long and surpass three hundred pounds. The more top predators we have in our system, the stronger our fisheries will be.

The best times to fish for gar are around dawn and dusk. My buddies and I, who've caught more three-to-four-footers on rod and reel than anyone from Texas to Tennessee, prefer the latter, which is conducive to drinking beers at night. We find a sandy beach with no obstructions where gar can be seen rolling, and we've had a lot of luck with shad for bait, which you can catch in cast nets or buy frozen at bait stores. When the sun goes down, the four main species of gar (alligator, longnose, shortnose, spotted) will follow smaller fish into the shallows. It also helps to check your bait frequently, and if you're using cut bait, change it every twenty minutes.

Baitrunner reels (also called baitfeeders) work best because they allow you to cast a long ways, and they don't get fouled like baitcasting reels. We prop the poles in spiral holders, flip the big switches so the fish can run, and use Carolina rigs which allow gar to take out line without feeling any resistance. Just put an egg weight on your line and tie on a swivel or a steel leader beneath that. If you use a swivel, attach two to three feet of fifty-to-eighty-pound braided line for a leader, and make sure that whatever line your reel is spooled with is strong enough to horse in a hundred-pounder.

The thing to remember about hooks is, the more metal there is, the greater the odds that a gar will get a taste of it and drop the bait. Also, you don't need huge shark hooks like old-timers used to use, which can rip a fish's stomach lining. Despite what gar guides commonly say about the metal eventually corroding away, if a hook gets lodged in a gar's stomach, it can tear through tissue or cause infection, which can sometimes kill a fish. Smaller hooks do less damage and take less time to disintegrate. So if you gut-hook a gar and manage to land it, snip the line or leader as close to the mouth as possible, and watch out for your fingers.

We've had our best luck with circle hooks the size of a nickel to a quarter in circumference. The logic is to let the gar run, and after they stop to swallow the bait, you set the hook when they run again (which, on average, only works 10 percent of the time). All you need is a big minnow or a hunk of cut shad, and when the gar takes off that second time, lock the bail and reel in fast. If the hook doesn't pop out of its mouth (which happens half the time), it's likely to lodge itself in the crux of the jaws, which is preferable to swallowing it.

And don't ever try to pry a gar's mouth open, because that can break its teeth. Tapping on a gill plate can sometimes encourage a gar to open wide, and then you can stick a piece of wood in there to assist in holding its mouth open if that helps in removing a hook. Otherwise, leave it be, and it will corrode away.

When you land an alligator gar, you'll need to take some measurements. Game and Fish will want to know its length, and you'll want to know its weight. Rather than stressing a gator gar out or injuring it with stringers and scales, there's a simple formula for figuring out how much it weighs. Take the length in inches, multiply that by its widest girth, multiply that by girth again, then divide by 800 and add 15. This equation works best for full-grown adults, but it's pretty accurate for juveniles in terms of estimating general weight.

Also, though gar are equipped with lunglike organs that can breathe air, if they start getting red in the fins, this means they're weakening and need to be set free. So take your pictures, count yourself lucky, and take solace in the fact that when you release and report an Arkansas alligator gar, you're helping to rebuild a decimated fishery.

That's what happened at the end of the fifties, when shooting rod-and-reel-caught gator gar led to a statewide extirpation and became the unsustainable norm in the state. This practice ended up making our riparian systems anemic. And now, with the recent proliferation of silver and bighead carp in our rivers, we need our apex predators to get as huge as they can as soon as they can, to help control destructive invasives that eat into game fish populations.

And here's the final secret: tell the AGFC exactly where you caught your alligator gar, but don't tell anyone else. Because if irresponsible gar hunters get wind of where to shoot 'em willy-nilly, we just might find their decomposing carcasses littering our shores again. And that would be a shame again. And we can do better than that.

## CHAPTER 3

# When the Blood-Gar-Moon Aligns with Earth and Mars

THE SUN HAD gone down, and a super-bright blood moon had just come up. It was a luminous orange orb with a black-cherry glow, passing through our planet's shadow in a total eclipse. Mars was shining redly beside it and was visible because the moon and Earth and Mars were in line. A family of foxes was yipping in the distance, and there was something eerily vibrant in the air.

Once again, Fishing Support Group was out on the sand. Goggle Eye, all skinny and sinewy and chemically composed of nicotine and beef jerky, was decked out in his pink sequined cowboy hat. A weathered navy vet who'd once been my grad student, he now taught college writing at our university. Turkey Buzzard, on the other hand, was a chemistry professor, all long and lanky and boldly bald, grilling and chilling in his lawn chair. Then there was Minnow Bucket with his sadistic glint. He was an English major turned payroll accountant for the City of Little Rock who could expound on how to skin a bear or belay into an Ozark cavern.

We were gar fishing once again on our secret stretch of the Arkansas River. It was the end of July, and we'd caught several gator gar in this spot and some big longnose as well.

Turkey Buzzard and Goggle Eye were using mono lines

because they cast farther than woven line. They had been doing well with shad and were using two-ounce sinkers on the bottom, some heavy-duty woven line above that for a leader, and two #4 or #6 circle hooks tied one and two feet above the weight. They kept the line tight, waiting for their bait to take off.

Minnow Bucket and I preferred braided line for its flexible durability. We also liked live bait on our Carolina rigs, so gar could take line out and not feel a thing. I had two stout poles set up in front of me. Up the beach, Minnow Bucket had two rods hooked up to alarms, one of which began blinking.

"You got a runner," I told Minnow Bucket right as his alarm went off, sending a squeal into the ever-reddening sky. That spooky blood moon was still rising higher, like a ghostly, gleaming, ocher eye.

If it were my rod, I would've lit off like a shoplifter, but Minnow Bucket was too cool for that. He ambulated up the beach, mumbled something sarcastic, popped the bail on his baitrunner reel, and let the fish run free. He was using a sunfish as bait, and we knew he had a gar on the line because it was heading downriver, straight and fast.

But three minutes into its run, it stopped, which was weird. We figured the fish dropped the bait, so we waited a bit longer, and then Minnow Bucket jerked his pole into the sky, setting the hook. The gar was on, and it was bearing down on the bottom. But as my eyes followed his line downstream, I saw that the fish was three feet from shore in a foot of water, which was also strange.

Minnow Bucket horsed it in, and then it was on the river's edge: a spastically splashing alligator gar, nearly four feet long. As usual, I got out in the water, blocking its escape. A sheepdog mentality always comes over me when one of my buddies is bringing in a gar. When I'm in that primal state, I've been known to lunge for gar, scoop them up, and carry them up the beach. My theory is, it's always good to get a fish away from the water before you start dealing with hooks and photos and high fives because then there's less of a chance of it getting away. So I grabbed that gar, hugged it to my chest, and carried it to higher ground, feeling that rush I always feel when battling a beast hauled up from the underworld.

Which, of course, is totally juvenile, but that's the goal: to return to that youthful perspective which adults feel less and less the more deadened they get by the tribulations of their times.

As Hemingway would've said, it was a good fish. But as I would say, it was a beautifully grotesque monster fish, all healthy and fangy and fattened up for the winter. It was steel gray with a checkered scale pattern from head to tail.

Minnow Bucket extracted the hook, which had penetrated the side of a jaw. I was glad it hadn't swallowed it, because whenever a gar swallows a hook, I always feel a pinching in my own intestines. Normally, this feeling lasts a few seconds, and then I focus on something else. In the meantime, that gar feels the sting of steel for days; for weeks; and sometimes until it goes belly-up.

But back to this particular gar, which I cinched beneath its pectoral fins with a stringer in order to weigh it with my semi-accurate fish gripper. If a gar is small enough, suspending it by its armpits (that's what it looks like) works pretty well. With the moon continuing to light the night, no headlamps were needed to read the numbers: it weighed twenty-seven pounds. Then we took some measurements, applied the magic formula, and it weighed ten pounds more, which meant it was somewhere in between.

When letting a gar go, it often takes a few minutes for the fish to get its bearings back. Sometimes you have to hold it upright because it's still spinning from the fight. This often allows you time to clean off clumps of sand mixed with mucous; but this time, the gar shot off like a lightning flash.

Ten minutes later, Goggle Eye got a runner, and Turkey Buzzard did as well. Both fish took out a hundred yards, then suddenly got off. And still there was something peculiar in the air, a kind of misty luminescence driving the foxes to yowl a bit more frantically.

Twenty minutes after that, Minnow Bucket's alarm went off again. It was the same pole, the same bait. He shuffled over there like an old man, grumbled something meant to undo his opponent's confidence, set the hook, and it was on.

This time it was a longnose, about three feet long, thick, and feisty. Its silvery, spear-shaped length was flashing back and forth as Minnow Bucket pulled it up onto the sand. Before I even knew it, I had a solid grip on the fish with both hands right in the middle.

So I'm walking up the beach, and the gar is thrashing like an exorcism demon-child. My hold, however, is totally viselike. I ain't gonna let this gar get away, so it can snap and lash all it wants.

Now imagine this scene in slow motion: The gar's snout was slicing the air from left to right, but on one of the returns it spit out the hook. A tooth then snagged the line, which wound around the tip of its upper jaw a foot above the super-sharp circle hook, the diameter of a half-dollar. Then that gar slashed again, whipping the hook through the air, and that hook went right into the palm of my hand and came out the other side like a scalpel through a chunk of cheese.

I dropped the gar, and it kept flipping and flopping furiously, yank-yank-yanking my hand around. Its gnashing jaws were chomping at the air, and that big old moon, now fully formed, was illuming Turkey Buzzard's gawking maw.

The fishing trip was suddenly over. The foxes shut up, the gar was released, no pictures were taken, and, as usual, the barb was just under the skin so couldn't be reversed or forced through because it was lodged in all that gristle and muscle and stuff. It was stuck stuck stuck like a stuck pig. Thus, I ended up in the emergency room.

Other anglers will confirm that the nightshift workers at hospitals love it when anglers hook themselves. They get a kind of giddy glee out of making jokes about whether or not the fish got away, and "who set the hook on who." That's what I had to deal with again, along with a new round of tetanus shots. The doctor numbed me up with Novocain, cut my flesh open to pop the barb through, clipped the hook right beneath the barb, and pulled it out the way it went in. Like usual, since I tend to get hooked every ten years, I was there until four a.m.

But here's the thing: I keep wondering how I could've protected myself better, and I keep coming up blank. Had I held it down on the edge of the water during its initial rush, that gar would've slapped around way more, and that would've been more dangerous. Therefore, I stand by my conviction that carrying a fish away from the water is always advisable. Plus, it's generally good to leave a hook in a fish while working on it in order to keep a line on it in case it breaks free.

Anyway, I finally decided it had been a freak accident and that sometimes there is no better way. Because that's the world I live in: a world of forged-steel monster hooks where you take your chances for what you love, and every once in a while, something goes wrong. That's the contract I made with myself, and that's the price others pay too.

So score one for the gar. And the blood-gar-moon as well.

## CHAPTER 4

# GETTING MYSELF AN ARKANSAS ALLIGATOR GAR

GOGGLE EYE WAS catching them. Turkey Buzzard was getting them. Minnow Bucket too. The whole world was catching Arkansas alligator gar, except for me: the author of two books on the species; the angler who's supposed to know them best. Sure, I'd caught them in Texas, in Thailand, and in nets, but never on rod and reel in my home state. That's why I had the fever. After a decade of constantly getting skunked, I had to get one—everything else be damned! They'd played with me, teased me, laughed at me, and I'd had enough.

It was a school night, a work night, so I couldn't expect any support from Fishing Support Group. It was the third time that week I'd been out to our spot on the Arkansas River. I found it earlier that summer, and Goggle Eye and Turkey Buzzard and Minnow Bucket had reaped the benefits: multiple juvie gator gar between three and four feet long. One night, the three of them even caught one each while I sat alone on a sandbar a few miles downstream, not catching anything, stewing in my own gar angst.

Again, the sun was going down, stars were starting to speckle the sky, and I was sitting on a camp chair trying to catch some bait. There are usually some bream (or sunfish) in this spot, but this night there were only little channel cats, which stick you with their needle-sharp fins. They were eating the crap out of my night crawlers, and I couldn't catch squat.

Luckily, I had four black salties, which are hardy, bronze, genetically engineered goldfish that are legal for bait in Arkansas. I also had frozen shad.

Then, right at dusk, my baitcasting rod ticked a few times. I sprang up and hit the button, allowing the spool to spin. But if it was a gar on the other end, it just wasn't taking out line. I fed it line, though, and it slowly took off.

After five minutes, I figured that it wasn't big enough to turn the spool, and I was wasting bait. So I decided to retrieve the circle hook, which I knew was too large for any punk just dicking around.

To my surprise, the hook took. There was sudden weight on the other end as I reeled in a cute, cream-colored shortnose with black spots on its tail, the barb right through its beak. Like all gars, it was smiling. But dammit, my bait was gone.

I unhooked the fish, threw it back, then put on a smaller, more reasonable hook and the third black salty, wincing as I punctured it right behind the dorsal fin. It's a feeling I've felt so many thousands of times that I've conditioned myself to tell myself the same thing every time: that it's only bait, that it doesn't think, that it doesn't feel, that its nervous system doesn't register pain like ours.

I had two poles out with minnows and one pole with a worm to catch live bait, the latter of which I had given up on. I'd already missed about twenty little fish that night, and all that concentrating just to catch some dinky cats I had to throw back was pissing me off.

What I really wanted was a gou, which is pronounced "goo" and comes from *gaspergou*, a Cajun word for freshwater drum. Gou ain't good for much, but when it comes to gator gar bait, they stay on the hook and don't expire like sunfish do.

ॐ ॐ ॐ

A FEW DAYS before, I'd been out here with Goggle Eye and had caught a foot-long gou that I'd chucked out with a chunk of shad because my new motto was "Add shad." The combo of a lively fish and oily excretions is always a winning combination.

In the night sky, my old friend Mars was right up there on the horizon beaming tangerinely in the same spot it'd been all summer. Over to its left, the full moon was coming up, shimmering with an amber glow. It was an hour past dusk.

Hearing a click, I released the spool lickety-split. It was a runner. Increasing in speed, then decreasing, then running hard and fast again, it took out over two hundred yards. It was a maddening run, but what a connection! It was on, and it was on good. Then it stopped.

I flopped down on the sand while Goggle Eye smoked a cig, waited about three and a half minutes, and when it ran again, I jumped up and set it. BAM! A furious fight then took place as I walked it backwards, hauling it in.

Goggle Eye said I did everything right; and I did. I got that gar up toward the beach, when something began zipping between us. It took a few seconds, but we finally identified it as my weight flashing around like a bat on my line, befuddling us.

We focused our attention on the weeds. The gar was rolling through some vegetation on the shore, and then it was right in front of us. It was five feet long and as thick around as a telephone pole, breaching a foot from the beach and crescenting like a banana. Its mongo moonlit head came up, the unmistakable head of an alligator gar, and its tail arose on the other end. What a sight! Both of us gasped as the hook popped out of its mouth.

But I wasn't shouting "NO! NO! NO!" I was shouting "YES! YES! YES!" That's the kind of connection it was, and that's the kind of sight it was: the kind that leaves an angler buzzing for days. Seriously! All those surging chemicals, they take a while to fade away.

∞ ∞ ∞

BUT LIKE I said, that was a few days ago. And out there alone on the Arkansas River, the Big Dipper above, twinkling from atmospheric pressure, I didn't have much bait in reserve.

I waited another hour, thinking about my gar out there: a hybrid alligator-longnose I had ordered on eBay and formed a bond with. After stunting his growth for ten years to keep him from outgrowing his aquarium, and having watched him go in and out of his jet-black spawning colors multiple times (which was evidence he was male), I'd brought him to this section of the river and released him. But what I didn't think about at that time was the bowhunters who typically shoot whatever they see and then leave their spoils at the launch. I'd released him a few years ago, and I was hoping he was three feet long by now.

Reeling in, I saw that my bait was gone, so I had to employ my last black salty. Avoiding its eyes, I stuck it through the base of its tail, watched it shudder, then cast it out.

Meanwhile, the worm-thieves continued nabbing my crawlers. I got down to my last one, split it in half, cast it out, and someone took it and got away. Putting on the last half-worm, I cast out again, then put that pole aside.

I wasn't catching anything, but it was nice to be sitting there getting bitten by mosquitoes as the hundred-degree day cooled down to the seventies. If I were at home, I would've been watching a fishing show, not worrying about the state of the world.

In another couple of years, I'd be driving back from Minnesota, listening to an apocalyptic novel by former President Bill Clinton written with James Patterson in which the banks are failing, the electrical grid is toast, and everything is going to hell. It would be March 2020, the month the country started sheltering in place. Folks on social media would be posting that the emerging virus was a mutant strain of the 1918 Spanish flu emerging from thawing Siberian permafrost. Such frightmare scenarios would soon start to scare the crap out of everyone, but the much more alarming details of the real situation would end up killing millions, thrust economies into tailspins, and culminate in an insurgency on American democracy.

But at that moment in summer in Arkansas, I was on a sandy beach drinking wine. I had two salties out, garnished with shad, and then I had only one.

That's when God gave me a gou. I didn't even recognize it. I thought it was a deformed catfish coming in, but it was a six-inch drum caught on my last sickly segment of worm. This meant I'd be out longer than planned. Because when you use up all your bait and you're graced with a gou, you take it.

I waited and waited, and after an hour, I reeled in. That weak-ass gou was pretty much dead. I didn't see how it could attract any self-respecting gar, but I added my last chunk of shad and heaved it out again. In ten minutes, no gar would touch it with a ten-foot pole.

Fifteen minutes went by, then twenty, while I sat there thinking nothing.

Then something clicked and I was reeling in with no resistance, which is curious because gator gar take bait out. This meant it was probably a turtle because turtles take bait toward shore. But as I reeled and reeled that slack line in, nothing took. So it must've been a catfish, but now it was gone. I reeled and reeled and still no weight.

Until a few feet from shore, right smack in front of me, something erupted, bending the rod. I could feel its weight, and I saw its shape. It was a gar alright! But I knew the odds. It was destined to escape.

Getting out in the river to block its escape, I saw a solid, juvenile alligator gar, almost four feet long and as fat around as a bowling ball. It was half in the water and half on the beach and thrashing as I circled it. Then throwing myself down on it, I covered that gar, I held that gar, and I wrassled it until it was pinned. It tried to squirm beneath my weight, but I wasn't gonna let it get away.

Sitting up, I held it tight between my knees. With one hand pressing down on its head, I used my other to unclasp my belt. I pulled it off, looped it under the front fins, and hauled the fish up the beach.

Holy hell! I finally had it. My first Arkansas alligator gar caught on rod and reel. It took a vexing decade to catch, but the ecstasy was worth the wait. It was closure. It was bliss: every atom in every cell singing, zinging to the stars!

That gar, however, had swallowed the hook, which made me groan out loud. Hopefully its stomach acids would quickly dissolve the metal away and the puncture wouldn't bother it. But you can never tell. There's no easily accessible data about how fast hooks dissolve, but there is a lot of talk based on speculation. In truth, nobody really knows how long it takes for hooks to degrade in gastric acids, so it's one of those things you have to force to the back of your mind, or thoughts of piercing steel will keep needling the hell out of you.

Shaking that thought away like I do every time, I clipped the leader, the gar grunting under me, exhaling its discontent. I then took some pictures, which are never any good when you're alone on a beach at night trying to restrain a frightened apex predator. Still, I got a few fuzzy shots and took some measurements that didn't matter. To me, it was a ten-foot fish, a thousand-pounder; a good, beautiful, wonderful fish; and a transcendental, angel-from-the-Arkansas alligator gar, which I placed in the water and released from my belt.

Then, brushing off sand as it slipped from my fingers, I watched it swish from side to side until nothing was left but a vanishing swell on the river's black skin. I didn't whoop, but this is what I said, dripping and covered with sand beneath all the stars of infinity flickering with golden light:

"Thank you, Arkansas."

And the sound of my voice, it really shocked me. It felt like I was saying "I love you," or "goodbye." It came from the gut as my heart hammered inside my chest, informing me that what happens between a person and a fish can't get more profound than this. And because there was nothing left to say, I just stood there in the moonglow, all molecules ablaze in immaculate light.

## CHAPTER 5

# Charlotte's Gar

L EA CALLED IN the morning, and the news was not good. Our ten-year-old niece, Charlotte, had been rushed to the ICU and was scheduled for emergency brain surgery. A tumor.

Lea was now back in New York State, Charlotte was in Chicago, and I was down in Arkansas, so there wasn't much I could do. I was bummed, of course, but I wasn't ready to give in to despair. The doctors were on the job, so I'd wait to see what developed.

It was a Sunday, and since Fishing Support Group was going fishing, I packed up my gear and hopped in the Jeep. Driving along, I talked with Lea via voice messaging. She was really upset—so upset that I should've been wiser.

When we got out on the river by Bigelow—Turkey Buzzard, Minnow Bucket, Goggle Eye, and me—we started casting along a jetty. The sky was bright and the bite was good. We were pulling in stripers and largemouth, which lessened the sting. We caught a bunch and moved on to a beach where we'd seen gator gar in the past.

It was a sunny October afternoon, and I wasn't fixing on telling the guys. I didn't see any reason to shift this burden to them. They didn't need that. Nobody did. This was a family matter, so I kept it to myself.

But I also figured I should be more communicative with Lea. Last weekend I'd gone fishing two days in a row and had disappeared from her radar, only to reappear when it was convenient for me. I'd gone to Lake DeGray to fish for pike and had ended up getting follows from three longnose. That last one, a four-footer, even came right up to the boat. It was hypnotized by the vibing fluorescence of my Mepps Musky Killer spinner. Swimming upside down, that longnose had rolled toward the flash, then took a snap, its eye fixed on the bright yellow tail. The snap, however, didn't connect, and in that split second, the lure came back to the rod. Reversing the direction of my pull, I snagged that longy in the mouth. It thrashed and got off, but what a blast!

It usually doesn't cause a problem when I lose myself in fishing, but when Lea is stuck grading forty papers thirteen hundred miles away, and considering what was happening in Chicago, I should've been more sensitive. But I wasn't—probably because I hadn't been fishing in weeks, except in my dreams, where I sometimes fish on a nightly basis. So, I'd been more than ready to get out there this weekend; the chance to fish for gar always exciting my inner kid.

When we got to the beach, I sent Lea a picture of me and my two largest bass to show that I hadn't gone AWOL. Big mistake. A text came back saying, "I don't mean to put a damper on yr day, but please don't send me photos of yr fun. I just can't take it."

Holy crap! For a moment, I'd totally forgotten about Charlotte. I wrote back, and Lea noted how it comes across that I don't let anything get in the way of my fishing. She was irritated, but she knew I cared, even as we volleyed texts back and forth with a lot of exclamation marks. Things eventually calmed down, but I couldn't help reflecting on what a jackass I was. Lea was right: there wasn't much that could stop my obsession.

Nevertheless, we cast out some bait, hoping for a gar or two. Like usual, I had a bunch of minnows that I'd caught in my trap, which I usually stab with a hook, then cast out and forget about.

But this time, pressing the barb in one side and out the other of a pretty green sunfish, it wasn't so easy to convince myself that subtracting one from the total population didn't matter. With its sparkly eyes and shiny sheen, that bream seemed a little more girly than usual.

In the meantime, the guys were laughing and clowning around, and I was too. But beneath my bantering veneer, I was stewing about who I really was: someone incapable of providing sincere support whenever I had a line in the water. But even worse, our super-luminescent niece was now face-to-face with brain cancer. To lose that little girl would be an unspeakable blow to the family, which now had to think about months and months of chemo, spinal taps, specialists, MRIs, loss of sleep, missing work, medical bills, insurance, etc.

But as all this was beginning, Charlotte was taking it like a trooper. She was giggling and singing and pressing on, as curious as always—like a few months before, when we lowered some chicken chunks into some crawdad castles; or the time I went pickerel fishing, and Charlotte asked Lea what kind of fish a pickerel was, so they pondered that together. They'd also discussed the word *empathy* and what that meant, and who Charlotte had empathy for, and Charlotte really got it.

And now Charlotte was showing people with years more experience how to approach one of the most terrifying situations there is with the most positive attitude possible—an attitude that most of us could never muster, especially after having seen what cancer can do.

It'd been four years since I'd seen this disease mutate my mother, twisting her body into something so contorted that I can't even try to describe it. She'd been in hospice, and my sister and I were waiting it out. My mom was gone, but her organs were there, wheezing and sputtering. It took days, and then her death rattle came gurgling up. We hugged her and cried as she faded away.

Basically, that's what was the family was facing now, and that's what I was mulling over out on that sandbar, deep in gloom. It was a shitty day.

But lo, a noodle started heading our way. It was an eighteen-inch tube of yellow foam with six feet of braided line dangling a hook baited with shad. We'd thrown out a bunch earlier, and this one was coming downstream. Goggle Eye said he saw a gator gar head come up, so we reeled in our lines and went out to get it.

It was Minnow Bucket's noodle, and Turkey Buzzard was driving the boat. Goggle Eye grabbed the noodle, and a tug of war ensued. Then suddenly there was no line attached. The gar had ripped the PVC pipe right out of the foam and was gone. This led to a huge communal swearfest because that trailing line could get tangled on something, which could drown the fish.

But after a minute of colorful cursing, Minnow Bucket said, "Hey, wait a second. That plastic insert should float because I filled it with insulating foam…"

"There it is!" Goggle Eye shouted, motioning over his shoulder.

It was thirty feet away, so Turkey Buzzard hit the gas and went tearing over there. Goggle Eye grabbed the PVC, and because the fish was too big to get in the net, we began towing it to shore.

Looking down, I saw five feet of fall-fattened alligator gar swimming along next to us. It was broad across the snout and the crosshatch pattern on its back was highly pronounced. You could totally see why those enamel-coated, diamond-shaped scales were once used as arrowheads by gone people from this region. But more to the point (no pun intended), it was a gorgeous, gorgeous, gorgeous fish! And the moment we pulled up on the beach, I was in the water grabbing it by the tail and guiding it onto the sand. All it took was one little shove, and it slid right up as if there were ball bearings under it.

Then instantly, we had it! And each of us had played a part in catching it. So after the high fives went around, we all posed while holding it.

My smile, though, was only for show. I was kneeling on the sand, holding a perfectly unblemished, fifty-pound gator gar in my arms, but just not feeling it. It was one of the greatest gar moments in Fishing Support Group history, but there I was, knowing what a jerk I was, and knowing that I would never change, and that my niece was going under the knife, and that the family was freaking out. It was a really, really strange sensation to have all that adrenaline shooting through me, but if I let myself feel what I was feeling, then I'd be a lousy human. So I couldn't allow myself to feel what Minnow Bucket and Turkey Buzzard and Goggle Eye were feeling as they hooted away and relived the details. For me, at that moment, secret self-loathing was the only emotion to entertain. And since this was something I was unfamiliar with, it was pretty damn confusing for my brain to be shutting down right as its cheering section was bursting into song.

When we let that gator gar go, it took its time swimming off. It didn't feel the need to blast away. It just sort of sashayed across the surface, telling us to feast our eyes.

We then used the unreleased alligator gar sex prediction app on my cellphone, which had come from Texas Parks and Wildlife. I entered the length from the tip of its snout to where the body met the tail fin skin (1,321 mm); then the length from the tip of the snout to the front of the eye (248 mm); then the length of the top of its anal fin (76 mm); and the app gave us the results: there was a 99.85 percent probability it was female.

A few days later, after things had settled down, I texted Lea about the gar. She was apologetic for having called me out, but having spent half my life formally studying creative writing, I was a veteran workshopper who knew how to accept feedback, and this was stuff I needed to consider in order to be less of an ass.

More importantly, the question wasn't whether Lea was ready to see a photo of the gar; the question was whether it would be appropriate to send the picture to Charlotte when she was dealing with blurred vision, missing school, hospital rooms, and all that new uncertainty. But Lea's answer was an emphatic "Yes!"

So I texted the photo of that grinning gar along with the comment that we had released it. I also added that it was a girl. And you know what that little stinker replied?

"You should've cooked that fish right up!"

Yep, that's what she said, no doubt chuckling.

And that's the moral of this story, in which a sweet, scared kid facing the most existential question there is never forgets her sense of humor and serves as a courageous example for the rest of us on how to roll with the weight of the world. Hence, I was moved to the point that I couldn't help summing things up with a simple, sentimental ending—the kind I usually try to avoid. But in this case, I listened to that voice that's often squelched by arguments we design for ourselves so we don't have to hear ourselves. And that voice, which I'd been hearing a lot more from lately, was telling me I needed to heed it, or remain stuck in my ways. It's main message being:

*You go, Charlotte, just like your happy gar, swimming around being free, full of possibilities.*

## CHAPTER 6

# CATCHING JACK IN MEXICO

WE MET CAPTAIN Salas of Juancho Fishing at six thirty in the morning on the Playa del Carmen beach. I was targeting sailfish, but the timing was not optimum because it was the end of December, when other species were more likely to be caught. As we set off on the Caribbean in a 60-horsepower fiberglass craft, the sun was rising over the blazing orange curve of the world.

Out on the ocean, tourist-hotel-condo-land now behind us, my brother-in-law and I began some of the most intensive jigging we'd ever done. Our guide was a cherubic native of the Yucatán Peninsula with a solid command of English, and he also had a first mate on board.

Using heavy-duty baitcasting reels on super short rods wound with hundred-pound braided test, the technique was to drop our foot-long lures straight down to four hundred feet. They were shaped like cigars and painted silvery white, each accompanied by a big hook which we'd reel in while raising and lowering the pole as fast as possible, smacking the water with ridiculous speed. When the multi-colored line showed red, that meant we'd come up a hundred feet, and it was time to drop again. Within fifteen minutes, we were two tuckered-out gringos wishing we were lazily fishing with live bait.

The captain and his mate, however, had decades of experience doing this, and they took over and kept up a manic pace. In less than an hour they received simultaneous strikes, setting the hooks three times each. Their arcing rods were passed to us, and we began the grueling process of hauling up and reeling in on the descent as dozens of feet of line screamed off our reels for every few feet we cranked in. We let the drags tire the fish out.

Mine came in first: an eight-pound almaco jack flashing bronzely with a shimmering olivine sheen. It was a blunt-headed, orb-eyed predator, built for speed with a spiky dorsal fin tapering down to a forked tail. Underneath, the anal fin was almost as long as its top fin, giving the fish an overall diamond shape. From the tenacity it had been dealing me, I expected it to be a four-footer, but it was closer to two feet long.

Then came Kraig's jack, a stubborn three-footer, three times heavier. When the mate brought it in, I heard Kraig utter his age with an air of amazement in his voice as if he'd expected a heart attack instead of the largest fish he'd ever caught.

Again, I had encountered a surprise new fish, and one I knew nothing about. Later, I'd learn that almaco jack are a highly prized game fish, their fisheries are pretty stable worldwide, and they can grow to a monstrous 132 pounds. Like barracuda, they can carry the poison ciguatoxin derived from feeding on algae eaters, which helps protect some populations from human consumption because no one wants to eat lethal meat.

What's most intriguing about this species is that they grow quickly and they grow huge, and they're being farmed in Hawaii and Mexico as an alternative to wild tuna. In fact, their flesh is often passed off as white albacore for sushi. The domesticated stock is good to eat, so there's a lot of hope for industrial jack ranching, which can help preserve bluefin tuna, whose populations are estimated to have plummeted 96.4 percent in the last few decades—a figure that might even be as high as 97.9 percent.[1]

Captain Salas took some pictures, we lowered our fish into the water, and they shot off like two bats out of hell. We then moved on to another spot, but Kraig wasn't feeling well. He'd been up all night battling the notorious norovirus, which was making its rounds on our family vacation, and he was losing the will to continue jigging like a maniac.

Fortunately, Captain Salas hooked us up with some bal-lyhoos, which are a common silvery baitfish with elongated under-jaws. The long, pointy beaks were removed and the bait-fish were skewered with a thick wire. The mate attached these rigs to our lines, and Kraig and I leisurely raised and lowered our rods, hoping to attract a grouper or wahoo or whatever else lurked 380 feet beneath us.

We did that for another hour, and I got the first strike. The fish was extremely strong, and I set the hook three times, just as I'd been told to do. From that moment on, I had a monster on my hands, taking out line ten yards at a time as I tightened the drag and got down to business: raising and reeling, raising and reeling. That lunker must've weighed a hundred pounds, and I was bringing it up, up, up. Two hundred feet! One hundred feet! Fifty! But before we saw any color, the line went slack.

"Christ!" I yelled. Usually I let these things go, but not today.

We then shot to another spot, the sun shining down on the scintillating sapphire water. The paragliders were coming out, along with scuba divers, snorkelers, frigate birds, and pelicans; but Kraig was going down. He was lying on the bow, trying not to throw a wrench into my fishing. Since his hotel beach was coming up, there was no reason for him to continue suffering. We brought him in, dropped him off, and got back out there.

Now it was hand lining time, meaning using a beer can wound with fishing line to drop bait to the bottom. We found a weedy, rocky area, and tossed out some ballyhoo chunks. Captain Salas and his mate began bringing in random kinds of snappers and various grunts. They were tropically colored, radiant fish, and they were fun to hook, even if I only caught one: a silly-looking, super-blue dory—also called surgeonfish because of the razor-sharp spines that pop out from their sides like switchblades. The captain threw that one back.

With a dozen baitfish gasping in our bucket (which never usually bothers me, but on this day it did), we then set off for barracuda, which I'd caught before in the Dominican Republic, Africa, and Tobago, so I wasn't that excited to do it again. I'd been there, done that. But as we circled a wreck, and as I took a look at an enormous fish cloud forming on the fish finder, the thrill of the hunt resurged in me. We were using a downrigger, which I had never tried before. Essentially, it was a large wheel on a long arm that dropped a cannonball-sized weight eighty feet, and we were trailing a foot-long snapper from that with two giant hooks in it. This bait was attached to a stout pole with 130-pound fluorocarbon test.

We trolled for about an hour, and my cup was half full. Sure, we'd caught two good fish that morning, but now it was the afternoon, there were only two hours of the charter trip left, and, by gum, I wanted another fish! One with fangs, one with heft! Because I was a spoiled American paying hundreds of bucks. And because I had spent years daydreaming scenes of Mexican marlin and king mackerel bursting from the surf, every cell in my body was telling me my chemistry needed this.

I'm rarely superstitious, but at that point I couldn't help considering some proactive tactics I'd used in the past, which, coincidence or not, might've connected me with fish. First I tried "magic pee," which had worked in Italy. But emptying my bladder over the rail failed to produce any fish. So next I decided to make a sandwich. Numerous times, breaking out the ham and cheese, I'd get a response while assembling lunch. But this time…nothing.

Then it struck. The thick pink line popped off the downrigger, and Captain Salas grabbed the rod. But that barracuda, it was off as fast as it had gotten on. He reeled in half the snapper, which meant that cuda had been a monster.

Damn! We just kept missing them. They even swiped a ballyhoo. We tried some more, and still nothing. So I decided to confront the albatross on board, which my guides were unaware of. Digging into my lunch bag, I pulled out a banana.

Captain Salas's eyes went wide.

"Maybe this is why," I said.

For anglers all over the world, jokingly or not, bananas equal bad luck.

"Could be," he shrugged.

"Sí," I replied and chucked it overboard.

The guides laughed as we cruised to another spot. We only had an hour to make something happen, and the chop of the water was growing rough. We were jumping five-foot waves and slamming down, when all of a sudden—

"Look! Look!" the captain shouted, but I couldn't see anything. Whatever he was pointing at was making him jump up and down.

"A shark!" he cried. "A huge shark! Look, look, right there, right there!"

I couldn't see it. He adjusted course.

"No!" he yelled. "A whale shark!"

Two minutes later, the boat was going up and down, right above it. The whale shark was cobalt blue and speckled with bright white constellations, and it was longer than a 1973 Plymouth Fury III station wagon—an XXL gentle giant, not even afraid of us. It was treading there, inches beneath us, the largest fish on the planet.

"Is that rare?" I asked.

"Yes!" the captain shouted, grabbing his camera and taking shots. "I haven't seen one in these waters for years. Do you want to swim with it?"

"No," I replied, content enough to gawk at its immensity.

Grabbing my camera, I hit the video recording button. Or so I thought. What I really hit was the rapid picture-taking function. Before I knew it, I had taken thirty blurred photographs in which the only things visible were two shades of blue—one light, one dark—and white spots everywhere.

Without question, meeting a two-ton filter feeder is a mind-boggling experience. Though I'd seen them in aquariums, this was a wild, peaceful, mega-monster in the flesh, surviving at a time when we're on track to lose a million species in the next few years, when any creature can get caught up in a chain reaction and be rendered obsolete, extinct, gone forever.[2] In other words, this astounding fish, which the World Wildlife Fund (WWF) lists as "Endangered," could vanish just like that and never come back. And there I was, fortunate enough to meet one in the flesh, when future generations might never get the chance.

Still, I wasn't catching jack, and I only had forty minutes left as we tore back to the first spot: jigging, jigging, jigging… nothing. Then we tried another spot: jigging, jigging, jigging… nothing.

"Okay," the captain said at the last spot, "we only have ten minutes left."

WHAM! He lit into something, set the hook thrice, and handed me the rod, which is a method I used to question. That is, if I didn't hook the fish, and then I reeled it in, that was a bit like cheating. But the way I see it now, I was out there to have a blast. That's what I'm always waiting for, that's what I'm always planning for, and in that moment, I was sure as hell not about to pass up an opportunity to play and land a monster fish, because that's why I exist.

Again it was an epic fight. The fish fought hard, but not hard enough. When we got it on board, we saw it was an almaco jack: shiny, stout, and twenty-five pounds.

In unhooking it, the captain tore its lip, causing me to grimace. Luckily, when stuff like this happens, I always have an internal speech at the ready to help me focus on other things. But this time, I heard myself audibly utter, "Nope…not this time."

The fish was released, and with only five minutes left, I was glad to hang it up. The captain, though, insisted on sticking it out.

"One more try," he said. "One more fish."

"Okay," I agreed, not expecting anything; but the jack gods were smiling on me. Again he lit into a fish, and again he handed the pole to me. But when I got the fish to the surface and the mate hauled it in, this one was different.

Captain Salas called it a "white amberjack," which I later found out was a coronado, also known as a greater amberjack. Its shape was similar to that of the almaco, but longer and leaner, with scimitar fins. Its maw was gaping, and it was glowing with a pearly gleam, opening and closing its jaws as if trying to articulate something. It only weighed seven pounds, but as I found out later, these fish are capable of reaching six feet three inches and weighing over two hundred pounds.

This amberjack, however, had been recently chomped by the ocean's top predator. Neither the captain nor I had felt the bite, but the freshly bleeding, claw-shaped wounds gouged into its belly and back let us know that on its way up, its flashings had attracted a shark.

Lowering it in, I hesitated in returning it to sharky waters, but at least it had a chance to swim for its life. It was in my hands, reeling with dizziness, but then it shot off, trailing two crimson ribbons in its wake.

A document from the United Nations' Food and Agriculture Organization would later inform me that the greater amberjack is a significant commercial species appreciated for its high quality meat. The Japanese have been successful at farming this fish, and there's a history of aquaculture facilities raising them in the Mediterranean, in Italy, Spain, Malta, Greece, Croatia, Turkey, and in North and South America too. Even Saudi Arabia is getting on board.

Farming mass jack sustainably is definitely something to consider more seriously, because here we are in the midst of another mass extinction, and the more fish we farm for humans on land, the more wild fish we protect in the water. And the more wild fish we protect, the more opportunities there will be for angling adventures, which can provide more than just a rush. Such experiences can educate us about what's really down there and what our real challenges are in conservation.

Nevertheless, farming fish is a double-edged sword. On one hand, it's an economic way to get food to market, but on the other, with all that overcrowding and fecal matter swirling around, fish farming breeds disease. Wild populations are also susceptible to genetic alteration from hatchery stock that lack key chromosomes and instincts for survival, which can weaken future generations of fish.

Meanwhile, still seeing that compromised amberjack dodging sharks in my mind, a personal concern arose. Once again, I was trying to convince myself that a moment of violence for a fish is defensible if it passes on a greater awareness to others. This is basically the internal speech I tried on myself earlier, and I still couldn't convince myself that it was okay to continue thinking this.

Whenever I hurt fish, my conscience automatically defaults to the notion that the pain I cause can be translated into something useful. It's something I always tell myself, because if I don't, it means I'm someone who messes with fish without any regard for their welfare. I realize now, however, that catching a fish in order to know it better without any consideration for the suffering I cause it comes from a childish impetus. It's just juvenile to believe that what we can gain from a fish's loss justifies torturing it.

Heading back to the concrete skyline defining the playa, this was an ethical question to consider. But I also had to confront myself on who I was to say what's ethical, when I'm a guy who kills gar for art.

I recently sacrificed a bowfin as well, for another fish print by the same artist. When I'd slid my blade into its brain, I'd immediately regretted it. The firewalls I'd previously set to protect me from such feelings just weren't holding like they used to; not when I burn through hundreds of baitfish per year, injure dozens of fish on a weekly basis, and lose noodles to underwater snags, leaving fish to asphyxiate, all so I can fulfil self-indulgent purposes, while using the excuse that it educates others.

Thus, more and more every year, I question my fishing ethics. And more and more every year, I keep switching off these thoughts like voices on the radio, in fear that if I listen too much, I might shut down these self-designed, monster-fishing missions that make me who I am.

But enough! Introspection like this can only lead to going vegan—or worse. So onward! Forward! Let's move on to other fish.

## CHAPTER 7

# PIKE FEVER AND THE CHEMISTRY OF ADAPTIVE
# FISHERY MANAGEMENT

T HE FEVER SET in when I caught a pike in Italy a few years back. It was a fish I'd known all my life and have been catching for over forty years, and it rekindled a lot of nostalgic reflection. Growing up in Minnesota, northern pike—sometimes surpassing five feet long, their ferocious, fangy, wolfish heads just waiting to erupt under an unsuspecting duck—had always been my favorite fish. They were the epitome of apex predators in the lakes and creeks I grew up fishing. But then gar came along, and monster fish after that. So when I caught that pike in the Italian Alps, it rekindled something in my DNA. Three years after Italy, my genes were screaming to get another.

I was living, however, in the South, where northerns are not a native species but had been stocked throughout Arkansas for decades. The state game and fish commission wasn't propagating this species anymore, but since pike were still in the system, I had to catch one, starting in Lake DeGray, a massive reservoir near Hot Springs.

Trolling spinners on the undeveloped side of the lake, I found myself with Armadillo Jeff. We were skirting what weed lines we could find beneath the bright October sky, but all we

got were three follows from three longnose, one which rolled
and snapped right next to the boat but failed to connect as we
cheered.

After that, I explored the coves of Lake Greeson but didn't
catch anything. Same thing on lower Lake Ouachita, where I
couldn't figure out why there were no pike hanging out in the
ferny, lush vegetation carpeting the bottom. It was their perfect
habitat.

Later that winter, back out on Lake DeGray, Big Larry (Grand
Poobah and founder of the Little Rock Kickball Association for
adults) kept back-casting way too close to my face. At one point
he almost snagged me in the nostrils. When I finally spoke up,
his wry sense of humor laughed back, "Did I hook you?"

"No," I answered, falling into his trap.

"Well," he shrugged, "then what's the problem?"

The problem was that months had gone by, and I still hadn't
caught a pike, so the fever was up to 104. And I'm not being
melodramatic. What I'm saying is true. When it hits you, it's
a chemical thing. It drives the content of your dreams. Hell, it
drives you to drive all over the state, buying lures and scouting
out spots. Like any addiction, pike fever builds and builds and
builds and builds, the obsession burning constantly.

I therefore decided to reset my expectations by going for
pickerel instead, thereby reframing the quest as a hunt for
mini-monsters in our midst. After all, both chain and grass pickerel were abundant in Arkansas, and through the years I'd caught
some in my minnow trap.

Starting out on Lake Barnett, I only caught a bunch of bass.
Then I went down to White Oak Lake, standing and casting in
the canoe. I didn't see a single fish, nor did I see the nearby Gur-
don lights, which, according to local legend, originate from the
swinging lantern of a decapitated railroad worker in limbo.

By spring I was paddling the coves of Dix Creek in Lake
Conway and casting along the lily pads. I'd found a video on

YouTube of a bass angler accidentally catching pickerel in this location, and I had contacted him for information. He gave me advice on water temperature and what color lures to use, but I couldn't seal the deal.

When summer came around and the fever was up to 105, I went up to Minnesota and relapsed back to northern pike. My brother-in-law had a couple of kayaks, and he took me out on White Bear Lake to a spot where he'd seen a four-foot musky, the grandpappy of the pike family.

Sneaking into the marshy grasses, we parked near a muskrat den and chucked out some bratwurst-sized suckers I bought at a gas station. We sat there for hours, watching a few painted turtles coexisting with a muskrat. The muskrat kept jumping in and collecting branches, then trundling them up to the top of his den, stepping on turtles and dragging brush right over them. But they didn't give a damn. They were all glad to hang out together, and so were we.

Sometimes bass would come along and just tread there looking at us with their upturned lower jaws and large, round inquisitive eyes. We'd look at them, and they'd look at us from only a few feet away, all of us hanging out together. Then a northern came along. It wasn't much longer than fourteen inches, and it had a funny-looking duckbill snout and a bluish hue. It was cool to just sit there and exist with it, and the experience of being zen with my target fish was worth as much as hooking one.

From Minnesota, Lea and I went on to Northern Wisconsin and stayed in Hayward, one of the three contested musky capitols of the world. It was the end of May and blizzarding, but I found a bridge on the edge of a lake and hunkered under it with a jumbo sucker on my line. I sat there all afternoon with snowflakes drifting down, but no pike came along.

I ended up back in Arkansas, the fever now burning like an acetylene torch. No other fish mattered in the world, and I didn't see how I could continue leaving a carbon footprint on this planet if I didn't resolve the urge to stare a pike in the eye and make sense of its baffling hold on me.

Weeks later, in the middle of the sweltering summer, I walked into my back yard and pulled up the minnow trap. As usual, there were a few sunnies flipping in there. But then I saw those slender silver contours and that raccoony accent to its eyes and knew exactly what it was. When the realization hit me, I actually felt a tightening in my chest, muscles constricting, pulling inward. When the water is warm and low on oxygen, pickerel expire easily.

That moment was not a triumph. It was the exact opposite: another casualty caused by me being me. That pickerel was stiff with rigor mortis because of my relentlessness.

‘‘   ‘‘   ‘‘

I COULD'VE DWELLED on that and continued to be bummed, or I could be proactive. Logically, if I wanted a northern pike, I should go north. And since Lea happened to be up in Madison for some sort of college reunion, and since the plan was for me to pick her up and then drive on to Chicago, and since I already had a Wisconsin fishing license, the answer was *duh*.

*Duh* because I grew up right next door to Wisconsin, and everyone knows it's full of pike. *Duh* because there are fifteen thousand lakes in Wisconsin packed with northerns, and rivers too. *Duh* because there are so many pike up there that Chippewa Flowage was begging anglers to take ten thousand out of their system to improve the musky fishery. In other words, Wisconsin had more pike than they could handle, and I had nothing, nada, zero!

So I shot up there and picked Lea up, we stayed in a yurt, and then met Kevin Moore of the guide service Muskies Etc the next day. Of course, I could've brought my own boat, I could've brought my own gear, I could've gone out on my own and tried my luck, but that would've lessened my odds. Plus, Kevin's rates were incredibly affordable, and he'd put me where I needed to be, in the right place at the right time. Also, he had answered my email immediately, sent pictures and information, and was enthusiastic about a plan he'd hatched to end my fever once and for all. He'd even bought my last fish book, which he read in two days and was eager to discuss.

When we arrived at the launch, Kevin's boat was loaded and waiting. Like Lea and me, Kevin was a product of the humanities. Whereas Lea had a PhD in English with an emphasis in creative writing, and I had an MFA in the same, Kevin also had a fine arts degree. He looked like a seasoned, optimistic hippy, and just like I knew he was our man when we started motoring down the Oconomowoc River, and I was looking through the crystalline water at all the perch and bass and water plants undulating in the current, I knew Oconomowoc was our lake.

We got to a spot, and I started casting, always giving the crankbait (a floating Rapala resembling a silver minnow) a few extra swoops beneath the boat in case a hesitant northern decided to lunge. Lea had never used a baitcasting reel, but Kevin gave her expert instruction. And get this: on her very first cast, a super-fat bass hit. The next thing we knew, it was in the boat. Call it luck, call it effective teaching, call it whatever; it was an impressive, green-sheened, three-pound largemouth caught on a crankbait half its size.

It was also a sunny day in the upper eighties and could've been humid, but the breeze was keeping us cool. Lea and I were casting off the bow, and Kevin was in the stern watching three rods set up in holders, each dangling a juicy, live chub. He kept us along a weed line, and the conversation came naturally. We learned that he had proposed the one-day nonresident fishing license to the Wisconsin Department of Natural Resources (WDNR) which I had purchased for Lea. Kevin also told us that he'd brought his daughter out the day before to scope out the lake for this fishing trip, and when I asked him how old his daughter was, he told me he didn't keep track of those things because they changed every year. We laughed at that, and the constant exchange of narratives established a rapport.

The next few hours, though, didn't yield more than a couple follows from a couple skinny longnose gar. They came out of the weeds looking like spotted sticks. I thought it was weird that they were plentiful in Wisconsin, but over in neighboring Minnesota I'd only seen one in my life: a pale, dead one in a logjam in Fort Snelling State Park. But apparently, along the I-94 latitude, longnose were common in Wisconsin, which made me wonder what the difference was: had Minnesota eradicated gar like they'd done in Iowa, as documented in Dennis L. Scarnecchia's seminal study "A Reappraisal of Gars and Bowfins in Fishery Management" (1992) or had Wisconsin done something special to preserve their most primitive native species?[1]

No answers descended from the sky as we kept fishing into the afternoon, and then moved to the other side of the lake. It was a bit past one o'clock, and Kevin said that a moonrise would happen at 1:34 and improve the bite. I didn't understand how the moon could affect the behavior of inland fish, but I was curious, and so was Lea. Kevin told us something about magnetic fields, and how we were now in a location where the wind was blowing toward us, which would shove a lot of phytoplankton our way and attract tiny fish that, in turn, would attract larger fish. And yep, there they were: schools of barely visible half-inch minnows swimming around in a bunch of green specks. But we weren't getting any bites.

"Let's move to another spot," Kevin said. "Whenever I start moving, that's when they hit."

Sure enough, right as he said this, one of the live bait rods began peeling out line. Kevin grabbed the pole, held it for a few seconds, and said, "Yep, we've got a customer." He handed it to me and told me to reel in fast.

The circle hook slid in, and the rod arced. A minute later, there it was: a little pike with a chipper expression, sliding right into the net. It was 1:31 p.m., almost at the peak of moonrise as Kevin reversed the hook, leaving a puncture that would soon heal up. We snapped some pictures and let it go. The Curse of the Pike had been lifted.

Within a few minutes, Lea noticed that one of the chub lines was at a different angle than the others. Kevin handed the pole to her, and she began reeling in. It was a remarkable bass, the size of a size-17 NBA sneaker, with vertical white stripes. Again, the damage was minimal as we took some pictures and let it go.

No sooner than the line was back in the water, another chub bit the dust. The pole bent, Kevin gave it to me, and this one had more heft to it. It was a girthier pike than the last one, this one nearly three feet long, exactly what I'd come to get. I could feel a buzzing humming through my flesh, working its true chemical magic. The fever was no more.

Then that northern was in my hands, and I was examining its alien sensory holes, coming right out of the top of its skull. It had oblong white spots gleaming on its side, a pattern so hypnotic I could've stared at it all day. But then we saw something else: down by its tail, it had been bitten, and the bite mark was not typical. It consisted of two scuffy, parallel lines, each about two inches long and an inch apart from each other. Having seen this pattern on fish in the South, I knew there was only one fish in this system that could've scarred a fish like that: a good-sized gar.

More importantly, that monster pike's maw was gaping at me with those full-grown canines I'd been striving to see. The outer row of needle-sharp teeth was surrounded by inner clusters of smaller teeth, hundreds of them, and their bristly spikiness was pulling me in. It also had jaws that were serrated like a survival knife—meant for gripping and holding on. It was a fierce top predator, an aquadynamic monster fish ready to do wicked battle.

I let it go, and the pike kept coming. I caught two smaller ones, and both fish were released in happy, snappy condition. But that last pike, the unhooking didn't go very well, and it was left with a hairline fracture in its snout. When I saw that, I bit into my lower lip hoping to feel a fraction of its pain. No such luck.

Lea then caught the smallest, cutest northern of the day. The live bait was doing the trick. But since I'd got what we'd come to get, and since my calves were now sunburned crimson, and since we weren't there for trophy fish as much as to beat the fever, we all agreed that the afternoon had been a success.

"That's good enough for me," I said, and we began heading back.

∞ ∞ ∞

But there was no hook, no substance to make this experience more than a low-stakes tale of some guy transcending an idea as absurd as pike fever. That's what I kept telling myself as we motored back to the launch with all those fish darting beneath us, so vibrant in the sparkling stream.

I'd asked Kevin if he knew of any unique environmental concerns for Wisconsin fisheries, and that question seemed to stump him a bit. It's a question I've asked myself about fisheries in Arkansas, and it perplexes me as well. I struggle to single out any specific eco-problems that aren't going on in other states, and I think this is what Kevin was dealing with too.

"Well," he told me, "lately, the larger pike seem to be going into deeper, colder water, which could be a response to global warming."

He also noted that many Wisconsin lake levels were up this year at a time when fresh water was becoming an increasingly scarce commodity in other states, and that the bass appeared to be growing larger because their growing season was now longer.

It was debatable whether this was a problem causing an impact on other species, but as we were both aware, scientific studies would eventually measure the effects of longer, warmer growing seasons.

Knowing that pike guides often switch to ice fishing in the winter, I asked Kevin if this was part of his business.

"The ice isn't very good anymore," he replied. "The shorter winters are giving anglers less time to do what they used to do before game fishing opens in the summer."

Since the ice was thinner and couldn't be trusted (the telltale sign of spring being a drunken snowmobiler going through the ice), Kevin told me that he now sold fishing equipment on eBay in winter.

He also said something about mayflies hatching later than usual, the implication being that traditional fish diets were becoming off-kilter with the changing environment. This got me thinking of musky.

The success of muskellunge fisheries was now producing quantifiable results across the country. Decades of stocking, outreach, and education had dramatically transformed this fishing culture. It used to be that catching a musky was extremely rare. When anglers took them out of lakes and rivers to mount on walls, a crippling effect rippled through their ecosystems. But now that catch and release is the norm for musky fisheries, those days are over and musky are becoming not only more popular to fish but also way more prevalent than they used to be (a few years ago, it took me about four thousand casts to finally catch "the fish of ten thousand casts"). So I asked Kevin if the eradication of northerns in favor of musky, like what was happening in Chippewa Flowage, was a concern in the central part of the state.

"Not really," Kevin answered. "But there is competition between northern and musky fry."

I'd read about this in a 2012 government document entitled

*Muskellunge: A Michigan Resource*, which documented how pike often outcompete musky because of pike spawning right after the winter ice melts. According to this document, "a musky's optimum growth rate occurs around 73 degrees Fahrenheit, compared to the northern pike's 66 degrees," so young pike are ready to start preying on young musky when they hatch.[2] Logically, Kevin figured that the warmer winters and warmer waters might start making more of a difference in the future.

Kevin also reasoned that zebra mussels weren't as threatening of an invasive species in these waters as fearmongering had made them out to be. He suspected that all the filtering they did made the water clearer. Meanwhile, invasive Eurasian milfoil was all over these lakes, and there were scrubbing stations at the launches and laws about draining boats and cleaning trailers to avoid infecting other waters. At the yurt, I'd even seen duckweed, another common invasive, which I'd never seen so far north before.

Whatever the case, still looking into the amazingly clear water as we motored back, things looked pretty good in Wisconsin. There were minnows shooting all around, and we'd met seven healthy game fish that day. This seemed like proof that the department of natural resources in this state was doing something right; or maybe it simply meant that the species here were lucky to not be vanishing.

"Maybe," I thought out loud, "despite all the fishery problems in the world, things are alive and well in Wisconsin."

Kevin agreed. I asked him why he thought this was the case.

"Slot limits on walleyes," he replied, "and increasing the statewide musky size limit."

SLAP! It suddenly struck me that there was follow-up I needed to do in order for my claims to be based on more than a few random observations. Sure, Kevin was an authority, and he knew his fish better than most, but I needed more than his suspicions backing mine to actually claim that Wisconsin was doing something progressive. I couldn't just use our general observations to make vague points about what fisheries could do better, because if my hunch was correct that the state was doing something right, I had to make an informed case.

This wasn't the direction I wanted to go, but it's what I had to do. Otherwise, I had as much solid ground to stand on as your standard conspiracy theorist. So with a sigh that signaled the start of more research, I resigned myself to the fact that I had to start digging deeper.

⚸  ⚸  ⚸

Fishery biologist Benjamin Heussner of the Wisconsin DNR, who considers himself fortunate to have worked on the Oconomowoc system for the past twenty years, was glad to respond to my July 25, 2019 email. He provided a highly detailed overview of fishery management tactics in the area and attached a few studies, which I immediately began reading. I learned that the WDNR, in partnership with private and public entities, was taking an active, multifaceted approach to fishery management that included everything from habitat restoration to creating refuges for fish.

But what really caught my attention in his email was an emphasis on monitoring cisco populations. Heusnner had replied that Oconomowoc had a "deep water habitat supporting native cisco populations," which is an important whitefish species that numerous game fish depend on as a food source. "Cisco," Heussner added, "are known to be an excellent forage species for predators such as northern pike."

A lightbulb went on in my head. This was not a top-down matter at all. If anything, the success of this fishery was a bottom-up phenomenon in which cisco, a species that depends upon zooplankton and other microorganisms, played a major role in sustaining the larger fishery.

Heussner also noted the Oconomowoc Watershed Protection Program, which was focused on reducing nutrients that create algae blooms and boost the growth of other plants, thereby decreasing oxygen and space for fish. This automatically made me ask how they were doing this, so I checked out the URL he had supplied, which took me to a document published by the City of Oconomowoc. It summarized how the city had embarked "on an innovative program called Adaptive Management to improve the water quality of the many lakes and rivers in the Oconomowoc River watershed."[3]

Ah, adaptive management, a concept once summarized by fish writer Ted Williams, who had explained the process in his 2007 book *Something's Fishy*: "you try something, collect and analyze data, then see if you got results; if you didn't get results, you try something else." That's what they did in Lees Ferry, a site on the Colorado River in 1991, and it quadrupled their trout population which is now self-sustaining.[4]

The City of Oconomowoc's goal with adaptive management was to lower nutrients, phosphorous, and pollution from storm water runoff. Through conservation practices such as incorporating cover crops, preventing leaves from entering gutters, monitoring residential use of fertilizer, and encouraging rain gardens and retention ponds, Oconomowoc had a plan.

Wetland restoration was also part of the city's overall vision. The idea was to "capture sediments, filter pollutants, and improve water quality" to enhance the area's recreational value.[5] Along with tactics for barnyard improvements and improved tillage, these methods were making the soil cleaner, which does the same for the watershed.

Returning to one of the cisco studies Heussner had sent me, I began to understand even more about how the bottom-up chain the WDNR envisioned went even deeper than I'd imagined. The study "Evaluation of Oxythermal Metrics and Benchmarks for the Protection of Cisco (*Coregonus artedi*) Habitat Quality and Quantity in Wisconsin Lakes" had come out in 2017. Here's a quick summary of what it looked at: After establishing that cisco require cold, highly oxygenated water, samples were taken from multiple bodies of water to identify benchmarks based on habitat oxygen levels. This sampling helped develop metrics for temperature and abundance, which act as early warning signs for lakes facing potential low oxygen problems. In other words, using cisco as indicators for the microorganic makeup of lakes was keeping Wisconsin waters healthy and strong. The study concluded that practices such as these can improve oxygen levels, offset warming caused by climate change, and prevent stress in fisheries.[6]

But as I noticed in Heussner's email and the cisco study, rather than saying flat out that adaptive fishery management was any kind of silver bullet, they were both careful to state that adjusting oxythermal conditions *may* produce positive changes in the chemistry of lakes.

Considering this, I knew I had to step outside my comfort zone (a term I've always despised) and tap into even more recent fishery research to really understand what ecologists and biologists and administrators are doing behind the scenes. Otherwise, I wasn't looking for solutions as much as I was relying on idealistic arguments that don't hold enough weight to substantiate what needs to be done.

Ultimately, that's what I caught on Lake Oconomowoc, and that's the direction I knew I had to go to.

Unbeknownst to me, however, there was another change in the works going on within my own micro-organics, and it had a lot less to do with adaptive fishery management than it did with adaptive *personal* management. Since my typical mode of operation was clearly shifting away from proposing solid solutions for environmental problems and toward considering the ethics of angling itself, it was definitely unsettling to see myself dropping what I'd spent twenty years fighting for in favor of something that seemed, at least to me, more philosophical than ecological. And hell if I knew where all this was going.

Thanks a lot, pike fever!

## CHAPTER 8

# AFTER THE GOLDEN DORADO
## A FISH OF PURE POETRY

"To children
  I wanted to show
   those dorados from
    the waters blue,
     those singing fish
      of gold."
        (Arthur Rimbaud, "Drunken Boat")[1]

ALEJANDRO PICKED LEA and me up at six a.m. in San Nicolás, Argentina, where we were ready to fish for the legendary golden dorado: a powerful, primitive, salmon-looking predator with a massive battering ram of a head. The "river tiger," as it's also known, is famed for hitting lures like the hammer of an angry god then going ballistic in the air. This carnivorously fanged spectacle of a fish ranges throughout five South American countries, and its gleaming, gilded monster madness is the holy grail of many international anglers seeking the ultimate freshwater rush—for reasons I was about to discover.

Knowing their conservation status has been in decline because of dams, and having read a radio-telemetry tracking study documenting how hydroelectricity infrastructure projects are blocking dorado migrations as even more are being built, I got straight to the point.

"Are there any fish ladders," I asked from the passenger seat, "to help them reach their spawning grounds?"

"Yes," Alejandro replied, looking a bit glum, "but they aren't working very well."

Alejandro was a dashing and fit thirty-something-year-old who'd gone to a Baptist college in Missouri on a soccer scholarship. He had an environmental science background, lived in Buenos Aires, and had become a leading guide for golden dorado.

After driving half an hour, the sky still dark but the sun beginning to muscle up, adding a blood-orange ruddiness to the horizon, we arrived at the boat. We then met our other guide, Matías, who had grown up in the area and knew the dorado well.

Following a bayou full of hunting egrets and diving nutria out to the Paraná River, we motored downstream to a goliath iron ore plant full of moored freighters, catwalks and cranes, and a rusty dust that permeated everything including the songbirds hopping on the shore. There were steaming cascades pouring down the clay banks from a power plant's cooling system, creating a dramatic, roiling turbulence that attracted our target fish.

For Lea and me, two poetry professors targeting an exotic fish in a not so exotic location, the day began as a relearning experience: for Lea, on casting a spinning rod, and for me, on casting a baitcasting reel. I'd forgotten how to use my thumb as a brake on what was essentially a musky-casting rig, and with the oversized crankbaits we were using, Lea had some trouble finding the right point of release.

We bungled around for an hour, our patient guides unsnagging our lines, telling us where to cast and the proper retrieval speed. By the end of that hour, we'd both regained our casting chops.

Still, bringing in a golden dorado was something else altogether. Alejandro explained how to set the hook and set it again, and how you have to reel in on the descent. After that, you gotta keep the tip down while always keeping the line tight.

So when one bashed my lure with the brutal force of a high school bully slamming a nerd's forehead into a locker (a memory I clearly recall from the receiving end), I set that hook and set it hard. An electric burst blasted from the froth, back flipping spastically four feet into the air. I set it again while the fish was in flight, then powered down on reeling in, both guides advising me to slow down.

When I got that dorado to the boat, I began guiding it around in a blazing figure eight while it shimmered beneath us, its horizontal black stripes adding an extra hundred watts of contrast to its steely blur. In the process, I lifted my rod too high. The hook popped out of its mouth.

Man! Having witnessed what we'd come to get, I was now completely adrenalized—so we got back at it. More bumbling and more retraining took place, and eventually, drifting through a series of barge-mooring columns and colossal cleats, Lea hooked a dorado and brought it in, all of us shouting instructions at her. She got it next to the boat where Matías lifted it in.

It was ours! Target fish landed!

But Lea, she wouldn't accept that she had done anything. She chalked it all up to luck, which I wasn't buying. She had honed her casting skills through trial and error, and there it was in the fish gripper, bleeding from its gills. This dorado, though, wasn't bright gold. It was just sort of platinum.

Photos were taken, and Matías tossed the fish back in the water, where it leapt three more times in rapid succession to show us that we couldn't break its fighting spirit.

We got back to casting again, this time upstream along some muddy banks traveled by cattle, gulls gliding overhead. The day was warming, the sky was bright, and I hooked three more dorados that got off. In the meantime, our guides had a line out with a live "anguila" on it, their common freshwater eel.

At one point, Lea noted that the golden dorado defies human instinct, which was a spot-on assessment. My urge was to always reel in with manic speed so they'd have less of a chance to get away, which is what I'd trained myself to do with bowfin and pike. But as my guides kept telling me, I needed to go "less loco" on reeling, and when I got them to the boat, I needed to haul them around and tire them out. Basically, to land these fish, we had to unlearn not only everything we'd ever learned in terms of fishing, but what felt natural.

After an hour, the guides switched our live bait to what they called a "morena," which was a shorter, fatter chub of an eel. When Alejandro stuck a hook through it, I felt absolutely nothing, except a minor sting from the fact that I didn't feel anything.

It was after lunch and Lea had had enough. She was sitting in the stern with her phone on one leg and a cerveza in her lap, and she was getting ready for some Facebooking time. But before she could open that beer, Matías thrust a pole into her hands and started yelling for her to "REEL! REEL! REEL!" and to "STAND! STAND! STAND!" Lea was pulled to her feet, stuff went tumbling everywhere, and somewhere in all that chaos, someone handed me her rod. I was holding it high while she got her footing, and out in the river a golden dorado was jerk-jerk-jerking the line. Lea was laughing her ass off as I handed her the pole, and she set the hook expertly.

"FAST! FAST! FAST!"

"SLOW! SLOW! SLOW!"

"SET IT AGAIN! AGAIN! AGAIN!"

"GO! GO! GO!"

A few minutes later, she brought the fish in, and Matías swung it into the boat. It was a dazzling, metallic golden dorado, its scalloped tail a brilliant blur of incandescent tangerine fringed with salmon pink, a rich black swath cutting right through the middle of it. Lea, however, felt sorry for the fish because it was bleeding from the hook, which didn't bother me at all, this being the standard price fish pay for me to get my kicks.

When we let that one go, it shot off like a torpedo, and a glorious golden one at that. I then hooked another dorado on a morena and again was given another barrage of instructions. I was bringing it in just as an osprey dove right smack in front of us, hit the water, grabbed a fish, lifted it, and dropped it back in. Then I caught a fifth, and a sixth dorado, both of which leapt in spasming spirals, performing insane, gravity-defying pirouettes, because that's the language of this fish, and that's the way they speak to us.

When you get a golden dorado on your line, the scintillating syntax of their skywork is just as expressive as the flashing of their flesh. It's an imagistic feast, an optical dance that I can only compare to poetry bursting from the breast. When verse is working at its best, when meter and rhythm twine to combine, there's a shift that can make for a larger effect. In the past, I've taught this trick as "the twist in the gut." It's a variant of what some poets refer to as "the volta," the turning point, the *aha* moment, the instant in which everything changes. But with the torqueing that comes from the twist in the gut, there are no words for this dynamic. It's something that can only be experienced in the intestines. I'm talking WOW! I'm talking WORD! I'm talking TRANSCENDENTAL! Because this is a fish which makes its own genre-busting rules that translate into something with the power to deliver a message which can only be felt at a gut level.

We let them all go, of course, bleeding or not. And the more we fished, the bigger they got, to the point that I couldn't imagine how the day could become any more of a head-spinning fantasy come true. So I called it a day, and sat down and had a beer.

Looking around, I saw myself out in the world, in a place I'd never considered going. The reason Lea and I were at the bottom of South America was because we'd asked each other where we could go that we'd never been, which led me to think of the golden dorado and what a blast it'd be to go after a fish so out-rageous. Lea had liked the idea too, and she wanted to know more about Argentina's history, which we knew would be challenging considering the thirty thousand fathers, farmers, brothers, teachers, students, and indigenous "disappeared" during the Dirty War. But we also wanted to indulge in the piles and piles of splendiferous meat this country was famous for.

Motoring back to the dock, it occurred to me that I needed to up my international travel even more, to see more stuff I'd never thought of, to learn more things I couldn't have learned if I'd stayed home. I also knew I was privileged to be able to indulge my passion and experience the metaphorical bycatches it always offers, and to be able to explore the world when others were literally eating dirt.

Another thought occurred to me as well: that I was *monster fishing the world*, which allowed for more than just fishing in the places I knew. This was something that introduced me to all sorts of cultures. In allowing me to visit museums, markets, restaurants, and to explore streets and streams I never could've imagined. This passion has always provided me a greater awareness of world history and politics, which is a bonus reason for why I fish.

"Do you mind if we fish for a bit?" Alejandro asked.

"No prob," I said, completely aware of how it feels for one's chemical composition to be under the control of fish.

Matías slowed the boat and they both began casting. It was clear that they had the fever, and it was a pleasure watching them enjoying their work and joshing with each other. They were flinging those lures with grace and precision between all the pipelines and flotsam and corroded junk sticking up, which we were now drifting through because we were back in the industrial zone. There were workers walking over us, cables strung here and there, and ships from Monrovia pumping ballast from their bilges.

Our guides didn't catch anything, but they decided to go out again as soon as Alejandro dropped us off.

After we docked and drove off in Alejandro's car, I knew I was lucky to have met those "singing fish of gold." The way things were going, with more and more dams blocking dorado migrations, their prospects for surviving another few decades were as endangered as their status, which is "Threatened" in Brazil and Paraguay. But in Argentina, Uruguay, and Bolivia, the International Union for Conservation of Nature (IUCN) hadn't yet evaluated the golden dorado on their Red List Index for tracking biodiversity loss. I had no clue why this was the case, but the fact that their sustainability wasn't being assessed in three major countries was not encouraging.

"I wonder why there's no IUCN status for golden dorado here," I said, then asked Alejandro if he thought their populations could be sustained.

He turned down the music, shaking his head. "I've seen the seine nets out on the river," Alejandro replied, "and upriver there are even more, sometimes strung from shore to shore. There are no regulations and no enforcement."

He went on to tell us that there's little environmental awareness in these parts, and since thousands of humans are consuming this fish, he was definitely wary of its prospects for survival.

"I know this guy," he told us, "who serves the dorado at his restaurant. It tastes excellent, but like I told him, 'You take one out of the system, sell it for two hundred pesos, and it's gone forever. So today we have dorado, but not tomorrow.'"

I muttered the words *short-term gain*, and that seemed to sum it up.

Still, another observation I had was the fact that the golden dorado we saw amidst the smokestacks were definitely a paler color, just like the shorebirds we saw tainted by the commerce of steel. This was basically evidence that short-term thinking was making animals in the area less healthy and wild.

Historically though, that's what happens whenever there's a rush for gold: the earth gets ravaged, the water and air turn toxic, and everything that once was natural is left a huge, ruined, mined-out disaster area. And the dispossessed, they get left with the debris of death.

I hope that's not the case with the golden dorado, but that's what this species is heading for if Argentina doesn't get it together. As Robert Hass writes in his poem "On the Coast Near Sausalito," "The danger is / to moralize." He was referring to the danger inherent in the "strangeness" of killing "for the sudden feel of life."[2] But an even greater danger, I'd say, is to *not* moralize about what the consequences are for burning through our natural resources, because if the ethics of conserving this fishery aren't considered seriously, then the most fantastically vibrant, ferociously explosive, poetically acrobatic monster fish in the world will be wiped out by indifference.

And that would be a tragedy.

## CHAPTER 9

# CHASING CHIMERAS IN THE SALISH SEA
## BLESSED ARE THE RATS

RATFISH! THEY'RE THE lowliest, homeliest, most despised monster fish I have ever met, and the reason I categorize them as a monster fish is because this three-hundred-million-year-old living fossil is literally from the order *Chimaeriformes,* named after the mythical Greek mash-up of a lion's head, a goat's body, and a serpent's tail—a fusion which doesn't quite match the anatomy of this freaky fish, but it's close enough to weird people out. The ratfish's tail is definitely snaky, and it has a big ol', bubble-eyed, rodent-looking face, which is why it's also called rabbit fish (its classification of *Hydrolagus* means water rabbit). As for the ratfish's purplish-gold, slime-coated, cartilaginous physique, it kind of resembles its cousin the shark, which is why it's sometimes called a ghost shark. Add to that a venomous dorsal spike, a bizarre clublike appendage on the male's head meant for clasping females for mating, and a pitiful bucktoothed grimace on its butt-ugly mug, and you've got one pathetic aquatic grotesque.

Ratfish! It's a creature I've known all my life, and a creature I'm always amused to catch and release since they have no food value whatsoever. Beyond sixgill sharks and the occasional massive rockfish, few predators dare to eat a ratfish, which is why they make up an alleged 70 percent of the biomass in the depths of Puget Sound. Back in 2010, it was estimated that two hundred million of these fish dwelled in these waters, which works out to "more than 30 rats for every man, woman and child" in Washington State. This info comes from Sandi Doughton's *Seattle Times* article "Rise of the Ratfish in Puget Sound," which is the most popular and comprehensive nonscientific profile of the spotted ratfish, a species that ranges from Alaska to Mexico.[1]

Historically, there are dozens of other ratfish species that have had utility. The Vikings found health benefits in ratfish liver oil, which they referred to as "ocean gold." For centuries ratfish oil was used for fertilizer, and for machine oil too. In World War II, pilots and other service members relied on pills made from the vitamin A in ratfish oil to keep their vision sharp. Other historic uses for ratfish oil (its liver can account for 80 percent of its body weight) include using it as a lubricant for watches and guns, and as a rust preventive. According to the website ratfishoil.org, "NASA even considered ratfish liver oil as a good substitute for Sperm whale oil, which was used as a lubricant in their space programme."[2]

But there's another practical use for this fish—and an even greater use at that—which we'll get to in a bit.

⚮  ⚮  ⚮

WHEN MY FAMILY gathered in early August to scatter my father's ashes and comb the beaches of Hansville, Washington as we have for half a century, I took this opportunity to launch a full-on ratquest. The first day, checking out the flotsam left by low tide, I stumbled upon my target fish. There it was, washed up in the kelp, half-decomposed and ignored by the gulls. The flesh had a grayish pallor, its eyes were missing, its innards were gone, but it still had that alien appendage protruding right out of its brow like a bulbous eye on a tubular stem. This meant it was male, and taking an even closer look at that appendage, I could see scratchy, toothlike spikes on the bottom of the rounded end, which work like micro claws to hold onto the lady rats.

I took a picture, kept on wandering, and found a fileted salmon to use for bait. I'd brought my heavy-duty travel rod along for dogfish, which are economy-sized sharks and my favorite fish to catch in the Salish Sea. This term for Puget Sound and its neighboring waters is being used more and more, and refers to the language of the coastal people of this region who fished here six thousand years ago. The "Salmon People," as some Pacific Northwestern ancestors were called, considered this fish the center of their universe. According to various creation narratives, salmon were put in these waters to nourish humans both physically and spiritually.

But with ten days of fishing ahead, I was going for underdogs. Hopefully I'd get a ratfish as a bycatch of dogfish, since they both rummage through the undermuck.

When I cast out at dusk, though, all I caught were sculpins, or bullheads as the locals call them. No matter. I still had over a week to bring a ratfish to fruition.

Then I got sidetracked by salmon. They were right off the beach, leaping in front of the rental house the following evening, and I had to get one. Using a hot-pink buzz bomb, it took an hour of casting, but eventually the fish erupted, and finally there was weight on my rod. Not giving it a chance to thrash off, I ran straight up the beach, hauling it right out of the water and up on the shore, thereby proclaiming it tomorrow's dinner: a healthy two-footer, all silvery and flopping on the sand. I'd never caught a pink salmon (also called Pacific or humpback) before, and admittedly, I abandoned all thoughts of catching a ratfish that night and concentrated on salmon instead.

ॐ ॐ ॐ

BACK IN THE seventies, my sister and I sat in the back of the station wagon, creating adventures with her stuffed rabbit Bun Bun and my modified Pooh bear Pugsly, who, with a shock of gray fur sewed to his head and his nose smushed in, looked like a grumpy old man. Our parents were up front as we took US Highway 12 through the Badlands; Miles City and Roundup, Montana; and then either headed up to Coeur d'Alene or down through Lolo Pass to get to Seattle. After a week staying with Meme and Papa, we'd drive out to Twin Spitz, where we always stayed in a musty motel near Hansville, for two reasons: first, for fishing and beachcombing; and secondly, because my father always argued with his parents, then got so pissed off that we had to leave.

Out on that floating dock, I'd fish my ass off, catch sculpin and piling perch (or pile perch) that squirted live babies right on the planks. Underneath us, the dock was covered in barnacles, and mussels, and tubeworms with crazy exploding clown hair that made great bait for anything. Down even deeper, there were Dungeness and red rock crabs, plus sea cucumbers and monstrous starfish with at least a dozen legs. We caught all these in our crab trap and on our rods as well.

Whenever I could, I'd be out there fishing, and my father was frequently with me. He might've had his bait in the water, but he was always more focused on playing the harmonica. He'd play Muddy Waters, honky-tonk, boogie-woogie, "When the Saints Go Marching In," but mostly the blues. When I had a question or comment, he'd only hear me half the time.

But I had no complaint, because I was where I most wanted to be, where fishing was the apogee, the best place to be, and where all I had to do to truly experience an otherworldly monster fish was drop my bait down to the bottom and wait.

Whenever I had a line in the water, my mind was always on fire envisioning monstrous skates and wolf eels and rockfish below. That's what drove me to fish and fish and fish and fish, there or anywhere: the visions, the creatures, the holy unholies I couldn't help imagining.

It's the same impetus that drives me now. But my father, he was out there to not have to answer to anyone or anything, including his parents, son, daughter, wife, or his infidelities that would soon break our family up. So I hated that harmonica, which might as well have been heroin, the way it removed him from the world. And I hated those same damn songs he kept repeating. But most of all, I hated what I couldn't understand: why he couldn't find escape by looking toward the fantastic, as I so easily did.

What scared me the most was the thought that I could become like him, sitting on that rocking dock, jagged black peaks right across the Hood Canal not inspiring anything—except, perhaps, an engulfing darkness to disappear into.

I mean, come on! This was our favorite family place, where I had caught "The Cabezon." I'd been six years old, jigging on the end of that dock, the melty smell of creosote hanging in the late summer air. My parents were out on the northernmost spit with my sister, collecting oysters and sand dollars, when my rod bent to the breaking point. But I hauled back and horsed it up. And when I saw its form emerge, I couldn't believe what took shape. It had huge toady eyes and amazing, fanning pectoral fins covered with zany, marbly, webby designs flaring out on both sides of that unspeakably hideous visage. And in its unbelievable mouth, the pint-sized head of a small sole was protruding from its bulging lips. I'd originally caught the smaller fish, which The Cabezon had chomped on to, refusing to let go.

I tried to bring the monstrosity in, but the reel couldn't take it. The six-pound line was about to break, and we didn't have a landing net.

"HELP!" I howled. "BIG FISH! HELP!"

Hearing this, my dad took off running in his blue shirt my mom had sewn. It had bright white stars all over it, and it showed off his hairy chest.

When he got to the end of the dock, he reached down and

grabbed the creature by a gill, which was an action I never knew was possible. He then hoisted it out and held it up, slime dripping all over the place. It was the ugliest, scariest, most repulsive, most beautiful creature I'd ever seen, and we'd caught it together!

But years later, The Cabezon lost its power. My dad didn't care if we fought another or if we even tried. For him, it was all about the harmonica, not being the hero he could be, which I knew he could be, because I'd seen him do it. But that dad, with his star-spangled shirt and hairy chest, hauling the monster up, was gone.

That's not the way I wanted to be, and I swore to myself I'd never be that way. I figured that if fishing ever became like that for me, then I might as well not even be.

And thoughts like these, they stick with you.

They make you who you are.

THE SECOND DAY in Hansville, I dragged my family into my drama. First Light Guide Service had showcased some ratfish on their website, and I'd hired Captain Mike Ainsworth to take us out: my brother-in-law Kraig, my nephew River, Lea, and me. Captain Mike told us that our odds were good for catching a ratfish while going for flounder and sanddabs.

We hopped in his boat, took off, and twenty minutes later we were right beneath the Space Needle, jigging in eighty feet of water. Kraig caught the first one: a brick-red rockfish.

"Cool," I said. "Let's keep it for Lea's paella."

But to my astonishment, Captain Mike told us this fish was now protected along with Pacific tomcod, two species I used to frequently catch. When I wondered aloud about this, he informed us that flounder and sanddabs were about the only legal fish we could take in these waters.

I later found out that lingcod, halibut, and cabezon have

short seasons in the spring, and that fishing for skates and piling perch was open year round. Things had really changed since I was a kid forty-plus years ago. In those days, no fish in the Sound were protected, and nobody needed a fishing license until 1978. Before that, in terms of recreational fishing, whatever you caught was free for the taking. But now there are restrictions on what kind of salmon and other fish are open, and there are specific seasons that close down when quotas are met. In fact, when I took a look at the fishing regulations for Marine Area 9 in *Washington Sport Fishing Rules* (2019), I saw that a number of common fish were off limits and that "all other fish" not listed in the publication were "CLOSED" as well, which is a conservation tactic I approve of.[3] That's how cod were brought back to the Grand Banks off Newfoundland, and that's how white sturgeon stave off extinction wherever they swim. Salmon fisheries have crashed on both coasts of North America, and closures have proven to be effective in bringing populations back up to snuff.

We got back to work, pulling in flounder after flounder, sometimes two on one line, and keeping the big ones for Lea's paella. Fourteen-year-old River was having a blast. Then I pulled up an octopus, which I thought was a small orange crab. It dropped off when I lifted it out of the water, but the captain caught it in a net. River got to hold it in his hands and let it crawl all over his arm, and after that, we let it go.

Moving on to another spot, we saw some porpoises and seals messing around, then hit the mother lode. Still, it was a mother lode of flounder with no ratfish to be seen, and eventually we had to head in. The family was bummed that I had missed my target fish, but I still had a week to make a ratfish crystalize.

ᕼ ᕼ ᕼ

But the next few days were ratfishless. Maybe it was too shallow off the beach. Maybe they fed later at night. Heck if I knew, but I kept on trying.

Then I hauled the whole clan over to Port Gamble, uncles and aunts and everyone, to see the eerie chimera on the second floor of the general store. Or, at least I'd remembered it as some sort of mutant ratfish from the *Chimaeric* order, but when I saw the sign reading "Skate or Sea Devil" I knew I had deceived myself. But it definitely was a monster fish with wavy, batlike wings and skeletal ribs. It also had two unsettling eye sockets, a beaky Muppet mouth, a single uni-horn protruding from its head, and a scythe-like demon tail.

"Is that thing for real?" somebody asked.

"Of course it is," some know-it-all answered.

Googling *skate* and *sea devil* on my phone, I was led to a series of images called "Jenny Hanivers." According to a 2018 article entitled "The Long, Strange Legacy of One of the World's Earliest Fake Mermaids," these intentionally altered stingrays "are shore-town oddities that hucksters have been billing as mummified dragons, mermaids, or other outlandish creatures since at least the 16th century."[4] So I wasn't the only one who'd been fooled by this faux devil fish.

⚇ ⚇ ⚇

FOLLOWING THAT, WE scattered my father's ashes, and then I fished for three nights off the beach. But we also went to a boat launch where Kraig caught a small salmon, and I caught squat. In the end, I had to console myself with watching the harbor seals, spotting ospreys, witnessing the insanely leaping salmon migrations, and being mesmerized by the misty morning magnetism which kept pulling my gaze out to sea, where I could never look at that strong, steely horizon the way I used to. Because now, in addition to my grandmother and mother being out there, my father was out there too.

Leaving Point No Point, Lea and I drove to Port Townsend. We still had a couple of days on Whidbey Island where our friends Karen and Danny had a house on the beach. They'd invited us out, and we'd had the good fortune to see a pod of orcas from the ferry, an increasingly rare sight these days. The salmon numbers were down, so the whale numbers were too, and every day in the local papers there was front page news concerning which orcas were MIA because of the degrading food chain.

Again, when we got to the beach the salmon were leaping, but my sights were set on lowlier fish. It was my last chance to get a ratfish, and for the past few rat-lacking days I'd been preparing myself for defeat. Resigning myself to giving up, though, was enough to make me push myself harder in order to catch what I was starting to doubt actually ever existed.

I didn't get much fishing in that first night, but the following afternoon Danny pulled a dinghy down to the beach and told me to row to the second buoy and fish there. It was forty yards out, and at high tide it would be forty feet deep.

It was sunny and bright as I tied up and broke out a package of frozen herring. I cut off a hunk, baited up, and dropped it to the bottom. Salmon were leaping all around me, but I was back to my primitive bottom-fishing ways, going for the most raga-muffin species in the mix.

It didn't take long to hook the first sculpin, and I was glad to examine it. With its ornate fins, comic froggy head, striated gills, and slick skin, that bug-eyed bullhead was a gorgeous, despised mini-monster, sparkling in the light of day.

Then I caught another one. And another. And another. They kept glomming on, and I kept tearing the hooks out, not giving a shit if I ripped their lips—because they were disposable. And way too many! And getting in the way of better fish. That's who I'd become. Because, so it seemed, sculpin were the only fish down there. Because ratfish were a myth, and I was a sucker!

I had heavy-duty tackle with me, however, so it made sense

to go for heavy-duty fish and to use those pesky sculpin as bait. So I grabbed one, poised my knife, and hesitated as I always do, wondering if this is the way it'll always be, staying the blade for a microsecond in which even the most hardened angler has to acknowledge that this is different from slicing an eggplant. It's a feeling that's always there, which I always accept when pressing down. That feeling then disappears like the surface of a wart you can slice away, even though the spore remains.

SNAP! I severed its spine, cut it in half, baited up with the tail end, and dropped it in. Thirty seconds later, something hit like a truck, bearing down on the bottom. The baitrunner reel I'd bought for cranking in French monster carp was bringing it in, but I had to be careful because I'd lost the ceramic guide on the tip, and the sixty-five-pound woven line was rubbing against the metal eye. I could feel the friction, which could weaken the fibers, so I was holding the pole as straight down as possible to keep the pressure off the fibers. Then I saw the sharky shape of a forty-inch dogfish heading into the net. Victory!

Holding it by the tail, I hoisted it up and let out a whoop as it thrashed. Danny and Karen's neighbor was watching through a telescope. He positioned his cellphone over the eyepiece, took a few shots, and ended up catching me in all my spiny dogfish glory.

Instantly, I was six years old again and back at Twin Spitz. My dad was clapping, my mom was taking shots with the Polaroid, and Pugsly and Bun Bun were jumping up and down. This was my consolation prize. What could be better?

A ratfish, that's what! But in that instant, I went with the dogfish instead, allowing its presence to fill my void because that's what we all do in one way or another when we lower our expectations. Nevertheless, the adrenaline was tangible enough to install a bounce into my step that lasted well into the next day.

∞　∞　∞

AS A SORT of canary in a coal mine, ratfish can act as barometers of water and ecosystem quality. This is the "greater use" I mentioned earlier, and the fact that their populations are so vast is evidence that something's out of whack, and that something needs to be done. Because if nothing's done, and we don't even try, then we're as worthless as ratfish are generally regarded to be. So I had to find out more.

Dr. Dayv Lowry, the senior marine fish research scientist for the Washington Department of Fish and Wildlife (WDFW), was happy to supply some ratfish answers to my ratfish questions. The first thing I asked in my email was whether the 70 percent biomass figure from Doughton's article nine years ago was consistent with current population statistics for ratfish in the Salish Sea. Ratfish artist Ray Troll of the band the Ratfish Wranglers had cited 75 percent on his website, so I was curious if the numbers were rising.[5]

Dr. Lowry responded by sending a report entitled *2019 WDFW Bottom Trawl Survey Cruise Summary*, which included a ratfish biomass estimate closer to 80 percent.[6] But as Dr. Lowry explained in his August 22, 2019 email, trawling samples come from mud and sand bottoms, whereas rockier areas have to be sampled by scuba divers and robot vehicles. In those spots, ratfish are rarely seen. For all habitats in the Sound, he estimated that ratfish make up "something like 50–55% of all bottom fish." Therefore, it appears as if ratfish making up 70 to 80 percent of the biomass is only true if we're talking about sampling done by biologists in trawlers, who concentrate on the deep mudflats where ratfish thrive. Not only that, half of all bottom fish (the percent suggested by Dr. Lowry) only accounts for bottom fish, not unbottom fish. Meaning the alarming numbers publicized by Doughton resulted from misread data being inflated.

Dr. Lowry couldn't answer why I was having so much trouble catching a ratfish, but he was able to respond to why there are so many. "There's a lot of good, deep mud—which they love," he explained, "that has lots of worms, clams, small fish, and other prey for them. In some cases, terrestrial nutrients from rivers, sewage outflows, etc. are a boon." That, combined with no fishing pressure whatsoever, explained why ratfish have flourished in the Salish Sea.

Okay, now we were getting to the heart of the matter. Ratfish abundance was directly linked to ideal habitat. But if that's the case, I had to know why's there a concern that ratfish are taking up space where rockfish and cod and other fish usually coexist. So I asked Dr. Lowry about the "Rise of the Ratfish" article, which claimed that rising water temperatures due to global warming were adding a new wild card to the equation. Doughton's article quoted Dr. Phil Levin of the Northwest Fisheries Science Center, who said, "the ratfish story is a byproduct of decades of insults to the Sound, not only from fishing, but declining water quality."[7] Thus, my question had to do with what those insults were, and what was being done to counteract the imbalance.

"The insults are many," Dr. Lowry replied, "and include fishing, stormwater runoff, sewage, increases in hatchery salmon, increases in predators that feed on hatchery salmon, toxic pollution from industrial sources, etc. etc. Programs exist to clean up and otherwise offset impacts from many of these stressors, but in the end, human population has brought profound changes to the ecosystem and getting back to a 'pristine' state is simply no longer achievable. New technologies have been brought to bear to reduce the worst effects, like removing PCBs, capping superfund sites, and improving sewage filtration, but slowing the degradation isn't reversing the degradation."

So that's the larger ratfish story: the reason there are so many chimeras ghosting around out there is because humans have helped create environments in which ratfish prosper and other fish don't. Hence, other fish in the system are currently experiencing everything from overfishing, to pollution, to changing demographics of species that can't hold to their vanishing habitats. And as Dr. Lowry clearly communicated, slowing the degradation that's happening now is not reversing the downward spiral. This means that the damage happening on our clock is *irreversible.*

Scientifically, this sad assessment, which reflects the damage we're doing with global warming, is the closest approximation of the ratfish situation I am qualified to make. Symbolically, though, I couldn't help but note one more possibility that I had to take advantage of: ratfish have evolved in such a way that makes them adept at hanging on. Not only are they well prepared to utilize human-created sedimentation for productive feeding and spawning grounds, and not only are the males equipped with specialized claspers on their heads, but there's one more grippy thing about this fish I was about to discover.

∝ ∝ ∝

THE NEXT DAY, I came up with a plan. It wasn't much of a plan, but since I'd been fishing for ratfish for nine days and this was my last day on the Sound, it was all I had. Knowing that ratfish feed primarily on crustaceans which they locate through noses noded with electroreceptors, I collected some common cockles at low tide. If clams couldn't do it, I had no idea what would.

Out in the rowboat that afternoon, I broke a shell open and cut off a muscly chunk. That piece of clam foot stayed on the hook so well that I caught three sculpins in ten minutes. During that time, I saw an eagle attack an osprey in flight, a curious otter came along, and several salmon practically leapt into the boat.

I fished for an hour, mostly catching sculpins while considering that vow I'd made to myself to study the hard science harder in order to understand what the experts were doing. Without question, communicating with Dr. Lowry was proof that I was following through on this commitment, but it still seemed like something wasn't connecting. And pulling up another sculpin, this one hooked through the eyeball, I knew exactly what it was: hurting fish to justify creating a greater awareness wasn't sitting right with me.

Meanwhile, Danny was casting from shore that afternoon, and so was the whole dang neighborhood. Lea and Karen were lounging on the beach, it was getting close to happy hour, and I was starting to hanker for a beer. And the more I fished, the more sculpin I caught. And the more sculpin I caught and released with injuries, the more hope I lost that I'd ever catch a ratfish.

*Alright,* I thought, *I'll try one last harebrained idea…*

Grabbing myself another cockle, I smashed a triangular window in it. That clam was the size of a baseball, and the gooey flesh was visible inside, and smellable too. If any fish could bust into this, it was the ratfish, which is equipped with shell-cracking tooth plates. Because ratfish have the highest jaw leverage known in any cartilaginous species, including sharks, they were the only fish in this system capable of breaking into a clam and getting hooked. But it would have to be a sizeable ratfish, and considering that the state record was only 3.9 pounds, the odds didn't look like they'd be in my favor.

I dropped the clam down, felt some knocks and tried to set the hook a few times, but after half an hour of dicking around I got so disgusted with my folly that I yelled, "Screw this!" and reeled in.

Digging the clam meat out, I hooked a chunk to catch a sculpin for dogfish bait. That's when three porpoises came porpoising by, laughing at me because I didn't have what it took to get a ratfish—because I was a ratfish loser!

A minute later, I pulled in a sculpin. And a minute after that, I had its tail end on my hook.

Again, shark week was on! It hit harder than the one I caught the day before, and I could tell it was a larger fish. I could feel the heft, the jerks, the thrashing in the strands. Pulling it up was like hauling in a manhole cover. Up, up, up it came, and again I had to account for the metal rubbing against the line.

Foot by foot, the dogfish kept rising. It was the burliest dogfish I'd ever fought. It weighed way more than the twenty-something-pounder I'd thrown back two years ago, only to discover I'd released the state record.

Then, right when it was under the boat, bowing the rod and giving me the business, the line snapped. In that flash, I saw the most mammoth dogfish I'd ever seen. It was nearly five feet long!

"AAAAAAAARRRRRGGGGHHHH!" I Charlie Browned, gripping my head and crying at the sky. That dogfish had ground right through the braided line and took off with the hook.

To hell with happy hour! I now had a burning objective! Tying on a steel leader, I clammed up and dropped to the bottom to catch another sculpin for bait.

Jigging, jigging, jigging, jigging.

Jigging, jigging, jigging, jigging.

Jigging, jigging, jigging—POW!

Something was on, but it wasn't a dogfish. It just didn't weigh enough, just didn't send those familiar vibrations through the line. Another stupid sculpin, I reckoned, so reeled in. But when it came twirling up, glimmering all coppery with white spots all over it, I recognized it immediately.

"RATFISH!" I yowled, and pulled it into the boat. I held it up, and the salmon anglers lining the shore exploded with applause. They'd been told that I was fishing for the most worthless fish in Puget Sound, and since they weren't catching anything, they now had something to cheer about.

"You got The Rat?" Danny called.

"Yep," I replied, "I got The Rat!"

Rowing back, I jumped out and showed it off. It was sixteen inches long, its smile curving toward its semitransparent nose. Those enlarged bubble eyes gave it a cartoony appearance, but with its vipery, extraterrestrial tail, that ratfish exuded a venomous vibe.

A crowd formed, photos were taken, and as it dangled there I suddenly noticed the most monstrous thing about this fish. It was something I never suspected nor had ever seen on any fish: in addition to that handy-dandy tool for assisting with procreation protruding from its forehead, down beneath its anal fins there were four sharklike testicles dangling in the wind. They were the color of liver and looked like elongated chicken gizzards, all spade-shaped and hanging from stringy tendons covered with tiny nubs. That ratfish had four nuts!

Dr. Lowry explained to me later that what I had seen were two bifurcated claspers, or penile organs which sperm travels down. But whatever the case, there I had it: even more evidence that the reason this monster fish has been around since way before the dinosaurs is because it's built to hang on in more ways than one; first, for purposes of procreation, and secondly, by flourishing in conditions that create wastelands for other species. This might be an oversimplification, but that's the ratfish story I discovered. And if ratfish continue to stick to this method, which they've been practicing for millennia as species come and species go, then (with apologies to Matthew 5:5) here's my sentiment on these sediment dwellers:

Blessed are the rats, for they shall inherit the earth!

But the earth they'll inherit won't have the biodiversity we've been taking for granted for centuries. Since many of these wastelands we're creating are irreversible, there are going to be far fewer rockfish, and there are going to be far fewer salmon, and there are going to be far fewer whales in our future. Because ultimately, there's going to be a lot more mud, and what that mud brings to bear.

## CHAPTER 10

# ROUGHING IT IN QUEST OF THE TRASHFISH TRINITY
## PART 1: THE FATHER

THE IDEA OF a "roughfish quest" (going after stigmatized species) came to me on Rondout Creek, a mountain stream in New York State's Mid-Hudson Valley. That's where our "New York Outpost" is, on the outskirts of the groovy, gluten-free hamlet of Rosendale where Lea lives most of the time and I live part-time. Our twenty-first-century commuter marriage used to rely on weekend air travel, back when we lived in a world of Ubers and taxis and Jetsonian walkways while meeting at conferences in between. But with the sudden onset of a worldwide plague, we were now driving cross-country a whole lot more in order to be in lockdown together.

For the last three months, we'd both been in Arkansas, fighting neighbors for bandwidth to teach from home. For the moment, though, we were back at the Outpost getting some stuff together. It was the beginning of summer, and I was fishing in one of my favorite spots beneath the Sturgeon Pool Hydroelectric Dam which I'd been trying for years with no success. What keeps me coming back are the massive, old-school common carp that scour the plant life and gravel in vigorous, healthy numbers.

Carp, of course, are not regarded with a lot of respect in the United States. Generally speaking, in this country they're considered a big, dumb, invasive species that destroy the nests of more elite game fish. In Europe, on the other hand, carp are fattened like hogs and are the most prized catch-and-release sport fish on the continent.

But I don't care where I catch them. Ever since I was a kid, those barbely lips have been calling to me to hook into their freakishly monstrous masses, which can sometimes surpass a hundred pounds. I've caught lunker-carp from coast to coast and thirty-pounders in France, and they've always rewarded me with action-packed, high-velocity, world-class battles that are as thrilling as taking on a muskellunge.

But back to my spot beneath the dam, which is as pristine as hell. The water is full of colorful boulders and skittering minnows and playful turtles, and eagles and hawks can be seen soaring above. But to get to that spot, you have to cut through some woods packed with poison ivy, which is what I did the other day. I thought I was being clever by wearing long pants over my shorts, which I shed when I got to the water. It would've been more clever, however, to have brought a lawn chair, because I ended up sitting on the soggy grass in a patch of hardly visible three-pointed leaves which I spotted too late. Nice going, Einstein!

But sitting there with the flesh-inflaming oil beginning to spread, that's where the idea came to me of designing a rough-fishin' mission to go after species typically considered crappy, no-good fish with little food value. A roughfish quest, however, would have to involve a definition of the species I was targeting, along with a reason why.

Saving the *why* part for later, I had no trouble whittling my species down. Whereas most authorities tend to include catfish, gar, bowfin, and suckers in the infamous roughfish canon, I envisioned an unorthodox "Trashfish Trinity" composed of the Father (carp), the Son (buffalo), and the Holy Gou (freshwater drum). And because there were some humongous carp rising and diving and slapping the surface out there, I started with the Father.

But watching one carp leap and others jump in response (which I figured was a mode of carpy communication, each splash telling the others where they were and what they were up to), I just couldn't catch any. All I had were night crawlers, which the channel cats were snarfing up before the carp could get to them. Thus, I needed to revise my plan, and I also knew I needed to research some new techniques. So I trudged on back with a stringer of catfish, not even bothering to put my long pants on to protect me from the poison ivy.

Why? I don't know, but there was definitely some hubris involved. First of all, for years I'd been staying clear of the stuff and had managed to escape the nasty rashes I usually get, so I told myself I was developing an immunity, which was total self-brainwashing. Secondly, with people dying en masse and losing their jobs and homes, and civil unrest erupting all over the country, I figured that, in comparison, this ain't jack. But mostly, I think my decision in this situation paralleled the whole debate about politicizing masks. To wear or not to wear? To give up one's "freedom" or heed the warnings of highly trained epidemiologists? Those were the questions of the times, and still are to this day.

But that attitude had been totally *un*-me. I mean, I kept hand sanitizer on my person and used it religiously. I also had a three-day system for quarantining mail, even though concerns about transferring the virus through touching surfaces were becoming fewer and fewer. I'd even publicly shamed an elderly lady for picking an onion up at the grocery store and putting it back. In other words, during that learning curve in which masks weren't mandated and there was a lot of confusion about how COVID was spreading, I was way more neurotic about protecting myself and others than most people, and I always practiced extreme, over-the-top caution. But when it came to the commonsense

consideration of whether I was going to take any chances with
my old nemesis Poison Ivy, who I'd had a severely toxic relationship with all my life, there I was marching right through it,
letting it brush my bare legs as if sheer confidence was enough
to shield me from reality.

Predictably, I became covered with patches of pus, some
hardened and scabbed over, some oozing freely for weeks. The
rash scarred my arms, it spread to my chest, and it was not a
pretty sight—which is why I've got to call myself out for such
dangerous arrogance, along with everyone else I see risking the
safety of others because of what they refuse to accept about the
new terms of service on this planet.

Untraditional fish writing for sure, but these were terrifying,
unprecedented times, and since that's what was going on, that's
what I had to deal with.

ᔓ  ᔓ  ᔓ

DOUGHBALLS! I'D NEVER really gotten a handle on this type of
bait so that's where I started. It didn't take long. After a few minutes of Googling I found an NPR transcript of a July 16, 2006
radio interview with Greg Wagner of the Nebraska Game and
Wildlife Commission. His doughball recipe was so easy and
intriguing that I had to try it. It was transcribed as one infor-
mal paragraph stating, "I'm in the kitchen, bringing three cups
of water to a boil, and I'm adding about, ah, three tablespoons of
strawberry-flavored Jell-O. And then I'm slowly adding, while
stirring, a couple cups of yellow cornmeal, one cup of flour. I
turn down the heat, and then still kind of stirring for about five
minutes. I let this dough cool, and then I refrigerate in a plastic
bag."[1]

After replicating this process, I took my oversized bubble-
gum-looking blob back to the poison ivy, which I knew was a
stupid idea. My rashes were blistering and bubbling, and going

back was not recommended. But that's where the carp were, and once again, the fever was rising.

My initial approach to catching carp had been entirely different. It had been early fall, I was eight years old, and they were running in the creek across the street. The water was shallow enough for the neighborhood bullies to chase them down and club them upside the head, but I had another plan. It involved a broomstick, a clothes hanger, and some duct tape. It was a highly primitive spear, and it didn't take long to make it in the basement.

That evening after dinner, I took the spear over to the creek. A few carp were making their way upstream. I recall chucking the spear and mostly missing but sometimes connecting. When I did hit one, the point would bounce off their scales, which were as thick as guitar picks and just as flexible.

After a while, I came to a pool where a few battered carp had been smashed by bricks. There was one gasping on its side, left by the bullies. Since it was a goner, I worked the sharpened tip between its scales, knowing that what I was about to do lacked any sense of sport. Applying pressure, the air bladder popped and deflated with a *hissssss* that went on forever.

Shuddering, I shook that memory off and kept on trucking through the poison ivy. I was wearing boots this time and two pairs of pants. I'd also brought along a can of corn because carp love corn, and I was naïvely convinced that catfish don't care for it. In baiting one rod with dough and the other with corn, my plan was to target carp specifically, so as to get a better understanding of using doughballs. I didn't expect to catch my quarry, but the research had to start somewhere, or else I was fishing for pleasure. And at this time in my life, fishing for pleasure was a frivolous thing of the past!

Arriving at the spot, I set up a canvas chair on the bank. Out in the current, the carp were even thicker than the day before. They were bursting and swirling like pods of dolphins, sometimes emerging in blasts of yellow, other times in dark brown with blood-red tones edging their tails. Their condom-looking lips were sucking on the surface, and I was ready to get down to business—because that's what fishing had become for me: serious business.

Stripping off a pair of pants and baiting my medium-action travel rod with five or six kernels on a dime-sized circle hook, I cast it out and let it settle. If I hooked a carp on this light rig, it would be one hell of a fight. The other rig, though, that was the one! I had a monster-sized baitrunner reel on it, spooled with some incredibly flexible twenty-pound P-Line that could horse in a tractor tire. It was mounted on an antique heavy-duty rod with wire eyelets that I bought at a junk store for ten bucks. It was maroon and gold and had a two-ounce egg weight on it so that the carp could take out line.

But the doughballs crumbled too quickly. I'd cast them out, and they'd dissolve in ten minutes. So after an hour, I switched out that circle hook for an equally tiny #4 treble hook. But those doughballs still kept falling apart.

Munching on a doughball and trying it out (it tasted like strawberry-flavored white bread), I decided to try one last tactic. Taking two skinny blades of grass, each about a foot long, I wound them around the marble-sized wad packed around the treble hook, tucking the strands under the barbs to keep the weave tight. Maybe it would hold.

Out in the creek, I saw a carp's dorsal fin rise. It was black and looked like a shark fin slicing the surface. I watched it cut across the top of the water for a few feet before descending, a fifteen-pounder at least. And all around it, every few minutes, another carp would come fluming up, its entire face visible before splashing down on its side. Meaning they were out there, lots of them, and they were active.

The night before, I had dreamed of stalking carp in this exact spot. I had a telescope with me and was watching them breach like whales, twisting and turning in the sky. I was using some sort of baited lasso.

Anyhow, after two hours and no solid hits, I started getting restless. Back in college, I used to go down to beaches on the Mississippi River and cast a couple of kernels out on a regular old J-hook. The carp came along, and that's all it took. But not today.

Then I saw the doughball line move a few times. Twice, I poised myself to set the hook, but since there hadn't been any follow-ups, I started taking notes on how I was failing. That's when something happened.

I saw it out of the corner of my eye. The line went tight, then dropped. Then it did the same thing again.

This was not what I expected. I imagined a carp would take it, and POW! We'd be off to the races. The spool would start whizzing, I'd crank the handle, and all hell would break loose. But this little fellow was teasing me by moving the line a few inches, then moving it again.

Still, maybe a carp had swallowed the doughball, and now it was nosing around in the vicinity. It couldn't hurt to give the rod a snap. At least that might make the bait get noticed, if it was even on the hook anymore.

Giving it a flick, the rod arced. There was weight on the other end. Dead weight.

*Must be a snag,* I thought, and began reeling. Whatever I hooked was just lying there like a sack of potatoes, probably some seaweed or a sunken limb. But then…vibrations! Definite fish-on vibrations shooting through the line! Something was on the other end, and it was moving.

No, it was torpedoing! Then suddenly I was leaping up and knocking corn all over the place. The fish was shooting straight and speedy like a carp, heading downstream, and I was bringing it in: an enormous, coppery blimp of a fish cutting along at sixty miles per hour!

Let's talk carp velocity. A 2019 article I'd read stated that a 50-centimeter carp (nearly 20 inches) can reach speeds of 3.85 meters per second (8.6 miles per hour).[2] But what that number doesn't account for is the factor of adrenaline. The speed of 8.6 miles per hour is a general cruising speed, not the velocity achieved when a spooked carp is accelerating to break a connection that can take its life away. So I'll affirm it once again, even if no one believes it: sixty miles per hour. That carp was blasting as fast as any car on any state highway winding through the river valley, and it was heading straight for a fallen tree.

This is the *why* I had avoided addressing earlier but realized in that microsecond. The simple reason I was researching carp was because of the totally tangible, hair-raising electricity that occurs when you hook into a "bronze bomber," a fish most American anglers consider a vulgar and eventless creature. But when a carp is cutting along at Mach speed, and when you have to act as fast as it in order to hold on to it, that's the *why*, that's the reason. When this happens, an actual, physical full-body blast travels through an angler's system. And in that moment, that energy was zapping through both of us, but for opposite reasons: the carp was trying to avoid the end of everything it's ever known, and I was at the zenith of why people fish. It's the same reason why crowds cheer, and why people strive to connect with something outside themselves when they're really trying to connect with something inside themselves—something that's triggered when trial and error finally evolve into that ass-kicking nanosecond when you find yourself throwing down with Monster Fish!

The carp only had a yard to go, and then it would be in the branches, getting tangled up. If that became the case, I might not be able to get out there and free it. So I kept hauling back, not allowing any slack.

ZZZZZZZZZ! The reel was working like a dream, and ye olde rod was absorbing the tension spectacularly. The carp was now inches from the limbs, but it was no match for the tackle it was tackling. I pulled the fish back, and it switched directions, now shooting upstream.

Jumping down from the bank and splashing in, I kept the pressure on. Reversing the carp's course again, I grabbed the landing net and brought the fish right into the mesh. Then it was on the grass, nearly three feet long with a bright orange, blazing belly, gilded to the gills and brown on top. I didn't have a scale with me, but I estimated its weight to be somewhere between ten and twelve pounds.

Unhooking the fish, I took my pictures. The plan had been to make carp dumplings like I used to back in grad school, but now I wasn't so sure. This carp had come from the cold waters of a mountain stream in the foothills of the Shawangunk Mountains and would definitely have a firmer, cleaner meat than carp from warmer waters, but it was just too pretty to sacrifice.

I suppose I was anthropomorphizing, musing on how its wide eyes and gasping lips made it look human. That thought, however, was immediately deleted when I saw a trickle of blood bead up under a gill. This brought to mind that carp I'd speared over forty years ago, and I just couldn't take the next step.

*And so what if it's an invasive species!* I thought. It was a non-native fish that we could live with, that had adapted to almost every niche of the continent and wasn't as harmful as other invasives. But mostly, this fish was just too beautiful to grind into fishburger.

Yep, I loved that silly, gorgeous, colorful fish, who I preferred to see as *my bro*. And whether it was actually male or not, what it really came down to was that I wanted it to keep on recreating its genes.

There's always something magical about helping to revive a fish, which I began doing. I was holding it with its humpback sticking out of the water, cradling it and assisting it in staying upright. It was slowly getting its balance back, but I decided to speed the process up by pulling it backwards, making its gills flare open, filling its system with oxygen. I did this a few times, moving it forward and pulling it back, opening its gills multiple times. This is how you jumpstart a fish.

Then something snapped in it. You can always see it happen: that instant in which it shakes off its daze and snaps back by slashing its tail and shooting off, leaving a billowing cloud in its wake. But because it wasn't fully recovered, it turned around and swam straight into the tall grass between my feet where it used the vegetation to hold itself steady.

I watched it for a few minutes, flashing back to that childhood carp: it was working its lips in the air, and the question of what to do with it was becoming as real as what I'd done to it. The next thing I knew, I was picking it up and hugging it to my chest. It was a nine-pound fish, and its reeking goo was getting all over my blue hooded sweatshirt as I took it home to show my father.

He was in the backyard wearing his denim jacket and playing the harmonica when I walked up slimed in mucus. There was no way I could smile. He looked at me and probably saw an expression not much different from that of the carp, still gurgling pathetically.

"Are you proud of what you've done?" he asked.

I can't remember what my response was, but that carp ended up back in the creek. It also ended up in my head—in the face of every carp I ever see—including this one in Rondout Creek.

A couple of minutes later, though, that carp was good to go. And so was I, contrary to what Zane Grey had to say in his book *Tales of Fishing Virgin Seas*: "Fishermen, no matter what supreme good fortune befalls them, cannot ever be absolutely satisfied. It is a fundamental weakness of intellect."[3]

But having just had an incredibly successful catch-and-release experience with a dazzling grotesque I never expected to catch right off the bat, I was euphoric! And because I had gotten a handle on doughballs, I was beyond satisfied. Because this time, as it swam off, I was proud of what I'd done.

## CHAPTER 11

# FLY FISHING THE IMPOSSIBLE GAR

F LY FISHING FOR gar was not at the top of my list of objectives, but since my international mission to monster fish the world had been smacked down by coronavirus, it was the logical thing to do. No one was flying on airlines anymore, folks were locked down in their homes, restaurants and businesses were dropping like flies, and it wasn't safe to be inside with other humans while the worldwide death toll was rising to half a million. This was definitely inconvenient for most, but I knew how to make lemonade.

I'd been trying to catch a gar on a fly rod for nearly a decade, and the maddening failures I'd been through were enough to let me know that I just didn't have the skills to finesse a gar via this technique. The last time I designed a quest for fly fishing gar, it totally bombed, and since this was eating away at me almost as much as the wounding of catfish I was doing on a daily basis by running lines out on the lake, I decided to give it another go—but this time with a rope fly.

A rope fly is a length of white nylon rope that trails its fibers in the water. It can be made at home (lots of videos on YouTube) or ordered online. It doesn't have any hooks in it, and when it's stripped through the water (pulling on the line, rather than reeling) it rises and dives like a minnow. A gar then sees it, snaps at it, gets its teeth tangled in the strands, and the fight is on.

Question: Why would anyone want to battle a species that has "earned little respect from Arkansas anglers," as an article in the *Arkansas Democrat-Gazette* characterized this fish in 2014? The unknown author of that article adding, "Venomous snakes and rabid skunks get as much respect as gar....Most fishermen despise gar."[1]

Answer: What other people thought didn't matter because this issue was between me and the fish I knew best. Having researched and written numerous "garticles" as well as two books on the species as a whole, having worked with the experts, and having caught various subspecies of gar all over the planet, it was a personal embarrassment that I still hadn't caught a gar on a fly rod, and this was sticking in my craw.

Not only that, but I saw gar as a common, misjudged, evolutionary, novelty fish. Having survived ice ages and dinosaurs, they've been around for over one hundred million years. And not only have gar been around longer than humans, but according to Johnny Carrol Sain's 2017 article "The Gar Hole: Repentance on the Banks of Point Remove Creek," they've been around sixty-five million years longer than humans and thirty million years longer than grass.[2]

Out on Lake Conway in Arkansas, where Lea and I had returned to hunker down and ride out the plague for the summer, there were shortnose, longnose, and spotted gar swimming around in the lily pads. Having fished these waters for a decade and a half; having found relief in the cypress trees and alligator grass; having lived off the fish I catch, always being rewarded by unbelievable leviathans, there's no lake in the world I've ever loved so much. So with my plans dashed for colossal skate in Scotland, it made sense to get out in my own backyard and put this aggravating grudge match to rest.

Thus, I broke out my dusty but trusty fly rod (heck if I know what brand or size), pulled the canoe out of the boat house, and got out in my cove. It was a hot and humid June afternoon, the sun was high in the sky, and the conditions were perfect for fly fishing gar.

As usual, I paddled out and stood up. My method was to stand in the center like a paddleboarder, take a paddle, take a cast, and work the weed line. Standing up allowed me to see fish on the surface, and it gave me more room to extend my casts compared to sitting down as I stalked the edge of the lily pads for a serpentine, armored grotesque with an alligator head on it.

Standing there, casting there, reflecting on gar, it occurred to me that there's another reason I find this fish worth studying: in a way, we're connected to gar because of our disconnection with them. There are few species on this planet more different from humans (except that we both breathe air) than this monstrous-looking carnivore which haters love to hate. The mindset that led to the practice of breaking off gar beaks harks back to the settlers, their dogmatically fueled misunderstanding of a species frequently labeled "devil fish," and the mobs that used to hunt down gator gar and publicly hang them for all to see. There are plenty of archived photographs of gars lynched for crimes they were suspected of having committed, and there are plenty of videos on YouTube of bowhunters shooting gar while calling them the N-word. This intentional, irrational torture, whether directed at humans or animals, always sickens me and brings out my unapologetic, outraged heritage harking back to Austria 1937.

Such dynamics relate to another we've all seen. The senseless, public asphyxiation captured in the image of a white cop cutting off a Black man's oxygen had recently sparked explosive protests all over the planet. This incident happened across the street from a bus stop where I used to wait every afternoon as a teenager to get to my after-school warehouse job. Having grown up in South Minneapolis, I was more than familiar with this culture of police brutality. I saw the Minneapolis PD beat the shit out of quite a few citizens, including me multiple times, and I can also attest to how some of my buddies got their teeth bashed down their throats by a prior generation of these same city cops back in the eighties for the crime of trucking beer through the woods. They were beaten within an inch of their lives, but they were lucky because they were white. Choke holds and kneeling on necks were approaches reserved for people of color back then, just as they are now. That's why the streets this summer were full of marching, chanting protesters declining social distancing to make their voices heard.

Anyway, because I had the luxury of finding my footing again, I was doing just that. The canoe seemed more unstable than I remembered, but most of that unsteadiness was me trying to remember how to "forget" again. What I mean by this is that standing up in a canoe involves a lot of not paying attention to unconscious adjustments for weight and movement. But the more I kept clumsily casting, the less conscious I became about trying not to fall in. And the more I screwed up in placing that rope fly where I wanted it to go, and the more I tangled that fly line in the gear at my feet, the less attention I gave to maintaining balance. After an hour out there, my balance came back naturally, and my attention became more focused on trying to refigure out the mechanics of the fly rod and the general technique of stripping in line.

It'd been a few years since I had a fly rod in my hands, and at this point, I couldn't cast more than twenty feet. But casting forward and whipping back, then back and forth and back and forth, and strip-strip-stripping the line in, I started getting into a rhythm. I was also working on flicking the rod tip to make the fly twerk through the water.

The problem, though, was that there were no gar to be seen, and according to the experts, the best way to hook a gar on a fly is to spot a gar, target that gar, plop the fly nearby, and hope for a connection, which wasn't happening. As usual, I was bumbling around, trying to get a handle on the basics again.

But that's what I needed to do to consistently fail in order to succeed. And looking ahead, I foresaw a lot of failures because, this type of fishing, it just didn't come naturally to me. I'd never done it in my youth, so it was as alien as bullfighting, which is why I kept at it.

ꝏ  ꝏ  ꝏ

It was time to go back to YouTube fly-fishing school. My search words were *fly fishing gar*, and they brought up a host of amateur anglers hosting their own how-to videos in the trendy style of self-produced fishing shows. It was sort of sad to watch these guys trying to fill a void in their lives by showing off their expertise, but because these videos had the most hits, it was likely they could help me out.

The first video I watched was posted by a self-proclaimed "Okie" who was "white trash fishing" for gar with his pal Rattlesnake Mike. They were in a spot beneath a dam, the water was moving swiftly, and they were casting rope flies into the current. I was mainly watching to see how they held their rods, and if they stripped the line in. It turned out they were reeling in, and they caught a bunch of longnose this way.

Then I watched some kid who fancied himself a comedian and kept plugging in "fun facts" about various species of gar. He had a lot to say about rope flies and how to target gar, but this was stuff I already knew. I watched him until I couldn't stand his pretending to be a TV personality any longer.

After that, I watched some guy in a kayak hauling gar in on traditional flies. It was pretty cool seeing the fish sidle up next to his lures and snap to the side because of their peripheral vision. When he hooked them, he'd strip the line in, which I decided I'd do instead of reeling.

The best idea I got out of studying those videos was to find some moving water and let the current work for me. If the water was moving, and if I was upstream of the fly, it could remain in the water longer and attract gar longer. And if there were gar swimming around in moving water, that meant they were there for a reason, like feeding. Plus, if they were already moving around, they'd probably be up for taking a chomp out of anything cruising by that resembled a baitfish.

So I went down to the Lake Conway Dam, where gar carcasses can be found all summer long littering the shores. The gar swim up Palarm Creek to get to the lake, and the spillway stops them. Shad congregate in that spot, so there are often a lot of gar in there, which bowhunters shoot up, then toss on the banks to stink up the entire county.

Sure enough, a few gar husks were lying there, flies swarming all around them as I got out on the concrete wall and began casting under the dam. The flow was assisting me as predicted, but because there were no gar, it looked like I'd be framing this outing as another practice casting session.

Some comic relief, however, happened when I stepped off the wall thinking it would only be a few inches down. Wrong-O! It was a five-foot drop to the bottom of that pool, and as I splashed in up to my neck, cellphone and everything, I couldn't help laughing at my klutzy self. Completely drenched and looking around, I scrambled back up on the wall. Nobody had seen my blunder. Anyway, I kept on casting, and finally got that rope fly twenty-five feet out.

Working my way downstream, I came to an area where some older guys were sitting on buckets and fishing with bobbers. I was a bit self-conscious fly fishing in front of them when it was clear there weren't any trout in these warm muddy waters. I also suspected they saw the flaws in my casting, but I kept at it until I got that fly thirty feet out.

In the end, it was a garless afternoon. But, as I tried to console myself, that's what makes for suspense. If I would've gone out there and got a gar, the story would've been over without any striving, which is the equivalent of a narrative lacking conflict. As I tell my students, that's not anything anyone wants to read. You gotta have hurdles to overcome, or no one's gonna give a damn.

&#x2053;   &#x2053;   &#x2053;

THE NEXT DAY was too windy to take the canoe out on the lake, so I launched the *Lümpabout,* which is a fifteen-foot 1950s run-about motorboat with batwing tailfins, a craft that I've been patching for fifteen years. I dug it out of a Missouri reservoir, where someone purposely sank it. It's spray painted with green and yellow stripes, and there's a 25-horsepower outboard on the back. More importantly, the bow can serve as a casting platform since it's two feet above the water and allows for room to maneuver.

Anchoring off the lily pads, I got to work. All former instruction was gone, and the wind was blowing at twelve miles per hour. Two and ten, the standard clock-based method for envisioning where to launch and release a fly, had become a matter of rookie intuition as I whizzed that lure back and forth, usually three or four times before releasing. I was getting pretty good at pointing the rod at where I wanted the rope fly to go, and half the time it was landing near the spots I chose. But other times, because of the wind, it would boomerang back and spin orbits around my torso until it finally came to rest in a knotted snarl, the apparitions of my former casting coaches frowning from the Phantom Zone (sorry Bill, sorry Drew).

This comedy of tangles went on for hours as I moved from spot to spot, observing the weed line from above. There were no gar in sight, but that didn't matter. I'd caught a spotted gar five years ago while blind-casting a rope fly along some random lily pads, but that was with a spinning reel. That fish had come up out of nowhere, and I was sure this could happen again.

In the meantime, with the wind at my back, I was sometimes able to zing that thing almost forty feet. My accuracy was also increasing as this failure to connect led to three realizations:

First, I'd gone out there to cast along the lily pads, but since there was no hook on that rope fly, I could actually cast right into them. This type of lure could be pulled through the plant life to areas where it would sink, and then I could make it swish and kick for any chilling-out gar looking up.

Secondly, I discovered that you can always watch the fly in the air. Just because you're back-casting doesn't mean you can't turn your head and keep your eye on the fly. I discovered you can always turn your head and make sure the lure doesn't get caught on something, which is preferable to being lazy and thinking you know where it is.

And thirdly, I could make the wind work for me. It was offering me the opportunity to get another ten feet out of my final forward cast, which began approaching fifty feet, so I should take advantage of that. And I did. And for the first time, I started getting an adrenal rush out of seeing the line unloop in the air and land further out than expected. Not only that, I was impressed by the strength my casts were starting to demonstrate, even though every time I missed my mark, Bill and Drew were slapping their foreheads inside mine.

Moving into an opening inside a lily pad field, the depth wasn't more than two feet. Some shad were popping, and there were occasionally fins swirling on the surface. I couldn't see what kind of fish were causing these disturbances, but then I saw a stocky gar hunkering under a lily pad. It moved off as I cast nearby, so that was a no-go. And then a lot more no-goes.

Again, it was another practice session.

$$\infty \quad \infty \quad \infty$$

THAT'S WHAT I told myself, but I wasn't buying it. All this screwing around wasn't getting me anywhere. I needed to take it to the next level, and I knew what was missing from the equation: mass gar. That's what I needed, a honey hole filled with tons of gar stacked on top of each other, raring to snap at whatever landed in their midst.

This meant contacting those in the know because, at this point, every cast that wasn't targeting a visible gar was a wasted cast. Practice was over. It was time to get on top of this by getting on top of gar!

I emailed Lindsey Lewis at US Fish and Wildlife. Without question, he was the state gar authority. He worked with the Arkansas Game and Fish Commission, with gar researchers at the University of Central Arkansas (UCA), and on gar restoration projects with the Department of Arkansas Heritage. He once held the state record for shortnose on rod and reel, and if anyone knew where they were concentrating, it was him.

I also got on a couple of chat rooms, one for Ozark anglers and the other for Arkansas hunters, asking where the gar were bunching up right now. The Ozark anglers replied immediately. Some guy named Dutch recommended "Pom north of Nemo on the east side in the great big flat cove," adding, "Don't throw them back." Ranger520vx echoed "Pomme," and an angler that went by "wily" suggested "strip pits in Kansas." Quillback said to go "between Big M and Shell Knob on Table Rock," where they're "pretty easy to find in the summer and early fall." Similarly, snagged in outlet 3 responded, "Lower Meramec has them." But these places were all out of state during a deadly pandemic, and no one was saying for sure where they were schooling in the present tense.

Then I sent an email to Cotter Trout Dock up in the Ozarks. Their website bragged about clients catching "Arkansas tarpon," so I inquired if they were guiding for gar at the moment. The Upper Buffalo was probably too shallow to float, but maybe they knew some backwaters. Of course, this was a last resort. I really didn't want to be dealing with the complexities of fishing with guides during COVID, and I was hoping to find a gar hole closer to home, hopefully in Central Arkansas.

Luckily, Lindsey responded later that day, replying that I "might try going to Aplin and taking the first dirt road to the right past the Fourche La Fave Bridge." He told me this road would take me to a low-water crossing on the South Fork of the Fourche where there are usually some longnose hanging out in pools and riffles.

Bingo! That's exactly what I was looking for: a new, off-the-beaten-path place not too far away. And since it was a sunny day, it made sense to hop in the Jeep and cross the Toad Suck Dam.

It was a stunning drive through the river valley, which was slightly obscured by a once-in-a-century dust storm called "Godzilla" that had originated in the Sahara Desert. The cloud was 3,500 miles long, and it made for a hazy light diffusing through the 95-degree heat.

Within an hour, I arrived at the spot: a concrete crossing over a crystal-clear creek that sparkled like a mountain stream, with plant life along the banks. But down in the water, there were no gar piled so thick you could walk across their backs (as the popular saying goes). I only saw bass.

Well, hell! I wasn't about to give up and go home. That would be the equivalent of crying for a wambulance. Nope, I was gonna get out there and see what's up, so I began heading downstream to get more mileage out of each cast.

The creek was only three feet deep. There was no one around and not one piece of litter. It felt like I was up in the Rockies or out in the middle of Nowhere, Alaska. It was just me and the trees and the minnows and the wildflowers and shaley shelves to step upon beneath that strangely soft-lit sky.

As I worked my way downstream, I couldn't help considering where I was and what I was doing. On the surface, I basically looked like that guy fly fishing a mountain stream in a thrift-store painting. But beneath that, I was in my head, still trying to make sense of the difficulty I was having in bringing myself to actually study the science I'd pledged to investigate more. I was still trying to make sense of my contradictory role as someone who harms what he's trying to protect. My approach was clearly not an environmental one. And because my identity was based on environmental advocacy and spreading that gospel, I was having trouble processing this.

But soon I started feeling the grace. Working that stretch, whipping that rope fly back and forth, then dropping it exactly where I intended, I started feeling like I was in that film *A River Runs Through It*. My line was unfurling in great, high, sweeping arcs. The woods were lush and the air was sweet. Being part of all this, it got to the point that my concerns about what's environmentally correct and what's not stopped mattering because—

WHAMMO! I suddenly had the epiphany that this is why fly fishers do it. That is, it's not about catching fish as much as it is about standing in streams with mountains towering all around you. That's what it's all about: the solitude, the grandeur, the chirping birds and dragonflies, the timeless, technicolored glory of connecting with something larger, something primal, something that generations of anglers know in the memory of their marrow.

Maybe that's a bit dramatic, but that's what I felt, and that's where I was.

Still, that's all I caught in that spot.

Or in other words, I finally got it.

☒ ☒ ☒

ON MY SIXTH day into this mission, I decided to fully read the Johnny Carrol Sain garticle I'd been saving, which I'd only scanned before. It was about how he used to bowhunt gar in the Point Remove Wildlife Management Area near Morrilton, until he reflected on his actions enough to change his kill-em-and-leave-em mentality. That thought aside, I was reminded of that labyrinth of lakes and streams only thirty miles away. It was a place I'd seen a zillion gar, most of them killed with arrows, putrefying on the shores.

So I shot out there to check it out. In half an hour, I was smelling them before I saw them. The scent was heavy in the air, thick with the sugars of gar remains breaking down. There's just something fruity about the funk of massacred gar. And these gar, they hadn't died for food at all, or even sport. They were just shot to hell and left to fester, their shells scattered all over the place, some run over and flattened by trucks, others buzzing with flies while the maggots went to town. It was a scene I'd seen plenty of times, but this time, it really pissed me off that innocent, harmless fish had suffered so some bowhunting bozos could get their freak on.

I started at my regular spot, where a ditch converges with the creek draining out of Lake Cargill. A decade ago, I'd seen a snake in this stream that was as thick around as a soccer ball and was pulling itself over a log. That copper-colored serpent went on for what seemed to be a dozen feet, leading me to believe it was a python someone released.

The cryptozoological legends in this state are another thing I can't get enough of. Most of these tales come from nineteenth-century Ozark storytellers who saw something they couldn't explain, so they came up with narratives involving the supernatural. Stories of water panthers and lake monsters and hoop snakes and wampus cats then got amplified, recycled, retold, and offered again to new generations. When I need a break from fishing research, I frequently investigate the details behind such stories. These folktales are another reason I've got a crush on Arkansas.

As I began casting along the bank, I didn't see that monster snake, but I saw a few northern water snakes. They were swimming around, three feet long, and brown and stripy, while nearby, rotting under the high, hot sun with their heads shot off lay the carcasses of even more harmless snakes.

Crossing a concrete bridge and looking down, I happened to see a nice, wide gar moseying out from under me. But by the time I peeled out enough line to begin casting, it had merged into the murk.

That's when this guy came out of the woods with an impressive stringer of largemouth hanging over his shoulder. He had nearly a dozen, some of them weighing four pounds or more. I waited on the bridge for him.

"Looks like a good haul," I told him.

He stood a bit too close to me, dark skinned and grinning back, his mask beneath his chin. Mine was in my pocket. No state mandates had been issued yet, but they were on the way. When I asked him if he'd seen any gar, he replied, "Yeah, lots of them. They're stacked up in there, fifteen thick. Thirty-pounders! Big ones!"

"I'd be glad to get a small one," I said.

"Take that trail," he advised, "and follow the bank. You'll see them."

"Thanks," I said.

"You catch a lot of gar on that?" he asked, indicating the rope fly.

"No," I said. "I'm not very good," a comment we both laughed at.

Moving on, I hit the trail and followed it into a ferny jungle. Cutting through the thorny vines, I found the creek, where a sunbaked mud bank allowed me to follow it downstream from an elevation of two to ten feet above the water. Because the sun was right above and filtering through the trees, there were a lot of sunny patches.

Then suddenly, I spotted a two-foot gar sunning on the surface. Before I knew it, I was letting out line in the air. This was something I hadn't done for years and had forsaken for the technique of uncoiling line at my feet. It was also something I used to be adept at, but a skill I'd forgotten. At that moment, though, it became second nature again. Each time I cast forward, I stripped out three more feet, and each time I cast back, I automatically released two or three feet more. The fly landed near the gar, but the splash spooked it, and it sank into the cooler depths.

I kept on going, occasionally seeing a gar or two. If there weren't trees blocking my casts, I'd take a shot. Letting the line out in the air was becoming more and more intuitive. And sometimes, when a gar was treading and I really wanted to cast to it, I'd find myself on the offensive, throwing more snap into it, not just pointing my rod tip where I wanted the fly to go, but stabbing the air to make it go there. And because of that extra bit of determination, that proactive, mission-fueled grit to get what I'd come to get, I started whizzing those flies right smack in front of those gar.

At one point, the rope fly landed a few feet short. The gar I was targeting couldn't even see my out-of-range lure, so I was about to start stripping it in when another gar arose out of nowhere. I saw its underjaw as it came up and slowly rolled toward the fly. Restraining myself from jerking the fly away, I tried tugging it toward me inch by inch. The rolling gar then took a snap, and I felt its weight. It was on!

But the electrical thrill that shot through my circuitry caused me to set the lure too hard. It popped right out of its mouth. Nevertheless, I had connected! And I was getting closer to meeting my objective.

Continuing on, I spent another hour gar-spotting along the creek, getting scratched up by the thorns and casting when the trees permitted. I went half a mile downstream looking for the place where that bass fisherman told me the creek opened up and the gar just grew on trees, but I never found it.

Heading back, I happened upon a skinny little gar chilling out on the surface. It was about ten feet upstream from me, and because it was looking the other way, I had the advantage. The bank was eight feet straight up, and since I didn't have to do any complicated casting, all I had to do was let out a few yards, zing that line back and forth twice, and release.

The cast was perfect. It landed right next to the gar, which turned and snapped, and the strands actually snagged its teeth. I waited a second before applying any tension, and the rope fly leapt right out of its beak.

That gar then followed a lure half its size to a point right beneath my feet, where it snapped again and missed. We kept that game going for two more minutes, me jigging the fly back and forth, that little fellow so intent on getting its prey that it didn't bother looking up to see a six-foot human standing right over it.

In those couple of minutes, it snapped a few times, and a few times it got those strands in its fangs. That gar was really intrigued, but the fibers kept coming free. After another minute, it deduced that what it was chasing tasted like string, so it sank down and faded away. Then I was back in the parking lot.

But because I had found the spot, it was now a matter of coming back and spinning the gar roulette wheel until it finally landed on my number. If I stuck to that tactic, the odds were I would connect. It might take a week, it might take the whole summer, it might take years, but I didn't care. So what if it was nearly a hundred degrees! So what about the ticks and chiggers! So what if my T-shirt was sopping with smears and sweat! I was committed to coming back, and those gar weren't going any-where.

&#x2180; &#x2180; &#x2180;

SOMETIME DURING THE following week of off-and-on rain, which kept me from returning, a reply came in from Cotter Trout Dock. The human who replied told me they sometimes catch gar while fishing for smallmouth bass, but they don't make intentional trips for gar. I was also told that the local fly guides didn't believe it was possible to catch a gar on a fly rod, the human adding, "We have some wire leaders to use with spinning rods for gar fishing, but I don't imagine you would be able to tie that on a fly rod."

Groaning from this news, I grabbed my fly rod (which did indeed have a steel leader tied to the tippet) and set off for Point Remove in quest of the "impossible gar."

It was extremely humid and sticky out, and the water was shallower when I got there, two feet beneath its previous depth. This allowed for more visibility.

Following the creek, there were absolutely no gar at all, which probably meant they were holing up somewhere cooler and deeper. So I went past the spot I'd stopped the prior time and eventually came to a wide open hole surrounded by what I can only describe as "quickmud," which could swallow someone whole if one was stupid enough to test it.

But in that hole, I saw a gar. Then another. And over by the shore, pretending to be a stick, hovering in a few inches of water, was another.

Holy garhole! I had discovered it. This was the mythical place that bass angler had told me about.

I was on the downward edge of it, about forty feet away. Without wind, this was the extent of my cast. I made several sloppy attempts to get that fly out to those gar, and they all fell short. I had to get closer.

But to get closer, I'd have to cross that soupy mud. If I made it, I'd be on a sandbar right in front of them sticking out like a sore thumb. But mostly, it would be foolish to plunge right into that muck.

So that's what I did, instantly sinking in past my knees, which wasn't about to stop me. I kept on moving, knowing that if I stopped I'd sink in further. If that happened, I'd get bogged down. And if I fell down, that would be it for me, because I was risking my life for gar.

Squishing and sloshing and slogging through, I finally made it to dry land, got down as low as I could, and crawled to the optimum spot. Since there was no way I could see them from that angle, I had to stand up. Maybe, I figured, if I stood as still as I could, pretending to be a tree, they'd buy what I was selling. It made sense to try this idea because that's what gar do; they make their prey think they're sticks.

For the next forty minutes, I stood there in the broiling sun, employing their own strategy. It was a hundred degrees, and the heat index was 110. Not only that, I was now on antibiotics for an infected tick bite, and my doctor had told me to avoid the sun because it would burn the crap out of my skin. But the way I saw it, a severe sunburn was a small price to pay for getting a gar on a fly rod.

Every once in a while, only moving one arm, I'd zip that rope fly back and forth, then release it into the gar hole. They were swimming around out there like no tomorrow, sometimes in packs of four or five, most of them not much longer than a foot and a half, but a few were nearly three feet long and as thick around as a can of Dinty Moore Beef Stew. There were spotteds and longnose and shortnose in there, all of them visible down to the markings on their tails.

Sometimes I'd land the rope fly a few feet past a gar and strip it in. I always tried to bring the lure up next to their eyes, but the line often crossed their snouts. Several times they felt it and zoomed away.

I must've made six dozen casts. The rope fly would land nearby, and the gar would phlegmatically roll toward the splash. Sometimes they'd snap. Other times they'd ignore the lure. I actually made a few connections, but it looked like the guides at Cotter Trout Dock were right. It was not possible.

The tree thing, on the other hand, was working. There was always a gar to cast to, and they weren't without interest in the fly.

Sweat was running down my ribs, and I was starting to feel dehydrated. It was bugging me that I hadn't brought any water, but what was bugging me more was I hadn't been studying the hard science for this quest, which I'd convinced myself was necessary to provide guidance for others. My fixation on the pain I continued to create for fish was definitely eclipsing this mission, but maybe this wasn't an either/or situation in which one approach negated the other. Perhaps I could address environmental concerns while dealing with ethical ones as well, etcetera etcetera.

This interior monologue went on and on as I stood stock-still in the dizzying sun. The gar were being fooled by my tree disguise, all except for one who followed the rope fly in, looked up, made eye contact, and—be it a hallucination or not—actually winked at me.

I started feeling woozy, blurs of light flashing in the sides of my sight, yet I kept on casting in this place which most would describe as inhospitable. With all the thorns and snakes and biting bugs and extreme heat, places like these are not manicured gardens conducive for family outings. But what I see in places like this are still-surviving, still-wild environments continuing to exist in an increasingly developed world, which is another reason I'm devoted to Arkansas. In a way, it's still the frontier, at least in terms of the habitats it provides for creatures that engage the imagination.

After about a hundred failed connections, I spied a pack of three small gar out for a leisurely stroll. I plopped my fly right in the center of their triangulation, and they all turned, arcing toward it. Because they were all going for the same prey, a competitive spirit kicked in. Each gar gave a snap of its tail, and as the rope fly sank, the three amigos followed it down.

Okay, I had to keep the line tight, and I had to keep that fly moving so it looked like a minnow swishing. Slowly, carefully, I stripped in a couple of inches—

ZANG! The tip bent, the line went taut, and the weight was definite. Fish on!

I was now at that point where I told myself I'd strip the line in rather than reeling, but something else happened instead. It was instinct informing me to do what I usually do when I hook a fish on a beach: run for higher ground. I didn't give it a chance to leap, I didn't give it a chance to thrash, I just towed it straight through the water and up onto the muddy sand.

POW! I had it: the impossible gar on a rope fly! Caught through a tactic that had taken a decade to finally make happen.

The gar was flipping and flopping when I grabbed it, a superbly perfect shortnose, thirteen inches long, fibers wound around its beak. It was silvery gray on top and white on the sides.

It took a few minutes to work the threads free, and in that time its tail turned red. This was a sign of stress, and I wasn't going to put it through any more. As I told that bass angler, I'd be glad to catch a small one, and I was. In fact, I saw no reason to stay there casting for more. Sure, there were heftier gar in there, but I was more than satisfied: I was buzzing, humming, crackling with electrical currents.

"Mission accomplished!" I told that slightly smirking gar and tossed it back from whence it came, now totally confident that my concerns about not hurting fish were as valid as my need to understand the science, for two reasons specifically:

First, because the goal of suggesting highly studied solutions to environmental problems is as focused on preserving species as treating fish humanely is, it was now clear to me that anything anyone does to help fish out is an act of ecological preservation. Period.

And secondly, because using rope flies decreases the likelihood of harming gar, this suggests there are other methods to discover for catching fish without hurting them, so I needed to get cracking on finding those.

Then heading upstream, I made my way back to the increasingly paranoid, scary-as-hell, new abnormal for everyone.

## CHAPTER 12

# MONSTER FISHING TEXAS
## TARPON ALLEY IN THE AGE OF CORONAVIRUS

THE SHITHAMMER HAD descended, not only on the world, crashing economies and bringing international travel to a standstill, but on my plans to monster fish globally. My plans for researching massive skate in Scotland had been smashed, and so had my expedition for goliath grouper in Florida. But after three months in lockdown, Texas was within reach, and I was hell-bent on finding out what lurked in Tarpon Alley.

So Lea and I, we got out of Arkansas, where corona cases were spiking like half the other states. The year 2020 was in the throes of earning its reputation as the most crippling year in world history in over a century, but because I had to get in some out-of-state monster fishing to satisfy the cells screaming inside me, we were heading down to Galveston, where the whole Houston area was experiencing a major surge in COVID.

At this point, the verdict hadn't come out about safety concerns for restaurants, so the grocery stores were mobbed with folks buying food to cook at home. Lea had made a bunch of calzoney things to either eat cold or heat up in a microwave so we wouldn't have to eat out. The idea was that we'd get to our hotel, then wipe down everything and only leave to fish Tarpon Alley, which is something I'd been trying to do for six years but kept having to put off because of death and other distractions.

Captain Mike Williams was legendary for hauling two-hundred-pound, state-record tarpon out of the Gulf of Mexico for nearly fifty years. He also guided for monster sharks, and there were sailfish and wahoo and other exotics in Tarpon Alley, a migration corridor he had discovered and mapped out. He'd even coined the term for this specific ocean current traveling the entire perimeter of the Gulf where there's a certain temperature range that tarpon follow. This pathway is generally recognized as a two-mile band running parallel to the Galveston beachfront with depths between thirty and forty feet. The hundred-plus-pound tarpon were now running, their super-silver, torpedo-like bodies culminating in upturned jaws capable of swallowing a Butterball turkey. And because there were also freakazoid hammerheads in those waters, and because all it took was a day's drive to get there, we hopped in the Jeep and took off.

I'd talked to Captain Williams on the phone and had asked him how he approached pandemic fishing. He told me he required masks to be worn on his boat, and that he kept a five-gallon bucket of bleach water on deck so clients could clean and sanitize. That's exactly what I'd wanted to hear, and because I'd have the opportunity to interview him about the environmental changes he'd witnessed in his five decades of catching and releasing more monster fish in this fishery than anyone in the world, I was ready to risk it.

Since mid-March, Lea and I had been living in a world of online teaching, social distancing, Zoom meetings, and buying $400 worth of groceries in one shot to keep us from having to go out. But it was another story in Texas, where stopping at a gas station in Beaumont and donning our masks (mine with a shark, hers with a collage of dictionary words), we got a lot of lingering stares from those whose eyes made it clear that they weren't gonna give up their God-given rights by wearing no mask. "Go back to where you came from," those stares blared, "and take your China virus with you!"

We made it down to Galveston, though, where another scene met our eyes: the crush of crowds along the seawall and nobody wearing masks at all. Moms and dads and kids were packed together, flowing in and out of gift stores and ice cream shops and sunglass huts while pedestrians swarmed like penguins on parade, bumping and brushing against each other. The hotel swimming pools were oversized Petri dishes full of splashing children and germ-coated beach balls. We could see throngs of customers crammed into seafood buffets while the beaches buzzed with boogie boarders and sunbathers. Everywhere, airborne aerosols were floating from spittle lips to nostrils sucking oxygen, which didn't up the comfort factor.

In other words, after an entire spring and half a summer of sheltering in place, after forty-five million Americans had lost their jobs in a recession and two million people had tested positive, and especially after 117,000 people in the United States had died from this virus (a figure estimated to double by September and double again by the end of the year), America was open for business again.

&#x2627; &#x2627; &#x2627;

AT SIX THIRTY in the morning we were ready and waiting at the marina, but it wasn't Captain Williams who met us there. It was some beer-bellied, coach-looking guy with a red-white-and-blue baseball cap who used to be a mortgage broker.

That was a disappointment. And so was the fact that he wasn't wearing a mask, nor was there a promised bucket of bleach water.

Choosing not to make a fuss, we got on board and wore our masks until it didn't seem necessary. Cruising out and into the Gulf, we were upwind of him and had enough space between us.

When we got to the spot, the sun was shining hard and hot, and my inner kid was buzzing with anticipation. Lea, however, wasn't feeling this exhilaration. The swells were raising and drop-ping the boat, and her seasickness pills weren't kicking in. But at least there were plenty of pelicans swooping down and dolphins surfacing here and there as we set up.

Pretty soon, we had three sturdy poles with oversized bait-casting reels in their holders, and we had three balloons out, each dangling a menhaden (a common silvery baitfish) eight feet beneath the surface. Our guide then felt it necessary to state his opinion on the "virus hoax" and the "rioting" of protesters. "Out of control" was the term he used, along with one of those bogus talking points about the flu being more dangerous.

Lea and I shared an eyeball roll but kept our mouths shut. In the interest of changing the subject, I began my questioning. What were the environmental factors affecting changes in these waters? Were the oscillating numbers of flounder and snapper in recent years making a difference with the fish he guides for? What about mercury and PCBs making blue crab and all fish in Galveston Bay too toxic to consume? And how about that big old oil spill in 2014?

The replies I received were pretty much one-word answers. He essentially confirmed what I had read, and we could see the tankers surrounding us, along with refineries and chemical plants and petrochemical smokestacks and vats. Further out, the oil rigs were visible too.

Still, I gotta give him some credit for calling our attention to the dredging vessels that degrade ecosystems by sucking up sand to replenish the eroding beaches. He also remarked on the dead zones forming in the Gulf as a result of nitrates and insecticides draining down from backyards along with agricultural runoff that depletes oxygen and kills off vast expanses of sea life. With all that coming down the Mississippi, choking out oxygen and suffocating fish, one of the world's largest hypoxic zones wasn't too far from us.

That's the stuff I typically study when focusing on fisheries. But this time, it didn't seem like this was the story. At that moment, I also had another concern: the dramatic swells affecting Lea. She was holding her stomach, but I'd seen her suffer worse. Especially in the Gambia, where we thought we'd be fishing on the river, but our guide took us out into the rising, diving ocean. Lea took a hit for the team that day, emptying her stomach multiple times, dry-heaving after that, then laying on the deck under the relentless African sun. Our guide had asked her if she wanted to go back, but she had opted to stay out and recover, which she eventually did.

Then suddenly, out there in Tarpon Alley, there were baitfish breaking all around us. Something was forcing them up. Something was coming through. The water turned white from all the flipping and foaming, and instantly a balloon went down. I grabbed that rod, the guide flipped the switch, and the circle hook did its thing.

"REEL! REEL!" he ordered.

As I did, Lea leaned over the rail and proceeded to chum for us. This poetic world traveler who'd been tossed by twenty-foot waves deep-sea-fishing with me in the Dominican Republic; who'd held it together in a taxi squealing through esophagus-dropping hairpin turns in the Andes; who'd always made the point that the word *travel* comes from *travail*; who, because her medication wasn't working, was now retching over the rail.

"It's a jack crevalle," the guide said when it came into view, flashing like a lime-green gleam because of the diffraction. It was a three-foot-long, thirty-pound blur and it was fighting hard, but I was more concerned about Lea.

"It's okay," she said. "Everywhere you travel…there's going to be some discomfort. It's part of the deal."

I kept on cranking in the jack, a species I'd already caught in Mexico. But when you got one on your line, you don't complain. And when a second one hits in the midst of this, hell yeah, you're going to fight that one too, even if you're targeting other fish.

When I got that first one up to the boat, the guide grabbed it, pulled it in, then handed me the other rod. I got the second one up, which was almost as large, and he lifted it in as well. But before we could get a picture, he tossed them both back.

"Now you've got your memory of catching your first jack," he told me. And with that, he brought in the remaining line, fired the outboards up, and headed back to port even though Lea was feeling better and was now ready to fish. But he didn't give a damn, and his policy was clear: if someone on board gets sick, the fishing trip is over—even if I'd already paid for two full days.

Whatever.

&#8747;&#8747;&#8747;   &#8747;&#8747;&#8747;   &#8747;&#8747;&#8747;

SINCE WE NOW had to spend a whole day doing something else, I tried to write. I also did some research on fishery problems in the Galveston area, then read a chapter from my Zane Grey book.

In one particular narrative, Zane's buddy Bob was hauling in an unknown fish, when dark fins emerged. The head of a tuna exploded on the surface, and Bob began pulling it in. A colossal shark suddenly breached, clenching the tuna beneath the gills. Bob fought as hard as he could, until he fell back with nothing on his line except a severed tuna head. A dozen enormous sharks then fought each other for that head, which Bob dangled over them. It was a hideous yet spectacular image, with Grey describing the sharks as fighting like wild tigers.

Oh man! That's exactly why we were in Galveston studying Tarpon Alley. This was another form of the dream I'd seen exponentially in my head, which I'd come here to experience. And looking around the air-conditioned room, Lea zonked out on her non-drowsy Dramamine, I couldn't sit there any longer.

Donning my mask, I left the hotel and crossed the street to see what the anglers on the jetty were catching, and to see if I

could nab a crab on the rocks. But when I got out to where people were fishing, something pulled me further out.

Against my better judgment, I entered a rinky-dink gift
shop. It was also the entrance to the pier. It cost twelve dollars
to go out there, and there were poles to rent, bait to buy, and a
full bar.

Now knowing what I had to do, I went back to the hotel and
rustled up Lea. We put on our sunblock and masks, went back to
the pier, and the next thing you know, I'm jigging shrimp off the
bottom to find out what can be caught off the beach.

We were each enjoying a preposterous margarita the size
and shape of a two-foot bong and checking out the pier-fish-
ing culture. It was an incredibly diverse crowd. People brought
carts out filled with lawn chairs and surf rods and radios playing
country music, and everyone was in good spirits. Folks were literally rubbing elbows, kids were running around touching stuff,
strangers were helping strangers unhook fish, and everyone was
acting like nothing was wrong in their various, glorious states of
denial.

But we had our own space all for ourselves because we were
the only ones wearing masks. Every once in a while, I even threw
in a cough or two.

The first fish I caught was a bluefish. It was a missile-shaped
predator with a strong underjaw full of hacksaw-looking teeth.
This mini-monster wasn't even a foot long, so I threw it back,
then caught a hardhead catfish which I jokingly named "The
Galveston Goonch." It had wiggly whiskers, but it also had
needly spikes coming out of its fins that could skewer a hand like
an exacto knife. I caught a few of those cats, and then some sand
trout with lavender sheens.

In the course of two more absurdaritas, I also caught a whit-
ing, which had a weird, lone barbel under its chin which lent to
a pitiful expression. That fish looked like someone was giving it
a wedgie, so it was easy to sympathize with.

I must've caught two dozen fish on that pier, which gave me a better understanding of what was in the neighborhood. Other people then added to that knowledge with the fish they caught. I saw a couple of technicolored Spanish mackerel snapping razor fangs. This fish was definitely prized, and cause for communal backslaps. Someone even caught an emaciated sand shark a couple feet long.

But the best fish I saw was something I'd been pursuing for years and still haven't caught. It was a stingray the diameter of a basketball hoop, with extraterrestrial eyes staring up from an uncanny head straight out of outer space. It was tan on top and creamy underneath and its batlike shape reminded me of those Teflon-coated stealth bombers.

It weighed over twenty pounds, and since it was too heavy to be pulled up on the line it had been caught on, the guy lowered a rope with some sort of bracket that caught the leader. He was able to pull the stingray up to the boardwalk, where it slashed around, swinging its bloody scythe of a tail, which I got too close to when snapping photos. But I tell you what, I'd rather be within inches of getting my shins sliced open than within a few feet of the unmasked, gasping crowd that surged forth as I stepped back, mask now below my chin.

Why? Because I'd been drinking margaritas, and I was letting my guard down. Realizing this, I slipped the mask back on and fished until we wavered our way back to our room and turned on the news.

Up in Tulsa, the president of the Divided States of America was about to hold a Juneteenth campaign rally in which nineteen thousand mask-hating superspreaders were getting ready to cram themselves into an indoor arena and yell and cheer with no social distancing whatsoever. Oklahoma health officials were wigging out because, as we kept hearing on the radio, "So many people are over COVID, but COVID is not over yet."

⚓ ⚓ ⚓

THE NEXT MORNING, I went out without Lea, who was still fuming about that guide. Not only had he forgotten my first name the previous day (which, incidentally, was his own), he'd kept calling her "ma'am," even after he'd been reminded what her name was.

The seas were less rough as we shot to a spot where I figured I should make my objectives known, so I explained what I was going for, which was any type of fish in Tarpon Alley that could be described as "monstrous." This is info I'd given Captain Williams, but it never made it to this guy, who couldn't care less what I wanted because he was there to do the exact same job he does for every client he takes out.

One interesting thing about the spot we arrived at was that it was along a floating belt of flotsam and sargassum, which is a ruffly, brownish-orange seaweed also known as gulfweed. It's actually an algae, and despite its name, it doesn't come from the Sargasso Sea. Rather, the Sargasso Sea (where both American and European eels breed) earned its name from this stuff. More to the point, I'd read that sharks follow sargassum because it attracts smaller fish which hide and feed in it.

It was thirty feet deep as we baited up with three balloons dangling dinner. Within minutes, the first shark struck. It took off, and I let it run for a few seconds. Then reeling in, the line went taut, and a four-foot shark leapt straight up.

I'd never seen a shark jump before, and the way the sunlight struck it from behind gave me a glimpse of its silhouette. It was totally black and totally snapping, and then it landed SMACK on the water.

I had my GoPro going, strapped to my head, which was a new type of technology for me. For the last two months I'd been getting a handle on using its video function while checking my lines on Lake Conway. Since I didn't have Lea with me today (who sometimes records the fishing action), I'd brought this camera along to document the experience. It's a tool that captures one of the primary reasons why I fish via direct, action-packed images of lunkers busting up from the underworld.

But back to that shark, which put up a ballsy fight. Unlike the dogfish I knew from Puget Sound (frequently compared to pulling up a log), this shark was all over the place. It was taking my line toward the props, but raising the pole and reeling in on the descent, I led it to the side of the boat. When I got it along-side, it suddenly ground right through the 250-pound mono-leader, and SNAP! It was off.

Nobody on board had touched the leader, but my guide declared it a caught fish. In my mind, though, it was a thirty-pound blacktip that got away with a hook down its throat.

We fished there for another half hour, and because nothing was going on, we moved to another spot. This one was forty-four feet deep and the water was rich in plankton. That's where I hooked another four-footer. It came boiling up to the surface, slashing and splashing and causing a commotion.

"It's a spinner," the guide told me.

"Can we bring it in the boat?" I asked.

"Nope," he told me, "too dangerous."

This is something I was used to hearing from shark-fishing guides, and it's something I accept. But because Captain Williams's website was full of anglers posing with sharks, I was hoping for a chance to get a shot. Another disappointment.

When I got the fish to the boat, the guide reached down and grabbed the line. He then hoisted the shark half out of the water, where it smacked against the boat. The light was hitting it right, and this time I got a good look at it, all white on the belly and bluish-gray on top. It had that classic signature dorsal fin, and its powerful jaws were gnashing away.

I was trying to get my cellphone out to take a picture, but before I could, it bit through the leader and flopped off. So again, another 250-pound leader bit the dust and a shark took off with a hook in it, which led me to wonder what these leaders are good for if they can't even hold a twenty-pound fish.

Then I hooked a smaller spinner, about ten pounds. The guide lifted this one right out of the water and severed the line. He wasn't going to take any chances trying to get the tackle back and said the steel would rust away.

The sun was now higher in the sky, which made it easier to see what was beneath the surface. When my rod bent double, I was psyched to feel what felt like a sixty-pounder. This one was a spirited fighter, peeling out ten feet of line for every five I reeled in. It took ten minutes of back-straining cranking to get it in, and then it was visible, down to its striated gills and what looked like a lateral line but was actually where its upper dark color met the white of its underside. It was another blacktip, minus the black tip commonly seen on the dorsal fin, but it did have a black tip on one of its front fins.

Not only that, it only seemed like a sixty-pounder because it had been foul hooked on a pectoral fin. So when I was pulling that thirty-pounder through the water, it had been coming in perpendicular to the boat, which caused a lot of drag.

SLASH! The guide cut the line, the shark swam off with a hook that no digestive acids could dissolve, and we moved on to another spot. When we stopped, there were thousands of menhaden everywhere, attracting dive-bombing pelicans and dolphins passing right under us.

Then another balloon went down. The rod was bowing and it felt like another sixty-pounder. I fought this one for another ten minutes, and when it finally came into view—

"A jack," he said.

It was flashing with an electric yellow luminescence, like when fish excite phosphorescent microorganisms which create blazing auras at night. But when that four-foot fish got to the surface, its color changed to alabaster on the sides and glowing neon-lemon on its fins.

It was the most monstrous jack I'd ever caught, and the guide let me hold this one and get a picture. Its head was the size of a baked alaska.

I let that fish go and got back to work. And it was work. My friend Catfish later asked why I wasn't jumping up and down and cheering on the YouTube video I posted called "Mark Spitzer Shark-Fishing Tarpon Alley June 2020." At first I couldn't answer that, but in reviewing the footage, I heard my own huffing and puffing increasing as the day wore on.

Part of this was because the equipment wasn't very good. Some of the eyelets on the rods were missing their ceramic linings, which didn't make for a smooth reeling in. Also, I had to constantly monitor the line on the spools and adjust where it went with my thumb or it would bunch up on the edges and grind things to a halt. And just as irritating, when I was reeling in and the balloon would go into the rod tip, that always added another layer of annoyance to contend with. Looking back, I don't understand why Mr. American Flag Cap didn't tell me to stop reeling so he could slide that hindrance down.

I caught three more thirty-pound blacktips and a fifteen-pound spinner that afternoon. In the end, it was seven sharks by my count (eight by his) and a jack.

Traveling back, it occurred to me that I was expected to give him a tip. But the tip I kept thinking of was left over from the day before and more along the lines of, "Hey, why don't you ask your clients if they want to go in before you decide that you know their health better than they do!"

I was also reflecting on the fact that the fishing hadn't been very fun, mostly because this guy was a dud. He was one of those guides I sometimes encounter who hook me up with fish, but he didn't care. He was in it for the paycheck, and maybe that's another reason I wasn't hooting and hollering when I brought those fish in. It was work. It was research.

And I didn't catch what I'd come to catch. And the sharks I caught, I never even got to touch one. I never touched jack except for a jack. It was like having some teenager at a pay pond bait every hook and unhook every fish: so uninvolved in getting messy that you have to question if that's really fishing. Plus, almost every shark line was slashed, leaving eight hooks in eight fish, which finally pushed me to seriously investigate how long hooks stay in fish.

What I discovered from the dearth of data on this subject was a 2010 paper by researchers from the Central Institute for Fisheries Technologies in India that concluded it took at least three hundred hours of salt-spray exposure for a barb to disintegrate.[1] An article on the blog *Begin to Fish* includes an interpretation of this study's data and states that this figure works out to three years in salt water, with a range of fourteen to fifty-one years for the rest of the hook to corrode in the ocean.[2] As for the rate of hook degradation due to gastric acids, a 2018 study of corrosion rates in sturgeon guts found that it took more than a year (399 days) for a standard sturgeon hook (which is smaller than a shark hook) to disintegrate only 34 percent.[3] The upshot being, whether hooks are stuck in the gut, or mouth, or throat, or anywhere, it takes years for them to rust away.

This never used to bother me. But now, something had gotten under my skin, even though what I felt couldn't compare to the red, raw, radiating burn of what was now lodged in eight fish who now had injuries because of my cavalier approach to getting what I want at the expense of what I want.

So when we docked, I thanked that guy and started heading off. But before I could get away, he offered me his hand to shake—on Texas's most record-breaking day so far: 4,246 new cases to be exact. This was at a time when fist- and elbow-bumping had become the norm because refrigeration trucks and ice-skating rinks were serving as temporary holding morgues for human cadavers piling up by the thousands. Not wanting to be rude, I accepted his hand and shook it. But as soon as I was out of sight, I broke out my Purell and washed my hands of what's-his-name.

ঔঔ   ঔঔ   ঔঔ

THE CLICHÉ "EVERYTHING'S bigger in Texas" sure wasn't true that day, at least by my standards. I'd been dreaming of ten-foot monster sharks and six-foot tarpon, but the fish I'd caught in that part of the Gulf weren't any bigger than the catfish I'd pulled from my own lake in Arkansas earlier that spring.

I have to remind myself, though, that I went to Texas to find out what lurked in Tarpon Alley, and I'd found a voracious, small fishery which reminded me of something else I'd read in *Tales of Fishing Virgin Seas*. When Zane Grey was fishing off the Galapagos Islands, he hooked a "game-fish class" shark that made him recall "the black-tipped shark of the Gulf Stream" and what he "had read about the mako-shark of New Zealand" (which is considered more vicious than the great white). Grey ended that passage by stating that he had discovered "a new kind of fish."[4]

Of course, it wasn't a new kind of fish species that Grey had discovered. He meant that in a figurative sense. What he discovered was how some sharks fight so hard and provide so much sport that they're deserving of being classified as "game fish."

And that respect, that's something I discovered as well, even if on a smaller scale. The blacktips and spinners I'd battled had proved to me that these were some of the most acrobatic fish to be caught in American waters. Not only that, but they're out there in huge, healthy numbers which reflect the robustness of a charter industry established to take advantage of a moderate-sized fishery sometimes offering larger fish.

Nevertheless, it strikes me that if Lea and I wouldn't have risked going out to investigate what's in Tarpon Alley, then we wouldn't have witnessed for ourselves the extreme divide between what some people *believe* is their right and what others *know* is unsafe as hell during a global pandemic. We also got a firsthand perspective on the growing division between people who embrace information provided by the sobering science of infectious disease authorities versus those who so easily accept the disinformation of political manipulation, the latter being enough to threaten all human life on this planet. Hence, it became clear to me that if you don't venture out and see such dangers for yourself, then all you've got is speculation—which might've been the safer route to have taken.

Driving back to the hotel, I realized that it was definitely time to stay closer to home. There were plenty of monster fish in my own backyard, and if there was ever a time to stay local, this was it.

Anyway, that night we watched *Jaws* again. A murderous menace was out in the ocean dismembering humans, so the chief of police had closed the beach. The mayor, representing the business sector, then overturned the chief's decision, and everyone dove in with their surfboards and snorkels and attitudes that all was fun and games.

And the rest, well…it's still pretty predictable.

## CHAPTER 13

# Translating Arkansas' Alligator Gar Management Plan into an Epic Monster Fatty

A MONKEY WRENCH HAD been thrown into my mission to monster fish the world, but I reminded myself that I already had. When the going was good, I'd pursued fantastic fish in Africa, Asia, Europe, Mexico, the Caribbean, South America, Canada, and all over the United States. I'd been able to haul in huge-ass sturgeon, demented piranhas, spasmodic tarpon, mammoth carp, elusive eels, berserk barracuda, and a mind-blowing bestiary of other jaw-dropping aquatics that few people on this planet have experienced. And because the driving force in my life now was the idea of *monster fishing the world and back,* and because I was back in Arkansas, I was accomplishing what I'd set out to do.

So now that I had come full circle and was lucky to be stuck in one of the country's most undiscovered, action-packed fisheries during a pandemic with a worldwide death toll of eight hundred thousand and rising, I had the chance to target one of the planet's first and foremost grotesques: the fish that got me started on all this; the fish that's never a disappointment to throw down with and always makes for a different story; but, primarily, the fish that always leads to unparalleled surges of adrenaline. It's just incomparable, the feeling that comes with that sudden first click, the spool spinning, the chemical burst informing you that you've locked on to a prehistoric predator.

That's why I was out on the Arkansas River fishing for Arkansas' first official state fish, thanks to a ten-year-old boy named Henry Foster from Fayetteville. He began his campaign in 2018 through a petition started on change.org. His message was, "Don't be a copy-catfish! Vote for Alligator Gar!" which he backed up with original cartoons to promote this massive, razor-fanged, gator-headed candidate for state fish.[1]

Henry's choice made sense to me, especially considering what alligator gar had been through in Arkansas. For eons there'd been no problem, but in the 1800s, settlers took aggressive measures to whittle gar numbers down through the use of guns, explosives, mob violence, you name it. Consequently, a whole bunch of bunk science arose from decades of refusing to recognize the value of gar. In the thirties, state agencies began coordinated efforts to wipe gator gar genetics off the map. Adding to this destruction, a highly destructive "sport" industry laid waste to this species in the fifties when international, big-game trophy hunters came to "The Natural State" to shoot 'em up. The result was a successful extirpation by 1960, meaning the state's top freshwater predator had been "cleansed" down to a non-reproducing number.

Since then, the most massive member of the gar family has returned to Arkansas because of the conservation efforts of state and federal agencies, universities, hatcheries, and the tireless work of assorted gar authorities with initiatives to educate the public. Still, I should also give a shout-out to global warming because the warmer the climate gets, the more precipitation there is; and the more rain there is, the more flooding there is, which provides gar access to their spawning grounds. Before 2010, the amount of flooding in this region had been limiting gator gar reproduction to an average of once every seven years. But in the last decade, there's been major flooding every spring.

Sometimes it's a one-hundred-year flood, but we also recently had a five-hundred-year flood. The cumulative effect of all this water in Arkansas being hundreds more gator gar supplementing their populations.

But back to Henry Foster's campaign, which got a lot of guff. There was this vocal state senator who argued against gar, claiming one had wrecked his tackle, so he sure as hell wasn't gonna vote for no trash fish like that. But there were also the commercial catfish farmers who wanted channel cats to be the official state fish and argued that catfish were entitled to this honor because of the commerce they created. Then there were the bass anglers and fly fishers who couldn't sign on to a lowly gar as state fish when their game fish brought in beaucoup tourists. But those fish, they were already state fish in other states.

Henry, however, made a unique argument for a unique fish that had never been in the limelight before, except when it was strung up in public squares to be gawked at for its man-eating mythology. Henry pointed out the great age of this living fossil and how cool it was. These were factors commanding respect along with the plain old fact that we brought these behemoths back from the brink. Also, they're in our waters right now, and at six, seven, and eight feet long, they're the second-largest freshwater fish on the continent, and they have a history of keeping rough fish (which destroy the nests and eggs of game fish) in check.

Toward the end of this controversy, the same state legislature whose greatest previous accomplishment was to pass the 2007 Apostrophe Act for the possessive form of *Arkansas* (thou shalt use an apostrophe S!) signed off on Henry's vision. But by the time that bill made it to the governor, the details had been tinkered with. For whatever small-minded reason, partisan meddlers had changed the language of the house bill to contain the word *primitive*, which left the door open for a more respectable fish to fill the contentious slot of overarching state fish at a later date. So even though the governor signed the bill, and even though alligator gar have been around millenniums longer than "the Arkansaw Territory" and the "Paleo" people who first lived here, our brand new state fish now had the adjective "primitive" slapped on it to remind folks that gar are second-class creatures that are not to be fully appreciated for what their monster fishiness can provoke in the imagination.

My reaction to that could only be *Screw 'em!* as I sat on a sandy shore, two full-grown sunfish on my lines. Each heavy-duty pole was rigged with eighty-pound woven line, and each had a Carolina rig on it with a steel leader and a quarter-sized circle hook. It was the end of summer, I was sipping a gin and tonic, the cicadas were blaring in the sweltering dusk, and I had a new mission: to catch a six-foot Arkansas alligator gar.

I also had Fishing Support Group's secret spot all to myself, where Goggle Eye had caught a five-foot-one gator gar earlier that summer. Turkey Buzzard had taken a hilarious photo of him releasing that fish, all masked up with his over-the-top, rhinestone-studded, hot-pink cowboy hat.

My plan was to hang out until a quarter past ten and then start packing up. If I didn't get a bite by then, my odds weren't very good. Most bites happen at twilight or dusk or right after sunset, but the one Goggle Eye caught had come in at six thirty in the evening. The summer before, Turkey Buzzard had caught a five-and-a-half-footer off this beach an hour earlier than that. But for me, the most magic time is always at night.

So I waited and waited, and nothing happened, except the purpling of the sky as a soft, piney scent drifted down from the tree line behind. There was also something pungent in the air, a decaying, rotting smell, more vegetal than animal.

Nothing was breaking on the surface and no gar were rolling. Then 10:15 came along. Then 10:16 and 10:17. Then 10:18. It was definitely time to go home. But at 10:19…*click.*

It was just one little tick from my big Penn reel that caused my whole body to snap, jump, leap toward the button. I hit it, and the spool spun free and began whizzing.

Holy crapola! It was a monster, the baitcaster unwinding at warp speed. The fish was taking out line, sometimes accelerating, sometimes winding down. It took two hundred yards out like it was nothing, and I could feel my heart hammering, the hair standing stiff on the nape of my neck. I was poised for the strike and ready to run up the beach: heart thumping, teeth gritting, all senses humming!

This is what it's all about: being connected to something so invisibly ginormous that bolts of lightning go screeching through meat. It had to be a six-foot gar, at least. Only a gar could blast so fast, so straight, so determinedly downstream! Then it stopped.

This was always the awkward instant, the moment in which everything itches like a rash. It usually lasts five to ten minutes, and then they run again.

I waited a minute, then another. But after three, I couldn't hold back. I knew it was a monster fish, and I knew I had a super sharp circle hook which would slide right into the crux of its jaws when I began reeling. So I did.

In my experience, gator gar are one of the hardest fish in the world to catch. Nine out of ten times you think you have a solid connection, you think you've got them on the line, you think there's no way they can get off. But if they weren't on in the first place, they were never on at all. That was the case in this situation. It had run six hundred feet for ten minutes straight and dropped the bait, which is always a letdown.

Deflated but still buzzing, I reeled in nothing.

Nonetheless, those are the odds I was used to, and that's what I had signed up for. Swearing my head off wasn't going to change anything. This wasn't the one out of ten. According to my math, I'd have to make nine more connections to bring a gator gar up on the sand. So the way I looked at it, I was once again one step closer to making my all-time favorite dream come true.

∞  ∞  ∞

UNDER THE LEADERSHIP of Eric Brinkman, Brett Timmons, and Jimmy Barnett, the Arkansas Game and Fish Commission has been on the cutting-edge in alligator gar fishery science for over a decade, sharing research with the international gar community through the Alligator Gar Technical Committee. This committed group of biologists, specialized ichthyologists, wildlife agents, hatchery workers, and university and private lab researchers, plus one rogue fish writer from the humanities, established Arkansas as a model for implementing the most avant-garde gar restoration work, especially in the area of data collection. Other innovative focuses of the AGFC's vision for rebuilding alligator gar populations included harvest management, habitat management, public outreach, and stocking projects. The mission statement of the 2017 *Arkansas Alligator Gar Management Plan* is, "*To manage and restore Alligator Gar populations in suitable waters of their historic range throughout Arkansas while providing a unique sport fishery*" (emphasis theirs).[2]

One of the commission's most novel approaches to sampling came from an obscure method for catching and releasing gator gar. They developed this approach a few years back, and there's a video on YouTube ("Arkansas Alligator Gar") that shows this method in action beneath the Felsenthal Dam on the lower Ouachita River. Fishery biologists throw out a float with three feet of steel leader and a standard size treble hook baited with hunks of buffalofish. They let the floats drift downstream, and when one goes under, they motor over, grab it, clip the line to a heavy-duty fishing rod, and the fight is on. Those lucky bastards then get to horse in hundred-plus-pounders till the cows come home. Measurements are taken, fin-clip tissue samples are archived to assess genetic diversity, and transmitters and transponder tags are attached. "Fish lice" (*Argulus*) are then collected and stored in vials for further study, and the gar are released.

The video ends with a still photo of a sixty-eight-year-old, eight-foot-two, 240-pound alligator gar caught by a commercial fisherman in 2004. The cowboy-voiced narrator, who sounds like he's making a barbecue sauce commercial, drawls, "The Game and Fish alligator gar team hopes fish like that will entice more anglers to respect the species and seek out alligator gar for their sportfishing potential."

After that, a voiceover from Brinkman adds, "This is just a really cool fish. It fights good…we have 'em here, we want to utilize 'em on a conservative basis to provide another opportunity for our anglers to go after a trophy fish in the state of Arkansas."[3]

This brings us back to the AGFC's alligator gar mission statement, which ultimately seeks to establish a unique sport fishery. That's the goal. But who's out there pioneering that unique sport fishery? Not many, that's who, because we're just getting started.

But there is one unofficial organization whose members are actively catching more juvenile alligator gar on rod and reel than anyone in the state. This group is Fishing Support Group, which consists of Turkey Buzzard, Minnow Bucket, Goggle Eye, and me. The AGFC was aware of what we were doing, and a few years ago they invited us to help gather data as citizen scientists. Brinkman equipped us with measuring tools, a scale, and a specialized net for weighing gator gar. Thus, Fishing Support Group's mission in recent years has been to support the AGFC's gator gar sampling and add to their store of data. But because of the floods—which have been helping gar out—elevated river levels in the last few years have been hindering our ability to provide assistance.

⚮ ⚮ ⚮

In the middle of summer, though, the rains relented long enough for the river to drop enough for us to get out there and try. And the guys and me, we were raring to help a fishery out.

But it wasn't that simple, mostly because Fishing Support

Group had suffered from some internal tensions during the previous year: Turkey Buzzard was mad at Minnow Bucket for reason X, Goggle Eye was bummed out at Minnow Bucket for argument Y, Minnow Bucket's wife was angry at Goggle Eye for issue Z, so Minnow Bucket had a beef with Goggle Eye. In short, we hadn't been fishing much. Turkey Buzzard and Goggle Eye had even formed a new fishing group with another guy. It was a group that I, in my petty jealousy, secretly referred to as "Club COVID" because of their sketchy social distancing methods, which came down to three guys being on one boat, touching the same stuff. In transit, they wore masks, but this carelessness still bothered me. Keep in mind that these were the days of latex gloves, when the Centers for Disease Control hadn't yet declared the curséd contagion primarily an airborne thing. But mainly, I didn't fit in very well with Club COVID, and they weren't inviting Minnow Bucket or me to fish with them. Hence, I got the sense that Turkey Buzzard and Goggle Eye were upset with me as well. So like all friends who become as close as family and then get pissed off at each other because their closeness allows them that, that's what happened to us.

Then, after a year of not fishing together, Turkey Buzzard surprised us all by suggesting that Fishing Support Group hit the beach for some gator-gar-fishing action. I was up for that, but after fishing in Texas and being in the heart of Galveston obliviousness (a region now shut down because of surging positive cases), I was playing strictly by CDC guidelines. I told Turkey Buzzard I'd be glad to meet them out on the beach, but I wasn't going to take any chances by shuttling anyone on my boat.

"No prob," Turkey Buzzard replied, so I went and bought two pounds of extra-large goldfish and black salties, which stay on the hook longer than sunfish and don't expire as quickly in the summer heat. Then I shot out to the launch.

Arriving early, I set up on the fine, white Arkansas sand, which is as pure and clean as any stretch of the Mediterranean.

It was a hundred degrees with stifling humidity, but the sun was on my back, and I had a patio umbrella for shade. Casting two heavy-duty rods out, I opened a beer and settled in.

An hour later, they came cutting across the Arkansas looking like a pack of bandits: Goggle Eye, decked out in that in-your-face, gay-pride cowboy hat (which is a compliment); Turkey Buzzard with a camo-colored neck gaiter pulled above his nose; and Minnow Bucket, sporting a no-nonsense black mask, that mischievous gleam in his eyes more visible than usual.

We set up along the beach, each of us twenty feet apart. As usual, Minnow Bucket spread out four rods on four holders with alarms, forty yards from each other. The rest of us each had two or three rods in front of us. Turkey Buzzard and Goggle Eye were using chunks of carp, which stayed on the hook because of the thickness of the skin. I was sharing my goldfish and salties with Minnow Bucket and adding frozen shad.

Out there in the dusty dusk, the ridgeline across the river radiating amberly, we began shooting the shit, just like old times. Because we had enough space between us, Minnow Bucket and I had our masks off, but Turkey Buzzard kept his on the entire time. Goggle Eye was somewhere in between, sometimes with his mask on, other times with his mask off.

"Hey," Minnow Bucket said an hour into it, "isn't anybody gonna help me drink these margaritas?"

He had a big old thermos full, but Goggle Eye didn't drink, Turkey Buzzard had been off the sauce for health reasons, and I was limiting my alcohol intake to one beer per day because I was on no-booze medication.

"Okay," Minnow Bucket said, pouring himself another drink, "I guess I'm on my own."

He hesitated, wondering if he should really drink his entire supply, but in true Minnow Bucket fashion, dove straight in.

Not too long after that, Turkey Buzzard got a runner that dropped the bait. He also caught an eating-sized catfish, and then a beeping started up. It was one of Minnow Bucket's alarms. He got up, and I followed him.

When he got to the source of the beeping, Minnow Bucket began reeling. He brought his line in, but there was nothing on it but his other line from further up the beach.

So we moseyed over to that rod, where Minnow Bucket, snarling under his breath, reeled in again. There was definitely a fish on this one, and after a few minutes we saw it. It was a longnose, about two and a half feet long and as metallic gray as a trashcan. He pulled it in without a hitch: a fine-looking specimen, but not our objective. I managed to pull the hook from the depths of its throat, it slid out easily, and Minnow Bucket let it go.

As the evening went on, Minnow Bucket finished off his margaritas. Night descended in a black shroud speckled with a smattering of scattered stars, and there was no moon out for light. We were all joking and laughing and ribbing each other as if there'd never been any tension, but then something shifted in Minnow Bucket. It was like he'd been slipped a roofie, or three. He was slurring his words and mumbling stuff.

By ten o'clock, Minnow Bucket was more than just drunk. Something was off. He was stumbling around and fighting to stay upright. Sometimes there'd be a conversation going on, and Minnow Bucket would break in giggling at stuff going on in his own head, then release what sounded like unintelligible Martian gibberish.

Turkey Buzzard chuckled and started a fire. He's always starting fires on the beach, even if it's a hundred degrees. He says he does it for the smoke, to keep the mosquitoes away, but I think he actually has some deep-seated need to start fires for the sole purpose of having a fire. This is one of life's mysteries that will never be resolved in our lifetimes.

Minnow Bucket, on the other hand, had progressed from shambling to stumbling to staggering and was now extremely vertically challenged, falling three or four steps forward, then catching himself and falling the same number of steps back. He was in a battle with gravity and seemed amused at how the universe was trying to pull him down, like a challenge from the laws of physics.

By eleven o'clock, Minnow Bucket was lying next to the fire, murmuring incoherently. That's where we let him be, sometimes waking and trying to stand. When that happened, Goggle Eye would insert himself between Minnow Bucket's wavering frame and the flames.

"I don't want you falling in," I heard Goggle Eye tell Minnow Bucket.

Again, this wasn't typical. We'd all seen Minnow Bucket fucked up before, but this was beyond fucked up. He was seriously out-to-lunch shitfaced, like fall-down-and-hurt-yourself shitfaced, like so shitfaced that something else had to be in the mix, but hell if we knew what it was.

At one point, Minnow Bucket decided to stumble up the beach to tend to his rods. I kept my eye on him. He was zigging and zagging, clearly off-kilter, until suddenly he shot straight into the river in a line that looked like the most recent graph of COVID cases in Arkansas: it was generally flat, with a bit of deviation here and there, but then it rocketed from 312 new cases per day up to 867. I rose to lend him a hand, but Minnow Bucket pulled himself out, scrambled for the beach, flung himself onto the sand, and passed out again.

Laughing at that, I told Turkey Buzzard what I'd seen. He shook his head in that what-can-you-do sort of way, and we continued fishing.

Sometime around midnight, we decided to pack it up. We started putting our gear in the boats, and that's when Minnow Bucket rose again, weaving toward us in the blackness. I couldn't see him very well, and then I heard a THOOMP!

"YACHH!" he cried. "I think I broke my nose!"

Turkey Buzzard was closer and had seen it happen. Minnow Bucket had done a face-plant right into his reel, and he now had a bleeding gash across his nose.

The upshot being, we loaded up, gathered Minnow Bucket's equipment, and made space for him to crash out in the bow of Turkey Buzzard's boat. Minnow Bucket crawled his way over, and Turkey Buzzard bandaged him up.

Goggle Eye and Turkey Buzzard then took Minnow Bucket back to the launch, trailered up the boat, loaded him into the truck, and drove his drunk ass home. They had to support him under both arms when they hauled him up to his door.

So much for "social-distance fishing," but for Fishing Support Group, at least things were back to normal.

∞ ∞ ∞

A few weeks after that "reel experience" (as Minnow Bucket later joked), I was back on the river, this time with Lea. We launched at Palarm Creek, shot across to a gravelly beach, and got set up. I had a bucket of extra, extra large goldfish, and I put two of those on two heavy-duty gar-fishing rods and cast out.

We weren't even there half an hour when I got my first run. The gar was heading downstream at a pretty quick clip, and then the second pole registered activity too. I let them both run and stop, and after ten minutes both gar dropped the bait.

Ah well, at least there was action, and there'd probably be more. So we grilled some Beyond burgers and waited for night to fall. And those were some damn good burgers too, with just the right amount of char.

My New Year's resolution had been twofold. First, in the interest of leaving less of a carbon footprint, no beef for one full year. I just couldn't support the unsustainability of that unconscionable industry anymore. And secondly, no tuna for a year since that fishery is stressed to the breaking point. And when the year is over, maybe I'll fall off this meat wagon. Or maybe not.

Then, again, it happened at dusk. First one runner, followed by another. After running twenty minutes each, they both dropped the bait.

Eventually, some faint stars came out with a bright half-moon tamping down their twinkling ambitions. The gin and tonics were driving home the fact that school would soon be starting up, and we were not looking forward to being apart for months. Both of us were scheduled to go back to teaching in the classroom, everyone masked and six feet apart. But for the moment, the river was full of gar.

Around ten o'clock, the sky light enough to see the lines on our palms, another gar hit. I was feeding it line, and it was taking its time, swimming casually downstream. It went for twenty minutes. When it stopped, I plopped down on a lawn chair and asked Lea for a refill.

Both the gar and I rested for ten minutes, and then the spool started turning again.

"What a lackadaisical gar," I told Lea, rising to set the hook. "Usually they run faster than this, speeding up and slowing down."

She didn't care. For her, it was about soaking up as much of the summer as possible before having to revise her syllabi. But she was also bemoaning the fate of each fat, happy goldfish gasping on the end of my line.

I braced myself and started power-reeling in. The moment the rod bowed, I knew the gar was hooked, so I ran up the beach to sink the barb in further. I was running and reeling like a maniac, cutting sharply back and forth and resetting the hook multiple times while Lea laughed (not with me, but at me).

That gar was on good, and it was resisting. When it got close to shore, I could tell it was a big one. Something long and silver started slapping around. For a second I considered letting it take another run because sometimes they're so full of piss and vinegar when you get them on the sand that you can't hold them down. But I had a feeling about this fish, and I knew I could tackle it.

Two seconds later, it was thrashing on the beach, its length between my knees, and I was pinning its head to the sand. It was a serpentine but solid longnose, only six inches shy of five feet.

Lea brought my gar-wrangling rope, which I wound around its chest and tightened, snaring it under the front fins. I then hauled it up the beach a dozen feet where it flopped some more. The steel leader was down its throat, a gurgle of blood was bubbling up, and Lea couldn't look at it.

Also, somehow, my left pinky got slit in the fracas. Maybe it was a razor-sharp gill plate, or maybe it was a razor-thin scale. Whatever the case, I'm used to getting a little cut up when wrassling gars, but this time I lost the very tip of that pinky.

In my experience, longnose are often the bycatch of gator gar, but I was definitely psyched to be dealing with this fish. This twenty-pounder I was measuring and weighing was rewarding the hell out of me.

"Can't you let it go?" Lea asked, advocating for a quicker release. Its fins were turning red.

"It's okay," I said. "They can breathe air."

This didn't matter to Lea, but I did get her to take some pictures before I put that longy back in the water and held it as it recovered. Blood was still trickling from its gills, and it was definitely spinning as I cleaned the sand off its slime. To Lea, I'm sure it looked like I was petting it, and in a sense I was.

A few minutes later, that gar swam off, leaving me strangely satisfied. All my molecules were pulsing with starlight from getting to do what I most love to do. Lea, on the other hand, felt like she'd witnessed a violent encounter.

And I suppose it was, considering the blood that gar lost and the flesh I lost as well. But because I was buzzing for the next few days, this injury was no cause for complaint. But it did cause me to acknowledge that there's always a price for indulging my passion.

Usually, it's easy enough for me to cause a fish pain, then release it and forget about it. But lately, this is something I've been dwelling on more and more, mostly from the comfort of my air-conditioned home with Wi-Fi and refrigeration. And as of yet, there's been no apparent adjustments to my standard operating procedure.

Meanwhile, out in the river, that gar was feeling the sting of steel, which I had lodged in it. And according to my recent research on corrosion rates, it would take years for that hook to disintegrate.

⚭ ⚭ ⚭

AFTER LEA LEFT for the New York Outpost, I immersed myself in fishing on my own. I'd been going hard-core for gator gar for a month and hadn't caught any, and I wanted to stick a fork in this project and turn it over before school began. But now school had started, and I'd been out on the river four nights in a row— flathead after flathead, longnose after longnose—and I was sick of this mission. Of course, I could easily stop forcing myself, but something kept driving me, probably due to a lack of something.

Having studied the work of psychoanalyst Jacques Lacan back in college, I was aware of how certain psychological forces drive people to repeat achieved and ascribed behaviors. But what I was missing in my formative years (which is what psychoanalysis from that period always seems to hark back to) wasn't something I could answer. Maybe it had to do with my father's harmonica, or maybe it had to do with how I'd vowed to keep fishing magical rather than descending into an antisocial funk like his. Or maybe it was simply about catching crazy-ass monster fish which can translate everyday life into staggering spiritual experiences affirming one's purpose on this planet. Or maybe I was a gar loser, which also involves the idea of "lack."

It was another glowing apricot dusk, cooling down from another hundred-degree day, and I was back at Fishing Support Group's same old spot. It had gotten to the point that, given the amount of runners who'd recently dropped my bait, I had to admit to myself that catching and releasing a six-foot gator gar was not probable. Because of this, I had lowered my expectations to a five-footer.

Still, having spun that "garoulette" wheel night after night, waiting for the ball to land on my number, I was holding out for the story I couldn't imagine, knowing that if I kept spinning, the odds were it would happen sometime in the next few years. So once again, I was lowering my expectations, this time down to four feet long.

Fishing alone during a pandemic provides a lot of time for reflection, and one thing I was reflecting on was the absurdity of my obsession with catching an alligator gar of specific proportions, which made me wonder what I was really fishing for. Because fishing for an exact number like 72 or 60 or 48, that's just ridiculous. It seemed to me that fish should be judged on the quality of their character, not some arbitrary number drummed up by someone with something to prove.

I therefore had to dig deeper because, as everyone knows, fishing should be for the sake of fishing, not proving anything to anyone. Fishing should have nothing to do with personal research or professional gain. Fishing is for kids.

Having forgotten my lawn chair, I was sitting on the sand sipping some wine. In front of me, I had two heavy-duty rods baited up with extra-large goldfish as well as a lightweight rod with a worm on it to add to my stock of bait. The water was so warm that any sunny or bass I'd put on the line would die within twenty minutes, but not those goldies. If it came down to it, they could stay strong for days, even with a hook burning through their spine.

Then suddenly, my baitrunner reel started whizzing. Holy hell! I had to get it! I had to finish this never-ending quest.

That gar was a screamer! It was heading downstream at top speed, peeling out line like a motherlunker. I was so amazed at how fast it was accelerating that it didn't even occur to me to pop the bail, and let it run free. I guess I thought this gar was too huge to feel resistance.

But a hundred yards into its run, it suddenly stopped and spit out the hook.

Man, I really kicked myself after that. I had lost The Screamer by standing there with my mouth hanging open. What a bummer! I reeled in a baitless line.

ଠ  ଠ  ଠ

THE NEXT NIGHT I was out there again, absolutely, completely disheartened. The sky was as dark as my outlook on ever catching a gator gar, and some honking goose wouldn't shut up. It was eleven thirty on a school night, nothing had bitten all evening long, and it was way past time to pack up.

My mood had no doubt been affected by some bowfishers who'd come along earlier. They came straight across the river with their generator roaring, and not too far from my line, in the same section I'd released my pet gar, they shot one right in front of my eyes. I could see the silhouette when they pulled it in, a longnose over five feet long. They called it some names, congratulated each other for killing it, and laughing up a storm, kicked it overboard. God bless America.

I cringed and got back to baiting my line, now reconsidering my thrill-of-the-hunt argument justifying why I fish. With the carp I'd caught in New York State, I'd claimed that the rush of latching on to a monster fish was the *why* behind my roughfish quest. With gator gar, I'd made a similar claim about the adrenaline surge being some sort of holy grail justifying whatever it takes to get to that point. This was the exact same mindset of those bowhunters, who were obviously after the same buzz as me.

Thus, it was starting to become a lot clearer to me that rather than sticking up for fish, these quests I design are really about me trying to feel something so extraordinary that the resulting rushes can't be defined. Sure, it looked like my goal was conservation-oriented, but because I wasn't acknowledging the consequences of my actions, this made me insincere. In the meantime, the intentions of those bowshooters were to flat-out kill, and mine were based on catch and release, but that doesn't matter when the results boil down to living beings feeling pain. In fact, it might even be more humane to straight-out shoot a gar in the brain than to let it go with a hook stuck in its gut that takes irritating years to dissolve. So again, this was something I had to account for.

"Sorry buddy," I told a sunfish, popping a barb through its back.

It had been trapped in my minnow bucket with eight others, two of whom had already died. I'd probably iced thirty bream that week to supply this never-ending crusade, and this one was either willing me to look it in the eyes, or I was challenging myself to really look at what I was doing. So I met its eyes, which caused me to clench my own.

But ten minutes later, it didn't exist, and neither did those bowfishers. It was just me…waiting for something…to change… until finally…a little click.

Releasing the spool, I let it run. It was slowly moving upstream, which is rare for a gar, and I could definitely tell it was a gar because it was moving straight and steady. I was feeding out line, aware that it was aware of me, but I kept my movements extra gentle so as not to spook it.

My other reel then started spinning, so I opened the bail on that one too. That runner took off downstream at a rapid clip, so I was feeding out two lines at the same time and feeling the connection with both big fish.

After the upstream gar took out two hundred yards and the downstream gar took out a hundred, I started seeing metal on both spools. There was less than a hundred yards left on both poles, so I walked them back to the boat and put the baitrunner in a rod holder mounted on my port rail. That was the downstream gar, and there was less than fifty yards left on that pole. I locked that reel, hoping the gar would hook itself, and I turned my attention to my more heavy-duty combo, which had about the same amount of line on it.

That fish had already run for fifteen minutes, it was still heading upstream, and it wasn't about to stop. When it got down to twenty yards, I had to steel myself to set the hook. Having done this a dozen times that week, it was pretty obvious what would happen. But when I struck, the rod arced, and somewhere out in the blackness, a tremendous SLAPPP! resounded off the rock walls lining the other side of the river.

I cranked and cranked and cranked it in, knowing from its massiveness that it was a hundred-pounder, at least. It was also a brawny fighter, not lashing out, not spazzing out as it kept the pressure on *on the surface*. For some reason, it refused to dive. It was using the top of the river to its advantage, splashing and thrashing like a bull, which was giving it more traction and creating more drag. It was like hauling in a log, as the saying goes, but in this case it was a super-strong, man-sized log, constantly powering away from me.

It took about fifteen minutes to retrieve more than two hundred yards, and I was huffing and puffing and straining my lungs, gasping for oxygen. It kept coming in, staying on top of the water, and then I saw a large, black, shape-shifting blob.

Grabbing my gar rope, I clipped the carabiner to my belt

loop and kept on horsing it in. It was right by the shore, the mythical six-footer I'd been after, all fattened up for the winter and as thick around as a propane tank: a striking, monstrous, broad-across-the-snout, exhausted alligator gar on that line between river and sand as I moved out and around it, keeping the hundred-pound line tight.

Then I was sitting on its back, and it was grunting. But it wasn't thrashing or snapping at me. It was too beat from being mammoth and fighting me with all that armor weighing it down, at least 120 pounds.

Working the rope under its belly, I tightened up and pulled it up the beach. The bright red circle hook was lodged in its top jaw, so I reached over to my tackle box and got a pliers and mangled it out. My 180-pound Kevlar leader designed for wels catfish in Germany had done its job.

That gar was too enormous to weigh with a scale, but I did the math. It was exactly two yards long and a yard around at its thickest. Thus, length (72 inches) × girth (36 inches) × girth again (36) divided by 800 + 15 = a whopping 132 pounds!

The light was bad, and I took a few pictures. They didn't come out very good, but that didn't matter. This was an epic experience I'd always remember, and the images ingrained in my brain would remain for decades.

I then dragged that gar back down to the river, put it in a foot of water, washed the sand off its slime, and sat with it as we both recovered. It was well behaved and not problematic. It got its bearings back and slowly swished away.

As for that other runner, it had severed the connection right in the middle and had taken off trailing a hundred yards of line. But again, out of sight, out of mind.

Then back in the boat, heading upstream beneath the glittering gold of the Milky Way, I suddenly heard a lunatic "WHOOOOP!" rising over the drone of the outboard motor. It was me, cheering and yowling with the coyotes. It was the sound of me realizing that I'd actually caught my six-foot Arkansas alligator gar. But it wasn't the sound of victory. It was the sound of me understanding why I'd been out there burning myself out and why this one meant so much more than those I'd caught before: because I caught this one by myself in the state I'd made my home.

But there was more to this epiphany, and it took another two days to figure out that the reason I'd been out there trying and trying and trying and trying, year after year after year after year, night after night after night after night, had a lot to do with satisfying my own monster-fishing ambitions. Still, it had more to do with the fact that to really speak on behalf of Arkansas alligator gar, I had to actually land a big one in order to be credible, or else I'm just yapping from the sidelines.

But whatever the case, and whether anyone likes it or not, I'm a gar writer in Arkansas who specializes in this species, and for over twenty years I've been translating the science into lay terms. Having worked with the experts, having fought for gar both publicly and privately, and having promoted humane gar-fishing tactics, I'm privileged to be an ambassador for gar who's in the position to send a message. So here it is:

I have been to the Gar Mountaintop, and I can confirm that alligator gar are the Gobsmacking Apogee of American Freshwater Fishing! And whereas the goal of the AGFC might be to create a unique sport fishery, there's an even better objective to strive for: the strengthening of this visionary fishery, which is well worth the effort, because strengthening it strengthens all fisheries in the state.

But to get to this realization, in striving to put a face on what I proclaim to love, I hurt what I love in the process. And in doing that, I burned through buckets of live bait, containing fish I tortured to death, because I am a hypocrite.

So instead of stating that Arkansas alligator gar can now take a bit more pressure and inviting others to get out there and experience this easily accessible fishery, I'm now turning a total 180. That's right. I'm saying let's not give in to the juvenile urge to compromise the health and safety of a great, old, beautiful fish in order to admire it. I'm saying let's be adults who are secure enough with knowing that they don't need to conquer a fish to comprehend how incredible it is. Yep, let's be content with what's enigmatic, and let's let the big ones swim—unmolested, undisturbed—in all their evolutionary magnificence without any need to risk harming any more for the glorification of needy egos.

In other words, let's just let them be…*Fantastically Phantasmagorical!*

## CHAPTER 14

# Roughing It in Quest of the Trashfish Trinity
## Part 2: The Son

N EXT ON MY roughfish list was buffalo: a wide-bodied, huge-headed, hump-shouldered bison of a bottom-feeder whose genus classification of *Ictiobus* is Greek for "bull fish." There are three species: smallmouth, bigmouth, and black. The state record in Arkansas is a 105-pound, four-foot black, shot with an arrow in Harris Brake. Considering that bigmouth can reach ages of over one hundred years, this freshwater ray-finned cousin could've been a centenarian.

Depending on region, the bigmouth has more nicknames than any other American fish. These include buffalofish, gourd-head, baldpate, marblehead, stubnose, redmouth, trumpet buffalo, white buffalo, bernard buffalo, bullhead buffalo, bullmouth, lake buffalo, slough buffalo, blue buffalo, buffalo sucker, round-head, bull-nosed buffalo, mud buffalo, chub-nosed buffalo, brown buffalo, pug-nosed buffalo, pug, and more.

All three species are commonly referred to as "buffalo carp," but that's simply wrong. Buffalo are not in the carp family. They're the largest member of the sucker family, and they only resemble carp because of their massive size and enormous, rounded heads that could pound a dent into a trashcan if a reason ever arose to ram one. That's why they're compared to bison, for the gore-potential their noggins conjure. But they also range across the prairies, especially when floodplains flood.

Through the years I've caught a few, mostly with worms and always by accident. The most memorable one I ever met was on Lake Conway. Hippy and I had thrown out a bunch of jugs baited with minnows, and when we paddled out to pick them up there was this two-liter tonic water bottle that kept shooting off every time we tried to grab it. It would go under, then pop up with a resounding CRACK! forty yards away. We chased that jug all over the lake and finally got it. Attached to the line was one buff buffalo: a fat, silver, boneheaded behemoth weighing nearly twenty pounds with an oversized Klingon brow. That fish was definitely a monster, and after we took some pictures, we were glad to let it go.

It had been unusual to catch a buffalo on a minnow because this species is primarily a filter feeder partial to microorganisms, vegetation, insects, and shrimpy things. Still, Goggle Eye had caught one with a shad once, and I had seen it happen.

Anyway, I devised a plan to catch me a buffalo. My idea was to take what I'd learned from using doughballs for carp, but with a few innovations and specialized noodles. To create strategic buffalo noodles, I bought six orange pool noodles from a dollar store and got some three-quarter-inch PVC pipe, then cut all of those into sixteen-inch segments. On each piece of PVC I fit a sleeve of noodle foam and drilled a hole all the way through both materials, an inch away from one end. As Turkey Buzzard noted, this ensures that if a fish pulls the line down, then the other end will pop up and signal a fish is on.

After that, I strung fourteen feet of 130-pound, size-15 waxed line (green so the fish can't see it) through each hole and secured the cords to the noodles. I pumped each hollow noodle full of insulating foam to make sure that even if the foam got old and lost its grip and separated from the PVC (as it did with Charlotte's gar), then the insert would float and could be recovered. Minnow Bucket suggested that the insulating foam also creates more buoyancy, and if this is the case, we suspected there'd be a degree more drag when a fish is hauling it around, which could help wear it out.

For the sinkers, I went down to Hatchet Jack's bait shop near North Little Rock. Last time I was there, there were two masked women wearing rubber gloves, but this time, all caution was gone with the COVID wind. Now there were two bearded dudes, both unmasked, even though a state mandate had been decreed that all businesses shall enforce mask wearing in public buildings.

I even stopped at a gas station bait store in Mayflower the other day, saw the sign requiring masks, then went in to find out what kind of minnows they had. Some employees were properly masked, but the girl operating the cash register couldn't be bothered. She let hers hang under her chin (a "chin diaper," in modern parlance) as she poked at her phone, exhaling invisible droplets that float around in the air for eight minutes. Nearby, a maskless truck driver was stocking the shop with Ho Hos and Ding Dongs, and an elderly woman without a mask was inserting quarters into some kind of slot machine.

Basically, there's no enforcement. I called the Conway Police to inquire if anything could be done since the country was at 4.5 million infections, and the numbers were increasing like wildfire. The cops told me they could only do something if a business owner reported people not wearing masks on their property. The sheriff told me the same thing. This meant the mask mandate was for members of the public rather than owners and employees, which doesn't make much sense at all when trying to control the spread of a virus.

But on to the weights, which were the "bank" type that look like a teardrop with a tiny donut on top. I bought a dozen two-ouncers because I wanted a lightweight sinker on each line that the buffalo wouldn't notice if they started dragging it across the bottom. I strung a weight on each line and tied a swivel to the free ends so the weights could move freely up and down between swivel and noodle like a Carolina rig, which had worked for me with that New York carp. If I dropped a noodle into a depth of ten feet, the weight would settle on the bottom, and there'd be several feet of slack line lying next to it. If a buffalo swam off with the bait, it would go a few feet, the line would tighten, and the needle-sharp tip of the hook would catch on its inner lips.

Because a #4 Eagle Claw treble hook had worked well for carp, I'd ordered a dozen of the same kind, but of the "soft bait" variety. These type of hooks are equipped with a metal spring around the shank to help hold the dough on, and I tied two feet of moss-green hundred-pound braided line to each of them. This line is light and soft, so fish don't sense it much in comparison to steel leaders or plastic lines, which are stiffer. At the other end of those leaders, I attached some heavy-duty barrel swivels with interlock snaps to clip to the noodle lines later.

Also, since they were doing some remodeling at Hatchet Jack's, they'd taken their taxidermies off the wall, and they were now up for sale. A lumpy, six-foot rattlesnake got my attention as well as a red fox with weird, yellow, gluey eyes that didn't look quite right. There was a dusty pickerel and a lot of bass, but then I saw the crappiest stuffed buffalo I'd ever seen. It was a two-and-a-half-foot, twenty-pound bigmouth, olive in color with a yellow belly, and its gaping maw was large enough to gulp down a beer can. All the fins were shredded to some extent and looking fringy, and it had a piece of masking tape on its stomach on which someone had written "$50" with a Sharpie.

There was no way I could not buy it. It was the fish I was targeting, and it would make a grotesque addition to my gallery of lowlife aquatic monsters displayed in the man-cavey space of our Arkansas house we call "the grotto room." There's an actual fish pond in there with two koi it, designed by the eccentric lady who'd dreamed up the Escheresque architecture of a dwelling so bizarre that only someone like me could've envisioned adorning its walls with a menagerie of bowfin and burbot and snakeheads and gar. So when I put that buffalo on the wall with its agreeable yet goofy expression, it fit right in.

I tried peeling off the masking tape, but because the paint started peeling off too, I left it on. So there it is on my wall, one of the trashiest-looking trashfish mounts anyone has ever seen.

Trash fish, however, are only in the eyes of the beholder. "Trash fish" is a label that implies a fish has no value. But that buffalo on my wall, it's clearly worth fifty bucks.

⚶  ⚶  ⚶

Following some YouTube doughball research, I went out and got a bag of cattle range cubes from a feed store. I soaked two cups' worth of those in water for a day, kept a cup and a half of the mush it became, drained off the excess water, and added four capfuls of anise extract, which has a licorice smell that works as an attractant. I then mixed in a cup and a half of bran straight from the cereal box and a tablespoon of red Jell-O mix. Whereas carp like their dough sweet, buffalo like it with more of a bite, so I threw in a tablespoon of garlic powder and a teaspoon of ground black pepper. In the end, I thickened it up with a third of a cup of flour, the idea being that the ball should be solid enough not to dissolve too fast in the water, but soft enough to break apart when a fish sucks it up.

I then took my premade leaders and formed pungent balls around the soft-bait treble hooks. These doughballs were the size of golf balls, and I put a dozen in an egg carton and wound the leaders around it. They sat snuggly in there, and I put it all in the fridge to solidify more.

As for the rest of the dough, I put it in a Ziploc bag to take out with the remaining range-cube mush to use as chum. And speaking of chum, I also took more cattle cubes along, plus two ears of corn.

The place I chose was Atkins Lake down by Pine Bluff because I'd read an article about a guy catching buffalo there. It was an intriguing oxbow right off the Arkansas River that, from an aerial perspective, resembled a twisting fish. Looking at this lake on Google Earth, I saw a public boat launch in the middle, and since the tail end was undeveloped, I had to check it out.

Hauling ass down there in my new used Subaru, I launched the *Lümpabout* around noon and shot to the spot. It was a cypress lake, about nine feet deep at the most, and there were quite a few blimpy blips on the fish finder. I could also see unidentified lunkers leaping here and there, and there were plenty of shad breaking the surface.

Choosing a location near the shore with a lot of tall grass and activity, I began attaching my baited leaders to the noodles. I tossed them out in a circle about thirty feet from each other, anchored in the middle, and chummed the whole area with cattle chow and corn cut right off the cob. It was September, humid as hell, even under the overcast.

An hour went by and nothing happened, and when I reeled in my heavy-duty gator-gar rod baited with a doughball, I found out why. The stuff had dissolved right off the soft-dough hook.

My answer to that was to bait the line with corn instead, which also didn't yield a thing. I let another hour go by, then went to check the noodles. All the bait was gone.

I was prepared for this. Since I had some corn shuckings in the boat, I could use corn silk to encase the bait. After all, winding grass around doughballs up in New York had worked for carp, and what's a little roughage to a rough fish? So I wound a web of corn silk around a few, then wrapped some of the other doughballs in ribbons of husks so they looked like tiny tamales.

All I needed was one barb sticking out, which I could use to pin multiple strands wound around the dough. Because buffalo are known for getting into flooded fields and eating corn right off the stalk, my hope was that this presentation would seem natural to them.

But still…nothing. Nothing but huge fish leaping clean out of the water in the distance, then slapping down with resounding SMACKS. At one point, a carp leapt right next to the boat, and I saw it turn over in flight, its belly white and fins tinged with gold.

One thing about noodles is that you can leave them there and come back later, so that's what I did. I explored the perimeter of the area looking for fish in the shallows, but most of the action seemed to be in six or seven feet of water. I also did some drift-fishing, trailing a bobber dangling corn on a small circle hook.

When the sun finally came blazing through the clouds, I broke out a patio umbrella for shade. But by five o'clock, I hadn't caught squat.

Giving up, I motored back to the launch and drove off in defeat. The doughballs had totally bombed.

⚭   ⚭   ⚭

KNOWING THAT OUR local commercial fisherman catches mass buffalo in an oxbow known as Portland Bottoms, I launched on the Arkansas River at Cypress Creek and took off downstream. The river was 265 feet at Toad Suck Dam, a measurement based on sea level even though the river rarely rises over twenty feet. This was the exact depth I needed to get into the area locals call "The Cut Off."

Heading in there, the depth got down to one foot. I raised the prop and throttled through, making my way into a long, sweeping backwater filled with herons and egrets and rolling gar. The maximum depth was six feet, and there were clouds of fish showing on the fish finder.

My idea was to take what I'd learned from my failure the day before and make adjustments, so I had added more flour to the dough to harden it up enough to stay on the hooks. I also figured I'd go linear this time and throw out my specialized buffalo noodles in a line running along the deepest shore, since fish often follow embankments.

The infernal sun was blaring down on my shirtless back, and every time I dropped a noodle in, I tossed out a handful of cattle food. Then I anchored up and cast out my corn rig.

The gar were coming up everywhere. I cast a few rope flies, but nobody gave a damn. Still, shad were popping on the surface, which is always a good sign. Carp were leaping as well. They'd jump three feet out of the water and shudder as if trying to shake something off, and maybe they were. And true to form, when they'd slap down, a couple others would answer back, splashing in the same semi-second.

After an hour of nothing happening on the noodles, I began checking them. The first two were baitless, so I rebaited and pulled my old tamale trick by winding some corn husks around the dough. But on the next ten noodles, the bait was still there, so I threw them back in. I had hit on the right consistency, which was drier and more like the texture of Play-Doh.

That afternoon of sweating it out ended with me putting my shirt back on way too late. I was sunburned pretty badly, had received no bites whatsoever, and had to pack up with the same result as the day before. My conclusion was that I lacked a key element of an equation that fishing celebrity Jeremy Wade lays out in his 2019 book *How to Think Like a Fish*. He writes, "Catching a big fish is very simple. All you have to do is put the right bait in the right place at the right time. You could even express this as a formula: $B + P + T = F$."[1]

Looking at it this way, it really didn't matter if there were fish all around me on the fish finder because if the place (P) isn't right, then the final product (F) is not possible. Because if buffalo are in this place (P) at the right time (T), then they'll snarf those doughballs right off the bottom.

So once again, it was back to the drawing board.

⚮  ⚮  ⚮

TWO DAYS LATER, I added more garlic powder. My tactic this time was to hit a sand beach where the doughballs would stick out rather than be obscured in the sediment. I envisioned scavenging herds of buffalo stumbling upon my bait, and there it would be, right in front of their hoovering lips.

Launching on Labor Day, right beneath the Toad Suck Dam, I took off downstream to a sandy area that Fishing Support Group knew well. We had caught some bait-sized buffalo there before, some off worms on rod and reel, others in cast nets while going for shad.

The river level was pretty dang high, but I eventually found a beach protected by a jetty. There was a forty-foot hole in the center of the cove teeming with all sorts of fish, and I laid a line of noodles on the edge of that in ten-foot depths and tossed out a handful of range cubes by each float. Then motoring over to a shady slope, I set my lawn chair up in a spot where I could monitor all twelve noodles. I also set two poles up in front of me: one with corn, and one with worms.

It was a lazy afternoon, and a bunch of buzzards out on the jetty were enjoying a reeking treat. A bald eagle passed by overhead, scrawwing its high-pitched cry.

It was comfortable in the shade. A breeze was blowing, and I caught a drum on a worm: a pretty little fellow with lilac coloring.

But sometimes I'd catch a whiff of something putrid. There

was a dead-fish smell in the air, and from my vantage point I could see a few fish skulls down the beach, bleached by the sun.

Hours went by, and I didn't catch anything else except one small cat. None of the noodles moved, and I reeled in my worm.

Hey! There was something hanging on the hook. It was a large scale with a bluish hue, which meant it could be a buffalo scale! This made me wonder if I could claim that catching part of a fish was equivalent to catching an entire fish. If I could, this exasperating quest would be over. But naw, that would be taking the easy way out.

I had to investigate, though, so I walked down to the water. Right by the shore, I saw a line of scales lying in the water. When I had reeled in, my hook had passed through them and had snagged a micro strand of tissue clinging to a scale. And the other scales scattered about, they were the right size and the right shape.

So I walked on down the beach to check those fish skulls out. There were four of them lying on the sand, along with some meatless spines with tails. But those fish heads, they weren't connected to anything. They were totally decapitated. And judging from the size of them and their upturned lower jaws, these were the skulls of bigmouth buffalo.

A lot of thoughts passed through my mind, the foremost being that someone had made a fire ring in this place (P), so maybe someone had been night fishing here and had caught a bunch of buffalo. So maybe I should come back at night…

Whatever the case, it was time to start packing up, so I got in the boat and motored around collecting noodles. As I did, I saw even more buffalo heads. A couple were floating by the jetty covered in fetid flesh. Then I saw one on the rocks that the buzzards hadn't discovered yet. It still had some meat on it, and the cut was in a perfect line right behind its gills. Whoever had cut its head off had probably used some sort of electric sawing knife.

Then I knew what had happened: it was Fishman, the only

commercial fisherman left in the area. In the past, I'd seen him bring out blue plastic barrels filled with the rancid remains of fish he'd cleaned, which he dumped straight into the river. Usually he did this right at the boat launch, so then you'd have to cruise through the stomach-turning stank, the water all tainted with oils and random bobbing bladders as he waved to you with a snaggletoothed grin, on his way to catch more buffalo.

Which were an extremely tricky fish to catch. And so far, they were kicking my ass.

ᘓ  ᘓ  ᘓ

I SENT MY friend Catfish an email. Having written numerous articles on buffalo, he replied, "Catching buffalos ain't easy in my experience. Even when you know you're fishing a good spot full of fish, you have to convince them to take your bait, and that's easier said than done." He added that they're in all the big rivers in the state as well as Lake Conway, where the state record bigmouth, a whopping fifty-pounder, had been caught.

*Well hell,* I thought, *I live right on that lake, and I've seen plenty of black buffalo spawning in the spring...*

Not only that, but because I went out there twice a day running lines for monster cats, and because this was a global pandemic, it made sense to stay close to home. Hence, it made sense to chum a spot in my very own lake.

Within a few hours, I was out there with a bag of range cubes, dropping them under the cypress I call "Lightning Tree," which had been shattered by a lightning bolt. And with the mantra "If you chum, they will come" repeating in my head, I began chumming on a daily basis.

I did that for a week, then hung two lines from two branches: one right on top of the underwater pyramid of cattle-cube mush I'd been building, and one on the other side of the tree. For the line on top of the cattle chow, I tied a foot and a half of hundred-pound test to the 130-pound trotline twine with a simple standard knot. That one had a soft-dough treble hook, around which I formed a really hard ball of dough. On the other line I hung a single octopus hook right on the bottom, baited with corn. That line was also trotline on the top, braided line on the bottom.

Nothing happened the first day, but on the second morning, the doughball line was gone, ripped right off the thicker line. Something had taken off with the hook, which, if swallowed, wasn't adding to its quality of life.

Holy crap! I was actually on to them now! This meant it was time to get serious with real fishing knots and actual swivels. No more messing around.

So that's what I did, and the next evening, there was definitely something on Lightning Tree. It was the corn line, and something was tugging it and yanking it and swimming around. My mission to catch a buffalo was about to crystallize before my eyes.

But when I pulled that line up, it was a measly channel cat, gurgling for mercy.

And the next night on Lightning Tree…another cat.

So I was chumming the catfish now.

ꝏ  ꝏ  ꝏ

AFTER A MONTH of chumming and nobody coming except every channel cat between Conway and Mayflower, and after a month of trying out baitholder hooks with extra talons for salmon eggs (seems catfish love those too) and experimenting with artificial maize baits made from marshmallow (supposedly having 400 times the smell of real corn) and trying out different doughball recipes, I was forced to reexamine Jeremy's formula of $B + P + T = F$.

What was sticking out to me was the P, because all I was

getting in my current location were channel cats, injuring half of them in the process, then letting them go. That's when it occurred to me that I was fishing in catfish territory and that trying to attract buffalo here was a losing prospect. The depth was about six or seven feet, with logs and branches all over the bottom, and buffalo liked shallower, weedier areas, with insects and micro-aquatics hiding out in the vegetation.

I was therefore forced to write off the past four weeks of compulsive chumming as "a learning experience" and to concentrate on a P that was more conducive to finding the F I was shooting for. In the meantime, because my buffalo lines were always out there, T remained a constant 24/7, and B was a matter of attracting at least one buffalo to beat a catfish to the hook.

For my new location, I chose a small cypress in my own cove, right along the lily pads. It was about four feet deep and mucky enough for carp and gar, and I'd seen a lot of mysterious humpbacks surging in the nearby alligator grass. This time I wasn't screwing around. I'd bought two fifty-pound bags of Purina Cattle Chow and a bunch of #10 cans of whole kernel corn weighing six pounds each. I paddled out to that tree and began dumping chum.

I had also adjusted my doughball recipe, adding minced garlic instead of powdered, and trying out red Kool-Aid rather than Jell-O.

And I chummed and I chummed and I chummed and I chummed. But the buffalo, they did not come. And the more I chummed and chummed and chummed and chummed, and the more the buffalo didn't come, the more channel cats I caught in the process. And the more channel cats I caught, the more I released with disfigured maws and mutilated eyes. I was definitely releasing more than I was saving to eat, and I was definitely injuring more than half the cats I was releasing.

Eventually, after two months of constantly chumming and no buffalo coming, the love was gone. I didn't even want to go out but went out anyway because I had set a goal and didn't know how to stop. It just wasn't fun fishing for buffalo anymore.

Once again, it was time to take drastic action. I didn't want to do it, but in order for B + P + T to = F, I had to change the constant that was keeping me from achieving F. That constant being P, I decided to cheat on Arkansas.

∞  ∞  ∞

I FOUND THE Buffalo Whisperer's website online, and it was a game-changer. I found that there's a Euro-style fishery for carp in Texas that had evolved out of the gear and tactics developed in England and France for targeting this fish. In the Austin area, an extremely gonzo buffalo-fishing culture had been born from this Texas carp-fishing culture, which essentially made the Americanized technique an offspring of European carp-fishing. Serendipitously, this realization lent even more credence to my idea of buffalo being "the Son" of the Trashfish Trinity.

The Buffalo Whisperer and his pals had developed a specialty in bringing in supersized smallmouth buffalo, and they were pioneering this sport in a chain of reservoirs in and around Austin's city limits. His website advocated "CPR" (catch, photograph, release) and boasted clients catching fifty-pounders.

Impressed by the professional quality of the Buffalo Whisperer's website (which often isn't the case with guides who care more about selling than spelling), and because his site was being regularly updated (announcing that the cooling of the autumn weather would increase the action), I was inspired to send him an email. He answered immediately, which is always encouraging, and soon we were talking on the phone. I told him all I wanted was just one buffalo, but he guaranteed me more than that, and of monstrous proportions. This was a deal I couldn't refuse.

The following weekend I descended into the belly of the

beast again. The gas station employees I saw in Texas didn't care about wearing masks, even if the virus was well into its second surge and more than eight million Americans had been infected. At that point, 229,000 lives had been lost in the United States, where a certain president had been making false claims that 85 percent of those who wear masks get infected. His flunky radiologist with no epidemiology experience, speaking on behalf of the White House Coronavirus Task Force, was parroting this misinformation.

The hotel staff at the Sleep Inn then said it all. Like pretty much everywhere, there were signs on the doors that masks were required, but once inside, no desk clerks or maids or other workers felt any need to protect their guests from the droplets their nostrils and mouths were spraying all over the place. You'd think this state would've learned something from the first surge, which maxed out their hospitals, and that they would've adjusted their behavior for the wiser, but Texas just didn't get it. That's why they were the second most spiking state in the country.

I went to bed, got up early, and met the Buffalo Whisperer at Lake Walter E. Long, near the airport. A bespectacled Brit with a salt-and-pepper goatee, he was wearing oversized waders and smoking a cig. His cheery wife Kristina was with him, and chairs were set up on the shore with three thirteen-foot carp rods on holders equipped with alarms. A padded fish cradle and landing net were positioned nearby, and there was a lot of professional tackle and gear at the ready.

Social-distance fishing was the mode. We all took our appropriately situated seats, and I unmasked. We had discussed the Whisperer's approach to pandemic fishing earlier, and he had assured me that he gets tested every week and takes precautions. I had my hand sanitizer and wipes with me, which I planned to use after touching any gear.

The Buffalo Whisperer had prebaited the area with a hundred pounds of cattle cubes, and I could see the silhouettes of buffalos porpoising a hundred yards out with spiky, sail-shaped dorsal fins. That's where he was chucking the bait.

It was amazing to watch the Buffalo Whisperer wade out and prepare to cast a tennis ball–sized wad of compressed grits mixed with creamed corn and other stuff, suspended on the end of his line. He'd let that hang behind him, both hands positioned over his head, elbows bent as he measured the distance and tested the wind, a power plant steaming on the other side. He'd meditate for a full minute, then let it rip. That bait ball would arc out into the sky and soar over the lake. It would pass over flocks of chattering coots and circling herons and land a football field away, right where the buffalo were rising and diving. Then he'd set the rods in their holders, adjust the alarms, and flip the levers on the baitfeeder reels so the spools could spin.

Each hook was attached to a three-foot mono-leader which was attached to thirty feet of fluorescent-green, thirty-pound fluorocarbon line. That latter line was meant to flex, and the rest was thirty-pound, dark-green, woven line, going back to the reel to the tune of three hundred yards. For each mass of corn and grits, there was a two-ounce weight in the center. In that conglomeration, there was a foot of line tied to that weight. At the end of that line was a specialized hair rig, which looked like a piece of dog food skewered to an equally round piece of foam strung to a hook. Just think two marble-sized orbs connected with a pin hanging from a small hook with two millimeters of thin fishing line between the top orb and the bottom of the hook. Rather than using a traditional boilie (a prepackaged bait), though, the Buffalo Whisperer used "tiger nuts," which can be bought at Cabela's. The Buffalo Whisperer had cured his in a spicy marinade, and the idea is that the piece of foam makes the tiger nut float above the corny grits. A buffalo then comes along and starts snuffling through the corn and sees the tiger nut floating in front of its face. It sucks that up, senses something's not edible, blows it out, and the hook catches on the inside of its rubbery lips. When that buffalo moves on, the hook sinks in.

It was a multicultural day at the lake. To our right there was an African American family waiting for catfish, and to our left there was a Romanian father and his ten-year-old son who also had the Euro-gear. Within minutes, they hooked into a big one and the kid brought it in. The father netted it: a thirty-pound smallmouth, compliments (in part) of the Buffalo Whisperer, whose chumming had attracted it. Then they caught a twenty-something-pounder.

As all this went on, our alarms kept going off, beeping and blipping here and there, but with no fish really committing. They were being finicky feeders, and we were waiting for a screamer. When it finally happened an hour later, that's when the "buffalo dance" began.

The Buffalo Whisperer picked up the rod, held it for three seconds, and set the hook. It wasn't a dramatic set; it was a moderate yank that went straight up, resulting in a bend at the end of the pole.

"It's all yours," he said, handing me the rod, and I commenced hauling back and reeling in. It was a hefty fish, and it was resisting, peeling out line and shuddering on the other end. It was heading to the left, so the Buffalo Whisperer told me to lower the rod and horse it horizontally, which got it to switch directions.

While I did this, Kristina and the Buffalo Whisperer brought in the other lines, sometimes passing a pole over or under mine. This cleared the field to bring in the fish.

When it finally came into view, I saw a giant lemon-shaped underwater blur of white light boil to the surface, then a mongo humpback and a flash of tail. I also saw the sickle shape of its dorsal fin as it tried to swim off. Tightening the drag did the trick, and it was too pooped to party by the time it slid right into the net.

Holy smokes! All I'd wanted was one buffalo to abate the fever, but this pearlescent, ballooning fish was much, much more than that. Lying in the padded cradle was a big, fat, gorgeous buffalo with a coppery back and tan-tinted fins. It had bulgy, buggy, cartoony eyes and humorous sphincter lips, and I wanted more.

The COVID crowds surrounding us pushed in to get a look. There were kids and moms and joggers and dog walkers and dentists, none of whom were wearing a mask as I kept my distance as good as I could. As I did, Kristina poured buckets of water over the fish, which was sparkling with a soft, burnt-orange luminescence in the rays of the rising sun.

Next came the weighing. It was fifty pounds, ten ounces!

Holy Toledo, the narrative had suddenly changed. No longer was the quest about trying to get my target fish. Now it was about a highly unique, world-class fishery existing right under our noses, which hardly anyone knew about.

∞  ∞  ∞

THE CURSE OF the Buffalo had been lifted, and there was a new moon that afternoon, a shining, white parenthesis, with the rest of the lunar circle as blue as the bright October sky. Anglers all over the world contend that when the moon is between Earth and the sun, that's the best time to fish. Most of their reasons have to do with tides, which affect oceans more than inland waters, but there's also the theory that when the sun is eclipsed for a day or two, there's less light at night for fish to feed by, so they're hungrier in the daytime. This might've been the case, because the fishing that day wasn't funny. It was damn serious! We were out there from sunrise to sunset, and in those twelve nonstop hours, this is what happened:

The next buffalo was a twenty-six-pounder and, even though it was half the size of the first one, it was just as much a fighter.

The one after that was a thirty-eight-pounder and more olive in tone. It had a darker tail, a salmon-colored lateral line, and it trembled like a dynamo, seizuring with fright. Having expended too much energy doing that, this one needed some support in the water before releasing. We named it Trembly.

Then I got a thirty-six-pounder with a white lateral line, and started to see that all these fish had different physical qualities which gave them their own character. Some had long, elegant lips, and others had features that were less pronounced.

I caught a twenty-seven-pounder following that; it was much more ivory-colored than any of the previous fish. A crowd of Hispanic kids came over, and one of them uttered the word "blanco" (whitey), to which I responded, "gordito" (fatso). Anyway, that one went down in my notes as Blanco.

Kristina joined me in naming them, and that's when the mother buffalo hit. I reeled it in, it took a bit, and it was the most jumbo buffalo of the day, weighing in at fifty-four pounds! Kristina used the adjective "chunky," so that's what we named that one.

The next day was a half day, and I caught a thirty-three-pounder named Blimpy. Then I caught one with a dark gold corona in her eyes. Kristina named that one Brown-Eyed Girl, a lovely fish weighing thirty-eight pounds. Then came Scuffy, the smallest smallmouth of both days, weighing twenty-three pounds.

All in all, as the world raged on with explosive protests and voter suppression, I ended up with 323 pounds of buffalo. But even better, none of those fish had been injured by us beyond a pierced lip, and they were always handled so gently and with such great respect that no anxiety was visible except in Trembly, who the Buffalo Whisperer said was an exception to the rule. In his fifty-five years of roughfishing, he'd never seen a buffalo react like that.

∂∂   ∂∂   ∂∂

I CAUGHT A lot more than that, however, especially toward the end of that second day when I began drifting back to my eco-ways.

"What has helped this fishery out," I'd asked the Buffalo Whisperer, "and what can help this fishery out?"

I asked this because he had realized the brilliance of battling buffalo, a fish which can get huger than most carp, and he was making something of it. In a way, the Buffalo Whisperer and his buddies were doing what someone had once done in Europe when they said, "Hey, look at all these monster carp here! Just think of what we can do with this!"

The Buffalo Whisperer considered my question for a few minutes, and then he replied, "The limited bank space on this lake and others in the area could be opened up more to ease fishing pressure. Some buffalo swim all over the lake and might never be caught in their lives, but there are always the more territorial ones who tend to stay in their usual spots. These fish get caught more than others, sometimes over and over again."

The Buffalo Whisperer figured that creating more anglers-only areas could be beneficial to both people and fish and could help strengthen this fishery and bring in more commerce for the city. But mostly, he saw a necessity for giving both people and fish the space they need to coexist, for practical ecological reasons.

"There's definitely a battle for space on this lake," he continued, pointing to the shore we shared with canoers, kayakers, kite flyers, wind surfers, and litterbugs. Having seen dogs rampaging across our lines and swimmers drifting into our space over the last two days, I nodded back.

Some confusion had been caused as well by Texas Parks and Wildlife posting incorrect signs about where people were supposed to fish at certain times of the year. This sometimes made park patrons think that anglers were taking up space reserved for swimming and splashing and carrying on.

That's when bowfishing came up.

"The bowhunters have access to this lake," the Buffalo Whisperer told me, "just like us. When they come in here and shoot fifty-, sixty-, seventy-pounders, those fish are then permanently removed from the system, so I'd like to see more regulations."

"Yeah," I agreed, "and those fish are predisposed to extra large genes. When we lose those, we lose our most robust genetics."

The Buffalo Whisperer shook his head and added that he didn't want the buffalo's top predator not to enjoy their sport, but since this lake was incredibly rich with this fish, he wanted to see the densest populations protected first. This made sense to me: to create dedicated buffalo preserves.

"These buffalo here," he added, "are descended from fish that got trapped when the reservoir was created, but now they don't get to reproduce. When they spawn, the stocked bass get all the fry. So these buffalo, of which none are younger than twenty years old, they can spawn all they want, but their young are doomed."

And what should happen right at the moment? A jet ski, that's what! It came out of nowhere, and the yahoos yahooing on it began spinning shitties right on top of our three baited lines. They were scaring the fish away, scattering the bait, disturbing the water, and generally being inconsiderate and obnoxious.

Seeing this, the Buffalo Whisperer started yelling and gesturing for them to get the hell away. I joined him in that, but suddenly he was facing the other direction. The party associated with that jet ski was right behind us having a COVID party.

"They can't hear you," Kristina told him. "They're deaf."

And yep, they sure were. They were crowded around a picnic table, moms and dads and kids and dogs, communicating in sign language. And a few of them, mostly tattooed men, were responding to my guide with fingers, fists, and painful, unintelligible expletives.

Tempers rose. A scene was made. The deaf men were pointing at an incorrect sign saying our area was not for fishing, and now the women were getting involved. They were pulling their husbands and boyfriends back, including Kristina, who was trying to calm the Whisperer down.

It was ludicrous! I mean, we were all there to have a good time, but because there were too many humans seeking recreation in the same place, we were clashing with each other. And the people we were clashing with were disabled citizens who had as much right to be there as we did. So if anyone looked like jackasses, it was definitely us.

The tension eventually de-escalated, and they moved to another spot. But that didn't stop the jet skiers from continually tearing around out there and scaring the fish away.

In Texas, where our president proclaims we're rounding the COVID corner, which is a flat-out lie fabricated to get him reelected.

In Texas, where dangerous aerosols hang in the air, then go up noses because masks are signs of "political weakness."

In Texas, where the hospitals are approaching maximum capacity again, and all our petty disagreements can never be resolved in a climate of mis- and disinformation.

But ultimately, in Texas, where the old-growth buffalo swim in hefty, healthy, dumbfounding numbers. And since these buffalo are here right now and comparable in size to the most prized freshwater sport fish in Europe, and since they're highly accessible and definitely setting a better example on how to get along with each other than we are, I say let's look at them as a resource to protect in game preserves as well as models to follow for our own behavior. That way, we can indulge in them while conserving them as the whole world goes to hell.

## CHAPTER 15

# CONSIDER THE LAKE CONWAY MONSTER CAT
## A LIVING, BREATHING, BLOOD-PUMPING MOSAIC
## OF THE MUCK AND MUD

M Y FRIEND CATFISH is always telling me there's a state-record catfish lurking in Lake Conway, and I believe it. I saw my first five-foot flathead the fall I moved to these shores. I was checking my lines in the canoe, and that badass cat was right on the surface, glaring at me with its beady little eyes on its massive, scuffed-up head. It must've weighed at least eighty pounds. The cypress branch I'd tied the line to was an inch thick and busted, only connected to the tree by the bark that hadn't been ripped away like a scab yet. And that catfish, it wasn't gonna take any BS from me. Slowly, phlegmatically, glaring daggers, it moved its head toward the tree, then whipped it the other way, ripping the hook right out of its mouth. The water erupted in thrashing foam, a gallon of which slapped my gape-mouthed face.

That was thirteen years ago. Since then, I've become even more familiar with such monsters in this Y-shaped reservoir, which is the largest state-made lake in the country, stretching nearly nine miles from end to end. It's 6,700 acres of lily pads, egrets, eagles, herons, ospreys, water moccasins, the occasional rogue alligator, and enough fish to sink a battleship. The average depth is 4.5 feet, and having run lines on it for over a decade, I've met my share of super-huge cats.

At first they were sixteen and seventeen pounds, and then Minnow Bucket and I set a line with some big bait and got ourselves a twenty-eight-pounder. Following that was a thirty-two-pounder. And once, after having left a one-pound goldfish on a trotline overnight, I paddled out to find a jet-black sixty-pounder. That catfish's head was the size of a microwave oven and hardly fit into the net, but I managed to get it in and haul the rest of the fish into the canoe. And yes, I let it go.

I've also met hundred-pounders out on that lake. Every fall for the last few years, they keep showing up at what I call "Monstercat Tree." The first one I encountered dealt me a tug of war I'll never forget. That bullcat was so powerful that it actually began pulling the canoe under water. I was in the stern, popping a wheelie in place, the bow completely in the air. In the end, it straightened out a size-8 circle hook and got off, leaving me a mass of shuddering guts.

The canoe soon became too much to handle. In my thirties and forties I'd prided myself on how I could power all over the place. But as I entered my fifties, a crippling injury put an end to that. I'm not sure how it happened—if it had to do with carrying my debilitated father around, or straining to shove my beached motorboat off a sandbar, or doing too many push-ups the wrong way, or the cumulative effect of all the above—but when Lea and I were driving through Louisiana, something snapped in my back. There was a searing pain up near my neck and a shocking burn radiating throughout my left arm, all the way down to my thumb. In the three days it took to get to the New York Outpost, that arm became pretty much useless. I was numb on that side, and the doctors were slow to diagnose. I got passed from specialist to specialist like a hot potato, and the more they scheduled appointments for x-rays and MRIs and spinal exams, the more that bicep atrophied. The tendons deteriorated, and I had to gobble a whole lot of pain pills. Turns out I had nerve damage in a vertebra so ended up in physical therapy. My upper left side was partially paralyzed, and I had to accept that there was no way to get out to my lines.

Six months of intense occupational therapy eventually brought my left side back enough to get back out on the lake. Squeezing balls, pulling ropes, lifting barbells, stretching every night, that's what did it. That bicep returned with a lot less muscle mass than in my right arm, but I was finally able to design my own PT. Paddling being an excellent, low-impact, upper-body workout, I knew the lake could help a brother out. Running my lines after teaching not only brought my body back, it also kept me from giving in to the great despair of the Meatwheel which can grind human spirit to mush.

The aluminum canoe, though, had to go. It was too heavy to keep shoving through the vegetation, which could cause more nerve and muscular damage. It made sense to take it easier on myself, especially when the winds were blowing at more than eight miles per hour.

My father had passed away and left me his kayak, a kind of boat I'd always despised. They made me feel uncomfortable, out of balance, too close to the water, and vulnerable. Plus, kayaks lacked space for fishing gear, and there's not much room for wrestling in monster fish. But I couldn't just leave it sitting in New Mexico. He loved it too much for that.

So I drove out and got it: a simple, tan, plastic, ten-foot Sun Dolphin. And as I drove back to Arkansas with it strapped up top, an occasional Ping-Pong ball would rattle out every two hundred miles and roll down the windshield when I stopped. That thing was shaking like a maraca, and when I finally got home, I found out why. My father had filled his kayak with Ping-Pong balls for flotation, which I promptly removed, filling a five-gallon bucket.

I couldn't believe it. Although my father had rebelled and deviated in his own ways, he'd strove to project himself as a practical parent to his kids. He'd get annoyed at me for transporting a bicycle in a canoe while floating down the Rum River (the idea being that after landing I could peddle back and get the car), and he couldn't even crack a smile at a dogfish rod I once built out of a broomstick, some radiator clamps, a pressure gauge, and a toy rubber dinosaur. Basically, he'd never been a fan of innovations that test the boundaries of what's considered appropriate. Nevertheless, he had filled his kayak with almost two thousand Ping-Pong balls—which actually might've been practical considering his Parkinson's. If the kayak ever flipped on me, I'd pull my knees in and roll out. But my father, he wouldn't have been able to do that so quickly. Knowing his grim sense of humor, I'm sure those Ping-Pong balls were there to ensure that if his boat turtled, his body would be more easily discovered.

It took me a few weeks to figure the kayak out: where to put the landing net, the right way to hold the paddle, the correct way to sit, the proper stroke, all that stuff. And during that process, paddling out to tend to my lines, I became pretty adept. The kayak was extremely stable and swift as well. It took less effort to glide on out to the cypress trees, and it didn't aggravate my spine like the seventy-five-pound canoe did with its seventeen feet of drag. I could even get out in fifteen-mile-per-hour winds with a lot less stress on my still strong but aging physiology.

Not only that, every time I paddled through the lily pads, communing with the muskrats and kingfishers, my dad was with me. He was in his beloved kayak just as much as his DNA, which couldn't be scrubbed from his grimy life vest that I now wore every day. I'd tried soap and various chemicals but could never get his sweat out. So as I tied on new tackle and fought the waves, he was always with me doing what he loved. That's how I chose to see it.

But last fall when the flatheads were fattening up, and I paddled out and saw my 130-pound limbline hanging from its branch and scribing figure eights in the lake, I doubted the kayak could take it. Pinching the line and feeling a definite hundred-pounder pulsing on the other end, I had to question the sanity of tackling a behemoth like that in such a puny craft.

In any case, I wrapped the line around my wrist, and that's when the fish shot for the bottom. It immediately started ripping me out of the cockpit. Bucking like a bronco four feet beneath me, the fish raced back and forth as I held on, my aorta screaming "NO! NO! NO!" while pounding to let it go. My brain, however, refused to listen to my heart: I wasn't about to loosen my grip, the kayak almost flipped, and that flatty gave one last thrash and busted the line.

After that, I upgraded my gear and used bigger, sharper, stronger hooks. I attached swivels, new line, and 135-pound wire leaders. And throughout that fall, the monster kept coming back. Or maybe it never left. Maybe I had found its den and was dangling bait right over it. Because that cat, it kept bursting knots and taking off. And each time that happened, a new white-hot blast of searing pain would shoot through its flesh from a hook that would take years to disintegrate.

The knots were always the weak spots, the place where all that tension between mega-cat and flexi-branch had to give. I must've lost five shark-sized circle hooks to that cat in three days. It got to the point that somewhere down there a pierced-out, punk-rock-looking flathead was swimming around displaying two jaws full of hardware.

And now the fall cometh again. So now I prepareth for that cat once again, knowing full well that tackling a monster flatty in a plastic kayak is nothing but a fool's folly. But that's the challenge I have to face because that's the mission I designed for myself: to catch a monster cat in a kayak.

Since a hundred-pounder would be impossible to get on board, I set my sights on the more humble goal of thirty pounds. It would be a challenge, but it could be done. And if I did hook a bigger one, maybe I could at least touch it. Either way, the prospect of wrangling in a whopper cat in a kayak, whether it be thirty pounds or a hundred, scared the hell out of me.

ᗡᗡ    ᗡᗡ    ᗡᗡ

ONE THING I'VE learned about catching big catfish is that using big bait increases your odds. So I went down to Hatchet Jack's and got myself some of those huge, juicy goldfish. The results were instantaneous.

It was a twenty-pound flathead shaking the limb, and it caused all sorts of chaos when I tried to tug it in. It even pulled the cockpit down, tipping the kayak on its side. A couple of inches more, and the lake would've been rushing in. I almost lost my paddle too.

If that's what a twenty-pounder could do, I couldn't help wondering what havoc a thirty-pounder could wreak. I also started envisioning every little thing in advance: like securing the paddle before pulling up my lines; pumping the aluminum tubing of my landing net full of insulating foam so it would float if it fell in during a melee; and tying backup lines to my heavy-duty limblines in case they should fail. And to lower the chances of anyone messing with my catches, I made new tags with my contact info clearly visible to show these lines were active.

Then visions of hoisting shot through my mind. I always had a spool of 110-pound trotline twine and a knife in the kayak, so I could always tie another line on and throw that over a branch to try to winch a monster cat up.

I ordered some 150-pound, plastic-coated leaders as well, and attached those with brand new circle hooks. I wanted plastic-covered leaders rather than pure wire, which could slice a fish's mouth all up.

And as all this went on, I paddled my paralysis off.

ᴔ  ᴔ  ᴔ

Catfish after catfish, they kept coming in, and not without injury. Every other cat I caught resulted in the loss of an eye. Those barbed circle hooks went right through their skulls, frequently exiting through an eyeball. For over a decade, I've been witnessing this while continuing to contribute to a catfish cache of Old One-Eyes swimming around in Lake Conway.

And here I am, having half-blinded hundreds of catfish while also teaching Temple Grandin's humane approaches to animal husbandry in my Creature Poetics class, an environmental creative writing course for both grads and undergrads in which they study texts that consider the ethics of how we treat creatures, then write poems addressing such subject matter.

And here I am, about to teach David Foster Wallace's essay "Consider the Lobster" again. And coincidentally or not, a string of questions coming up in that essay is "Do you think much about the (possible) moral status and (probable) suffering of the animals involved…what makes it truly okay, inside, to just dismiss the whole thing out of hand? That is, is your refusal to think about any of this the product of actual thought, or is it just that you don't want to think about it? And if the latter, then why not? Do you ever think, even idly, about the possible reasons for your reluctance to think about it?"[1]

For me, the answer is no, I don't, or won't. At this time, I'm having enough trouble just dealing with the thought of not consuming tuna and beef.

I'm also having constant conversations with Lea about how she thinks I'll change my live bait-massacring ways and become a more sincere defender of fish. But when that topic comes up, I always wave it away.

After sticking live bait for nearly half a century, I've become numb to this issue. Using live bait doesn't faze me anymore. I tell myself my mind is made up, that this is who I am, and that I'm not going to stop being who I am—because if I do, the person I've made myself into will implode.

But because of who I've made myself into, I also know that this is the most profound way in which I refuse to grow. So call this a paradox, or call it ironic, or call it whatever. What it really is is an intellectual failure on my part that affects what I love. And since I'm not doing jack to resolve this issue, I keep asking myself what this makes me.

An opportunist, that's what! Who's eager to hurt animals in order to excuse it as research. And perhaps, as DFW suggests, I'm someone who doesn't consider my reluctance to think about what I don't want to think about: mainly, the fact that my actions cause bloody gashes, missing eyeballs, and open wounds to fester with infection. Torture and death, of course, are also frequent results.

Admitting this prompted a lot of questions, starting with, How would I like to be treated like that? And hasn't the Holocaust taught me anything? And how can I advocate for human and civil rights while refusing to acknowledge the pain I inflict on animals? And are these just idle thoughts, or do I stop short because my inner caveman comes out and clubs my conscience over the head, grunting "ME WANT MEAT!"?

These issues led me to discuss such ethics with my Creature Poetics class, using examples like Robert Hass's lines "Creature and creatures, / we stared down centuries."[2] My questions to my students were basically, "Why is he bothering to stare at a fish?"; "What can you see in the eyes of a fish?"; "Is he anthropomorphizing or being dramatic?"; and ultimately, "Centuries of what? Centuries of why?"

I'd shown my students a poem I'd written about that hundred-pound catfish I battled out on Lake Conway, which ended with the lines "and that, my friends / is as close as anyone / can ever get."[3] "Get to what?" was the question I put to them, and the answer was obvious. But framing Man vs. Fish as a spiritual experience, I had to confess, was a blatant act of romanticizing that can't justify endangering a fish, injuring it, ripping an eyeball from its socket.

The same question came up when I brought in a live lobster for my students to consider. When I did this two years ago, it had worked out well. I got a lively one from the tank at Kroger's, which my students handled and passed around. We had a blind student in that class, and everyone was psyched to describe the squiggly, wiggly details to him while he held it in his hands. But this year, no live lobsters could be found in Conway or Little Rock, so I'd ordered one straight from Maine. It arrived with a dismembered claw and a soggy, groggy, lobotomized demeanor. It was limp and pretty much lifeless. Passing it around in its Styrofoam sarcophagus elicited an entirely different communal reaction, which my student Annie Grimes summed up quite expertly:

### Tell Me That the Lobster Is Fine

*with the plastic yellow bands around his claws*
*with the bed of crumpled paper and white styrofoam walls*
*tell me that he doesn't dream of the ocean*

*the salty rush of water through his gills*
*the sun casting a ballet of crystals upon its surface*
*tell me that he is incapable of dreaming*

*that his puny lobster brain functions in waves*
*memories washed away like layers of a beach*
*skin cracked open and scraped clean*

*like a king's plate after a fresh catch*
*dripping red his stench of the sea*
*tell me that the lobster is empty*

*that breathing is neither here nor there*
*with his shell gone soft and green like moldy bread*
*tell me that the lobster is dead already*

*with his claw detached and deteriorating*
*holding onto nothing here in this box*
*tell me that the lobster was an orphan*

*just a stupid, idiot lobster without a family to miss him*
*without poems to write*
  *or portraits to paint*
  *or songs to sing*
  *or jokes to tell*
  *or books to read*
  *or movies to see*

*tell me that the lobster was nothing.*

Clearly, I traumatized my students by bringing that lobster in, but in challenging them to challenge themselves, they were now challenging me. In the same way Annie was trying to tell herself that the lobster was nothing, I was trying to tell myself the same thing: that the hundred-pound catfish I kept hooking was nothing. It didn't feel. It wasn't sentient. And because its thoughts didn't matter, I could sleep well at night. And all the fish I've ever hurt, they don't matter either. So there's nothing to feel guilty about because what I do is justified, because it passes on a greater awareness. And the fact that I ate that blah-tasting lobster doesn't matter because things live, and then they die. That's the natural cycle of things.

Telling myself this, I couldn't help pondering if accomplishing this monster-cat mission could lead to a decline in harming fish, or if I'd keep on telling myself their suffering was nothing. Without question, catching that monster gar on the Arkansas

River had led to a remarkable laying down of my rod. Because I had put that mission to rest, I no longer felt the urge to burn through live bait to get another gator gar. These days, I had no desire whatsoever to fish for that species. Having satisfied that goal, I was content on that front and glad to not be ripping stomach linings and busting teeth, which made me a better human (or so I told myself).

But giant gar and giant catfish, those are two very different things. And the catfish issue remained unresolved.

Still, if catching a goliath alligator gar could lead to me becoming a more humane steward (at least in terms of gar), then maybe catching a monster cat in a kayak could do something similar. Maybe, I considered, that's what I had to do to back off on catfish in order to really, truly understand them with genuine empathy.

So I kept on running my lines.

⚓ ⚓ ⚓

AFTER A MONTH of maintaining heavy-duty cat lines on a twice-daily basis and constantly adjusting tackle that kept costing smaller cats their eyeballs, my father and I paddled out to Monstercat Tree. I saw the line wound around it, and there was definitely something on. The moment I touched the line and felt the tension, I knew this was the one.

It took a bit to pull the line away from the tree and off the bark it was snagged on, and that's when the fish started jerk-jerk-jerking with a familiar bullying tug. It was definitely larger than any cat I'd ever fought in a kayak before, and when it erupted on the surface, so bright and silver and explosive, I thought it was something else. But all that chrominess was the water playing tricks on my eyes.

That splash scared the bejesus out of me. I didn't know what it was, I didn't know how big it was, and its force was so intense that something in me wanted to release it lest it release its fury unto me. But all that setting of lines and catching of bait and years and years of daydreaming this exact moment commanded me to hold tight as it thrashed like a mastiff shaking the crap out of a rat.

When it came up the second time, I could see that it was an impressively thick monster cat. It had a brassy, brownish, speckly pattern and two muscly humps pushing up from its bulbous back.

It was on the surface, and I was swearing my head off, trying not to flip. Getting that cat to go headfirst into the net was not going well, mostly because the limbline I was holding vertically was preventing me from getting the net over its head, so I had to get it from underneath. I missed a couple of times as it pulled me around in semicircles, but I finally got the mesh under it, and it swam right in.

Then I had to get it into the boat, and pulling it up was only pulling the kayak down. But leaning the other way, I compensated for the weight and managed to hoist it up and over. Another ten pounds and I might not have been able to get it in, but it slid right into my lap. Holy moly, I had my monster cat!

It was lying there in my lap, nearly four feet long with those fins. God, those fins! Those splayed-open flexing fins, all massively fanned and baroquely imprinted with scrolling wiggles and gilded squiggles. Not a rip, not a tear, glistening and glittering!

And the skin! That slimy skin was scintillating with ornate golds and burnished bronzes in play with bituminous blacks and olivine greens. It was a Pollocky pattern in which kaleidoscopic pathways could be followed with the eyes.

That animated camo pattern instantly recalled the thistle leaves and climbing vines I once ran around Europe trying to find in illuminated manuscripts. I was an undergrad studying grotesque iconography in medieval art history. It was a highly immersive independent study that involved Jungian psychology, because you can't study monsters without asking why we create scapegoats in the imagination, where images we fabricate fill in for what we can't understand. Back then, I was going to museums and archives and researching specific missing links, in search of depictions of what's generally termed "wild people": those hairy half-humans representing a primal connection to wilderness, so are often found hanging out with unicorns, monkeys, and long-necked birds.

But in this catfish's mucus, the wildlife was of a different nature. There were fish lice skittering around like bumper cars, looking like itty-bitty contact lenses with cilia-fringed legs for propulsion. And in that slime, you could see a living, breathing, blood-pumping mosaic of the muck and mud from which it had come, where it's going, and how that strangeness draws us in.

Okay, maybe I'm trying to make more of a fish than it really is. And if that's the case, I should call myself out for embellishing. Because let's get real: swirly patterns like this are natural, not fantastic.

Well, I did take some pictures, and one is the background on my desktop now. And looking at that optical feast every day, I can definitely say there's something psychedelic about that cat. But there's also the question of if the lost eyeballs and lives it took to finally get to this fish were worth it—which I still can't answer.

What I can say is that targeting a mega-flatty in a kayak led to one stupefying masterwork of a monster cat as well as one of the most astounding, breathtaking, holy shit–inspiring specimens I have ever seen in my life.

But out in the kayak, in that jaw-dropping instant when I suddenly saw what was inside its wide open mouth, I knew there was work to do. Opposite from where my hook had gone in, there was an injury where another line had shredded its mouth. The flesh was swollen and chopped up, and shifting the fish around, I saw a standard silver trotline hook lodged in its inner cheek, a foot of string wound around it.

That catfish then became a well-behaved patient waiting for me to do what I would, which was break out my pliers. I then began reversing both hooks. This took five minutes, drifting with the wind, working inside that massive maw.

And what an awesome maw it was! You could've fit a soccer ball in it. And behind the upper and lower lips there were rows of super-sharp needly teeth, thousands of them. Brushing a finger against a patch was enough to open dozens of miniscule, scarlet scratches.

Inside that cavernous gorge, you could also see at least three different colors contrasting with each other. There was the liver-colored tissue leading to the lower palate; a vast, bright white expanse rising up from that; and a sort of electric saffron, stegosaurus spineline heading into two tunnelly corridors delving into its gut.

My battery-powered scale wasn't working, but I know a forty-pounder when I see it, and this flabbergasting fatty of a flatty was exactly that. And because I had my GoPro going, you can see this entire monster-cat smackdown for yourself on YouTube (*avec* some colorful language). Just enter "Spitzer Catches Monster Cat in Kayak" and strap on your safety belt.

Anyhow, heart hammering, endorphins zipping, I positioned that fish on the edge of the kayak. Then giving it a little shove, it slid back into the murk as my father and I cheered from above.

AFTER WEEKS AND weeks of running heavy-duty lines with heavy-duty tackle and heavy-duty bait, my monster-cat kayak mission had been accomplished, leaving me coated in the glorious goo of meeting such a stunning grotesque, and having the honor of releasing it. And because of COVID, I'd been graced with the opportunity to stay at home and bolt down on what I love while thousands of humans died like flies each day as if they were nothing.

Meeting such an inconsequential goal, though, during such a dire time didn't lead me to lay down my lines and become who I wanted to be: someone who can suddenly quit sticking baitfish that plead with their eyes; someone who can reject the navel-gazing urge to spin pain as victory; someone who has the compassion to change his mass-mutilating ways.

Therefore, I had to put myself on the stand and demand to know whether my refusal to think about the suffering of animals was the product of *not* thinking for the sake of conveniently remaining who I know myself to be, because that's my identity. And if that was the case, then I had to ask myself if my reluctance to change was due to the fear that if I changed my identity, then that's the same as throwing away everything I've ever worked to be. Because if this was the driving factor for why I continued to fish, no matter the consequences, then my refusal to evolve was more about me being afraid than about fighting for fish and the planet we all depend on.

But ultimately, despite these self-interrogations, there was just too much left of catfish season to cease running lines. Catching that technicolored smorgasbord of a monster cat hadn't cured my fever one lick. If anything, it encouraged me to go for more. And because the urge was still burning, I still felt the need to prove that there were hundred-pound predator cats lurking in my own backyard. Proving this, I figured, would make me more me than not being me. Because not targeting monster fish, that's not me.

So as the mythic Big One continued to elude me, I continued being me. And that hundred-pounder, it's still out there calling to me.

But something else is calling as well, and I'm not so sure I like what it's saying.

## CHAPTER 16

# ROUGHING IT IN QUEST OF THE TRASHFISH TRINITY
## PART 3: THE HOLY GOU

'VE BEEN CATCHING freshwater drum all my life, which are commonly known as "sheepshead" in parts of the North and "gaspergou" in parts of the South. Having lived in Louisiana, where it's still not uncommon to see old Black men in Baton Rouge selling "Coons 'n' Goo" from pickups under the overpass, I came to think of drumfish as "gou," "gasper" be damned.

One might ask what makes a gou monstrous enough to qualify as a monster fish—because if you look one in the eye, you're going to see one pitiful, sorry-ass fish staring back at you. They have this disappointed expression on their wide-eyed faces, their lower lips hanging open as if stuttering, "B-b-b-but why?"

My answer to that is because they're there, ranging across half of North America, a seemingly unremarkable fish of just a few pounds, kind of hunchbacked and silvery with a purply sheen. The big ones can grow to mammoth proportions and look pretty rough. The larger they are, the fuglier they tend to be, with lumpy, battered, pugilistic mugs that conjure visions of toughened drunks in smoky barrooms waiting for another beatdown. I've seen plenty such lunker drums dumped at boat launches, some surpassing thirty pounds. The world record is a whopping fifty-four-pounder caught in Tennessee.

Hence, I set my sights on a super-gou; or to be consistent with my Trashfish Trinity theme, the Holy Gou.

I set out by fishing for everything under the sun. That's how you get a gou; it's how I used to catch them with worms under the I-35 bridge in Minneapolis that collapsed in 2007. I used to go there in college and be rewarded by inner-city carp, bowfin, catfish, bass, but mostly gou. I even cooked one in a hubcap for my father once by simmering it in beer.

That gou didn't taste like much, but since then I've learned to cook them in crab boil. You throw the meat in with a bunch of vegetables, let it stew, drain the spicy water off, and pour cocktail sauce on top. The meat has a chewy texture and tastes amazingly like crab.

But there's something else about gou that makes this homely grotesque a mythical creature to pursue. As Rob Buffler and Thomas J. Dickson put it in their book *Fishing for Buffalo,* "In the spring of the year, a low rumbling noise emanates from certain lakes and rivers....An angler hearing this mysterious rumble and accompanying grunts cannot find the source at first, but after careful listening will realize they well up from under water."[1]

This is the sound of the male gou's mating call. To attract females, the males make a grunting noise by vibrating muscles against their swim bladders, which is why their Latin classification is *Aplodinotus grunniens,* that latter word meaning "grunting." Thus, other nicknames include grunt, grunter, grinder, croaker, bubbler, thunder pumper, wuss fish, and gooble gobble.

Here's another fact about gou: they've got these calcium conglomerations underneath the flesh on each side of their heads that are sometimes called "lucky stones." These otoliths (ear stones) are commonly thought to be the source of the grunting vibrations, but what they really do is help fish balance in bodies of water that are hard to see in. A century ago in the Upper Midwest, lucky stones were rumored to be good luck charms. According to naturalist William Henry Hudson, they were used by fishermen and sailors to stay safe from storms, ward off illnesses, provide an advantage in card games, and help a guy get laid. Before that, they were made into jewelry and used as currency by various precolonial populations surrounding the Great Lakes. Supposedly, if you hang one around your neck, it will cure a hangover.

Still, I had to ask myself if what I was looking for in a gou was a trophy gou, a mutant gou, a monster gou, or some sort of gou narrative. It was too early to tell, but because I had to start somewhere, I went straight to my local fishmonger.

ॐ ॐ ॐ

There was a manhunt going on when I pulled up to Fishman's shack. The Mayflower Police and Faulkner County deputies were gathered round, nobody masking and nobody social distancing, thanks to a soon-to-be-twice-impeached president not stressing the urgency of a national crisis now surpassing nine million COVID infections and rising. The world was eight months into quarantine, but one runaway teen wasn't down with being in lockdown. She'd been seen hiding behind a dumpster, so the police were scouring the area.

It wasn't the optimum time to ask, but I did. Fishman had always been friendly to me and had provided info when I was studying alligator gar. He gave me a crooked-toothed grin and said, "Launch at Toad Suck, go down to the fifth rock, and fish there."

Translating "fifth rock" as the fifth jetty, I got out there on a sunny autumn afternoon and spread my jugs and noodles out. I was using bream for bait because they were schooling up in the boathouse, and trapping them was easy. Having caught tons of gou on small sunnies, this was a proven bait.

Waiting it out all afternoon in the *Lümpabout*, occasionally a float took off, and I'd chase it down. It was always a catfish, and I caught a shimmering, sixteen-pound blue, all pretty and chubby. They always fatten up in the fall. Fishing Support Group likes to go jug-fishing at that time, using baited lines connected to plastic pop bottles. We round up a bunch of cats, then have a fish fry over at Turkey Buzzard's. But because of the epidemic, those days were over now, which is why I was on my own, waiting for a gou.

And waiting and waiting and waiting for a gou. All day long, I waited for gou, pinning my hopes on another target fish by creating pressure on myself to meet a specific objective, which always makes fishing less fun. These missions I design for myself, they used to provide a sense of purpose. But lately, as in my quest for buffalo and a six-foot Arkansas alligator gar, these self-imposed monster-pursuits of highly specific monster fish were burning me out and taking away from the mojo of enjoying my all-time favorite pastime.

By the end of that day, I took solace in a couple fillets, which I took home and made into a catfish curry. I was actually proud of how it came out, but unfortunately, I couldn't invite anyone over to share it with. Nope, not in the world this world had become.

&#x2694; &#x2694; &#x2694;

A WEEK LATER, feeling more pressure to get a gou, I declined going out on the river with Turkey Buzzard and Goggle Eye and shot down to the southeastern corner of the state to put an end to what was becoming an increasingly infuriating gou quest. Luckily, it was the peak of fall colors, maples were bursting in brilliant orange, yellows were flaring here and there, and ochers and russets were calicoing the rustling woods. It was the time of year I love most, and I was heading down to a lake named Wilson Brake, where Chuck Piker had caught the state record gou in 2004. It weighed forty-five pounds, and he'd caught it on six-pound test.

Trailering my motorboat, I cut through the cotton fields, winding through terrain I had never explored before. This was part of the lower Delta, with radio stations coming out of Mississippi on an unseasonably warm November afternoon.

The brake was off Bartholomew Bayou, looking like a siren salamander from above, looping back toward its tail. It was an oxbow full of cypresses and cormorants and wisps of Spanish moss. There was also a lot of alligator grass, and no doubt some gators too.

Baiting up my noodles and jugs with frozen shrimp (which was the closest I could get to crawfish, the gou's favorite food), I motored out and threw them out along the boat lane. I then found some shade and proceeded to grade some research-based poetry regarding cryptozoological legends that my Creature Poetics students had written. My students had investigated mothmen and windigos and mermaids and cactus cats, and I was amused.

It was eighty degrees and the floats were moving around. I caught a few cats and let them go. I also caught a couple of tough-looking bullheads: one black, one yellow. Since one had swallowed a treble hook, I cleaned them both in the boat to make a sweet and sour bullhead stir fry.

A couple of hours went by as I vacillated between being rewarded by this time alone and being damn sick of being alone. It'd been months since I'd seen Lea, and playing it cautious by not fishing with friends was also taking a mental toll. Basically, the only voice on tap was my own, and its repetition in the virus vacuum we'd all been living in had become as annoying as my father's harmonica, always playing the same songs. Although I usually fare better than most in keeping myself entertained, like billions of others I was a social being in need of interaction, stimulation, and ideas that had not been hatched up in the isolation of my own brain.

By sundown I still hadn't caught a gou, and once again this

was pissing me off. Turkey Buzzard had texted me a photo of a gou he and Goggle Eye caught that afternoon, which didn't make me feel any better. They had asked me how my fishing was going, but seeing their genuine smiles beaming in the JPEGs they sent, I was too grumpy to respond.

I then hooked a fish and was reeling it in. When I saw it was a bass, I began lambasting it with every vile name I could think of, which stopped me in my tracks. This wasn't me! Something had changed drastically.

After motoring back and loading up, I decided to have a talk with myself. I was driving up toward Pine Bluff, explaining to myself that I understood my frustrations. Having just spent a leisurely day exploring an area I had never been before, which had been interesting and relaxing, I wanted to know where this attitude was coming from. I had my suspicions, of course, but lately, the childlike wonder that used to be a factor wasn't a factor anymore. When I'm on a fishin' mission now, I get so serious about achieving my objective that I forget what fishing's really about—which is staying engaged with the world, having a stake in the world, and hell, just having fun.

Well, I replied to myself, I love fishing for the same reason most people do: because it provides an excuse for getting out and getting away while communing with creatures along the way.

Okay then, I continued, let's try to put a positive spin on this. You had a nice day, the weather was good, you met some cool fish, and you wouldn't have experienced this if you hadn't gone for gou.

Seeing that I had a point, I decided to change the narrative: gou wasn't just another quest; it was simply a reason to go fishing and not worry about what I did and didn't catch. That's how I needed to look at this. Essentially, gou was giving me permission to travel the state, to search out new bodies of water, to spin my mental gou-roulette wheel and see where the ball landed, then go there. And because of this, I was actively interacting with the place I lived so was getting to know it better.

Which is Arkansas, a place I've always loved. Probably because I'm not from here, so there are always new things to discover. Geographically, Arkansas has mountains and prairies and plains and swamps and even some semi desert regions, plus rivers and lakes and bayous galore. But it's also a place with incredibly inventive cultures, especially in terms of literature and music: from traditional hill folk verse born of Appalachia, to the ingenious prose of novelist Donald Harington, to the "true grit" of Charles Portis, to the swamp-rat poetics of Frank Stanford, to C. D. Wright, and Jimmy Driftwood, and Johnny Cash, and Lucinda Williams, and all the artists Arkansas has to offer. From the Ozarks to the Ouachitas, from the Delta to the mastodons, from the crystal currents of the Buffalo River to the petroglyphs of cliff dwellers, this place is full of history and natural phenomena. From the wampus cats and hoop snakes chronicled by Vance Randolph, to the Civil War, to civil rights (Daisy Bates, the Little Rock Nine), to Bill and Hillary Clinton establishing Arkansas' place in contemporary politics, this state keeps teaching me, especially in the area of monster fish: monster grinnel, monster gar, monster cats—what a blast that Chance had landed me here!

Driving through Pine Bluff, a realization began to mutate like a rogue variant of the virus: gou isn't the goal of any quest; rather, it's an absurd objective providing a way for me to return to myself by allowing me to connect with the world at a time when going global isn't possible but going local is—and I'd be a fool to not take advantage of this.

Consequently, the silly mission of getting a gou was now giving me hope that things would always stay this way, that I'd keep on driving and fishing and exploring and discovering. As long as I failed to catch a gou, I'd have this let-it-all-unfurl attitude to drive my drive all over the state in a state of Holy Goulessness. So yahoo for gou!

Because this talk had gone better than expected, and because my gut was now growling, I pulled into a Burger King drive-thru. It was packed with two lines of idling cars, and it took fifteen minutes to make it to the ordering spot. The optimism I'd tricked myself into was beginning to fade, and it took another fifteen minutes to get to the pay window.

As I sat in my Subaru trying to think of a snide response to send to Turkey Buzzard and Goggle Eye for catching a gou meant for me, I could see the workers working inside. They all had their masks tucked under their chins, and they were all exhaling nitrogen. The droplets from their nostrils were floating through the burger-flavored air, dropping down onto Whoppers and fries, then going straight into paper bags destined for customers.

Ten minutes later, totally on edge, I finally made it to the pick-up window and received my spicy chicken sandwich combo. It had taken forty minutes, and the thought of eating those COVID fries was enough to make anyone lose their appetite. But at that point, the void in my esophagus was calling the shots.

I debated whether I should really eat this meal, or if I should drive an hour to get home, then make a sandwich. Or maybe I should chill out, be more understanding, just roll with this, and be real with myself by accepting that hunger is only a temporary First World problem.

That's when it hit me: this is exactly what I'd been doing with fishing. Meaning pretending I have to prove something, getting all rigid with my passion, and stressing myself out to get a gou— when all I really had to do was be honest with myself and go fishing for the juvenile joy of it.

Back on the highway, I took my first bite, struggled to chew, then managed to swallow as another thought smacked me in the face: going for gou was not going well. In fact, it was sucking! And the reason it was sucking was because I wasn't out there angling *for* the Fantastic. If anything, I was hiding in the harmonica. Yep, that's who I'd become, and that's what fishing had become for me.

Realizing this was enough to make me swerve onto the shoulder. I couldn't take another bite and had to fight to stay in my lane. There was no difference whatsoever: I now fished as obsessively as my father once played the blues. And the more I did this, the more I cut myself off from others. And when I was in that zone, fishing alone, not listening to anyone but myself, this was self-sabotage.

Two miles later, I couldn't stomach it anymore, so threw that sandwich out the window.

&#9901; &#9901; &#9901;

THE NEXT WEEKEND, a sunny Sunday in mid-November, I drove up to Oil Trough near Batesville. My destination was the White River Monster Refuge, an area I'd studied for an investigation of the Arkansas-specific cryptid for which this stretch of river was unofficially named. Back in 1937, stories of an alleged whale of an unidentified swimming object brought international attention to this region, which had been laid to waste by a devastating flood, especially economically. In order to bring in tourism and rebuild infrastructure, an event was created to bring in some bling. A professional diver was commissioned to harpoon the rumored leviathan, and network news broadcasted the hunt to the world. The myth grew, the stories continued, and in 1973 the state legislature passed a law protecting "Whitey," thereby making it illegal to "kill, molest, trample or harm" the monster in its refuge.[2]

It was a place I'd always wanted to visit, but when I got to the old ferry road, which was now a boat ramp, the river was pretty intimidating. It was deep and dark and muddy and roiling with a current that made me reconsider launching. A nuclear plant was steaming on the other side, which didn't add to any feeling of security. But mostly, it was the turbidity. Add to that the slick-as-hell mud which my Outback kept sliding down as I backed the trailer into the river, and my Spidey sense was tingling off the charts.

After launching, which was way more complicated than expected, I shot upstream, still trying to process what I had admitted to myself in Pine Bluff. I had no idea how to dissociate my militancy for fishing for gou from my father's withdrawal into the harmonica, but I figured I'd think about this out on the river.

Shooting upstream, I made my way to a bend I'd scouted out on Google Earth. There was a long, sandy stretch there protected from the fifteen-mile-per-hour winds. The plan was to throw my jugs 'n' noodles out upstream of this beach then set up on the sand.

But when I started throwing out my lines baited with shrimp and shad, the weights refused to settle on the bottom. The floats were rapidly floating downstream, so I scurried around, picking them up and throwing them closer to shore. As all this was happening, the *Lümpabout* was spinning in circles, and there were snags and deadheads jutting up all over the place.

At one point, I had three or four out-of-control floats surrounding me, and I was twirling downriver while pulling them in, untangling them, then throwing them out again. I was drifting toward a logjam, and I had to make a move and do it quick.

Firing up the engine, I heard a FUMPP! and turned to see that I'd caught an old pink noodle in my prop, and that noodle was now obliterated. From the vibrations, I could tell that its line was wound around the propeller too.

Suddenly, there was something sizeable right under the boat. It was like ten feet long and swishing upstream, releasing two parallel trails of bubbles. I managed to maneuver around it, and—I shit you not—whatever it was, it sure looked like a living thing, all shouldery and massive and undulating under me.

It was ten feet upriver of me, and ten feet from it, one of my jugs began to bob. It was a one-liter plastic bottle, and damn if it didn't slowly start going down. Belligerently, almost even mockingly, it resisted for a few seconds before vanishing before my eyes.

Then, about fifteen feet to my right, one end of a noodle shot upward. It hovered there, standing at attention on the water's surface, and then it went straight down, sucked under like nothing.

This spooked me big time. Not only that, but looking over at the shoreline, I was shocked to see that I was back at the launch. The rushing current had swept me half a mile in less than ten minutes, and I really didn't have the gas to be motoring up and down this river to rescue runaway noodles 'n' jugs.

I resigned myself to anchoring in an eddy where I could spot any floats heading for the hills. I'd only been able to toss out half of them, but that was enough for me.

In the meantime, that eddy defied all logic. It kept spinning me like a pinwheel, and the jugs I threw out kept catching on underwater limbs. Two jugs by the boat instantly got tangled in each other, and by the time I freed them, a number of others had disappeared upriver without a trace.

I graded some poems out there but didn't feel very safe. The White has a history of making people hallucinate monsters, and now I was seeing why. That oldies hit "Spooky" from the sixties kept replaying in my mind as I decided to cut across to the other side.

The spot I picked was in the wind, but it was also in the sun. I pulled up on a muddy bank, cracked a beer to calm my nerves, and threw out a worm on my lightweight rod. I was giving up. And as I sat there giving up, I looked at the mud on the bank and saw a super-smooth rock, about the size and shape of an oblong baseball. But the thing was, there were no other rocks in that mud, so it was sticking out like a sore thumb.

Wondering if it was a giant egg, I finally got out, picked it up, and, yes indeed, that's what it was. But it was hollow, nothing inside.

A shudder ran up my spine, telling me to run, but something more rational was telling me to stay. I had a number of lines in the water doing my dirty work, so it would be foolish not to wait and see.

I waited a bit, then checked my worm.

Awww crap! It was snagged on the bottom. Great! Having reached my threshold, I began swearing my head off at the river, before deciding to break my line. But to my surprise, as I pulled back, something budged.

I horsed it in, and it came in like an anvil. There was no way it could be a fish because there was no vibing in the line. It had to be a log, or maybe it was a snapping turtle, or perhaps it was a descendant of that "monster turtle" I read about, from a Quapaw legend dating back to 1893, according to somebody's Aunt Lizzie.

Then I felt a familiar flex and saw a flash of silver passing by. It was shaped like a gou and heading upstream, so I was thinking *Yes! Yes! Yes!* which I quickly revised to *No! No! No!* because catching a gou could end my "fishing for the sake of fishing." But when I finally hauled it over to the boat, I saw it was a buffalo!

I netted it, a seven-pound smallmouth: the fish I'd spent months and months failing to get in Arkansas, so had gone to Texas to catch in spades. And I didn't even ask for this or expect it. So I laughed.

It was a fine-looking fish with a highly keeled humpback and puckery lips. It was gray with black fins and hints of yellow on its belly. Its most amazing trait, though, was that its scales were as swirly and squirrely as the river it had come from, weaving and winding all over its body. And these patterns weren't in random spots; they entirely consumed this fish. From tail to gills, a carnival of wavy wonkiness was going on. Some scales were shaped

like turnips, others like boomerangs, and others like parame-
ciums. I'd seen such blobby patterns on mirror carp before, and
this looked similar. Still, I couldn't help thinking that the nearby
nuclear plant had lent a hand.[3]

But in that moment, with the sun going down, I decided
to eat it. Placing it in a cooler filled with water, I set up a battery-powered aerator. Then, finishing my IPA, I went upriver to
get my floats. But they were gone. All of them!

That was fine by me since I'd caught a remarkable fish. Not
only that, but the tension I'd felt on the White was now being
replaced by visions of crispy buffalo ribs. So when I finally got to
the ramp and released a long, audible sigh of relief, my thoughts
turned toward pizza—which I ordered for pick up in Beebe and
ate on the way home. Because pizza is perfect pandemic food.

ᘒ　ᘒ　ᘒ

As I wrote to Lea in a text, "Such a purty fish. Feel bad about
killing it. The ghosts of fish haunt me more and more."

Without question, this was true. Having fished with the Buffalo Whisperer and having learned to look at members of this
species as unique entities with diverse personalities, I poised my
buck knife over its brain. That trippy, psychotropic fish had survived a two-hour drive in two square feet of water, and it was
just as lively as it had been when I'd set it in there. I'd read that
buffalos were experts at existing in low-oxygen conditions, and
this was proof of that.

Beneath me, one shiny ebony eye was staring up at me. It
was looking right into my brain, and it was doing what any sentient animal would under such conditions: it was appealing for
empathy from its executioner.

More than any other fish I'd ever been with in this situation
(no doubt thousands), this fish was affecting me with a peculiar, not-so-comfortable wiggliness. It was speaking to me, and I

heard it loud and clear. So I did what I always do: I steeled myself and told myself that this fish is food. And since its thoughts mean nothing, and since it's better to know where your food comes from rather than buying it off the shelf without any reflection, that's what I told my gut, which winced when I pressed down.

It felt like I was doing a fellow creature wrong, but I fought that thought like I'd fought the White River—or my concept of that river during some moments of self-doubt. And when that buffalo spasmed, so did I, in the pit of my stomach.

Then I cut her belly open, and the tangerine roe came spilling out, signaling the termination of tens of thousands of eggs now incapable of adhering to submerged vegetation to continue this fish's legacy. I shook my head. It was the same thing I always confess to myself when I'm responsible for killing what I often pretend to defend, and this time, it wasn't so easy convincing myself that I was doing this for food. This time, I was being honest with myself, and I was still shaking my head.

Nevertheless, I kept on cleaning it, astounded at how easy it was to cut through the upper ribs which were flexible and light. I'd assumed it would be like cutting through the blade-dulling ribs of a carp, which is why I had a pair of tin snips at the ready but didn't need. It was easy to fillet the flesh off the skin and cut the red meat off.

The next day, I tossed those ribs in some hot sauce mixed with a whipped egg, dredged them in a mixture of cornmeal and flour, and put them in the deep fryer. And those golden ribs, I'm sorry to say, were way better than just damn good. They were sweet and crunchy and flaky, not muddy tasting at all, and the best buffalo ribs I had ever eaten in my life. They were exquisite!

But if they were worth the life of that paisley-scaled fish and its spawn which could've become equally incredible, I'm still struggling to answer that. But I can say this: Despite the fact that those buffalo ribs were some of the freshest, juiciest morsels of fried fish I ever ate, everything fried tastes the same. And fried food these days, at least for me, stops short. And more and more, fried food was leading me to conclude that there's more you can do with meat than just bread it and fry it, American style. Thus, there was one more test to do.

I had some backstrap left, and because this was happening during a pandemic (nearly thirty million actual infections, according to Johns Hopkins), I wasn't about to go running to the grocery store to shop for food when I'd soon be leaving for the New York Outpost. I was going to use what I had on hand, and what I had on hand was a garden to harvest before the frost.

Buffalo Butternut Squash Curry! The idea just came to me. It was so appropriately quirky that I couldn't not chop a squash into half-inch cubes, brown those in olive oil, then throw in the sliced-up buffalo and some whole cloves of garlic. I stir-fried all that in a cast-iron skillet, added two cups of water, and let it simmer next to the white rice. Then I broke out my curry, which was Japanese (yes, that's correct). I'd found it at my local Asian market in the form of what looked like chocolate bars. Breaking one up and stirring it in, I turned off the heat and let it all settle before serving myself two big scoops over rice with golden raisins sprinkled on top.

OMG! That deep orange, tastebud-igniting concoction was a super-rich, brain-boggling ecstasy that spun my head like a top! And again, since nobody was inviting anyone over, there wasn't anyone to share it with. Nor did I have anyone to share my discovery with, that buffalo is one of the cleanest, best-tasting, freshwater fish that I've ever had the pleasure of savoring. I'd even go so far as to say that it tasted like crappie, but without the fishy taste.

I write this partly as a friendly dig on Turkey Buzzard, who's a crappie fanatic, but I also write this straight from the solar plexus. That is, this declaration is sincere, but it leaves me in a conflicted state. On one hand, I'd hate to see more buffalo taken out of their systems, and on the other, there's an undiscovered continent of possibilities to explore more with buffalo. Generally speaking, we haven't yet begun to understand what we can do with this sweet, salivacious, abundant fish that has so much to offer in terms of sport and sustenance.

That's why I say let's farm buffalo. Yes! We know how to do it, we've been doing it for millennia, and aquaculture is a productive and relatively inexpensive way to get a lot of food to a lot of people while protecting wild populations. And I'm sure they grow fat and fast as well.

However, there's little information available about farming this fish. A quick Google search will show that buffalo have been an important food source in the past, but as the online magazine *Louisiana Sportsman* noted in January 2021, this fishery is now smaller than it used to be, and the market "has remained ethnic." That's a veiled way of saying what the article later says: "Back in the day, smallmouth buffalo were the most desirable of the three buffalo species. The best of the catch, sold as 'No. 1. white buffalo,' were marketed in the northern United States and were principally consumed in the Jewish trade," whereas bigmouth and black "were sold as No. 2 grade" in the South, with 83 percent of that market being African American.[4]

As *Communications Biology* reported in 2019, bigmouth buffalo were also once a key staple of Native American cultures.[5] Minnesota is only one of many states representing the fact that buffalo were once as central to the diet of the Ojibwe and other Indigenous peoples as bison once was for the original nations of the plains. There are multiple lakes named for *niigijiikaag* (Anishinaabe for "buffalofish") and *Kandiyohi* (Siouan for "where the buffalofish come from") in Minnesota alone, where the city of Buffalo is named for this species. In other words, for centuries predating the states, numerous North American cultures relied on protein from this fish.

Still, the modern mainstream has not yet taken advantage of the possibilities this food source has to offer. And maybe it shouldn't. But maybe it should.

∞ ∞ ∞

That's what I got from gou, including one more buffalo—and an extraordinary mutant at that—which ended up in photographs I sent to my colleague Dr. Reid Adams, a fish biologist at the University of Central Arkansas. He speculated that the nonuniform scale pattern might be attributed to "prior injuries and regrowth," but he contacted buffalo expert Dr. Henry Bart at Tulane University for a second opinion. Bart replied, "I have seen scale pattern irregularities like this on buffalofish specimens before, though never this extensive…I wonder if this fish had a problem during early development when scale pattern was first setting up." This sentiment was echoed by the Buffalo Whisperer, who told me he'd seen some smaller buffalo with similar scale patterns, but these occurrences were rare. He believed it to be a nonlethal birth defect prevalent in specific populations.

Therefore, it looks like I ate a unique genetic anomaly, the likes of which had never been documented.

More important, at least for my purposes, was a personal discovery gleaned from going after gou: the revelation that I didn't have to get a gou. Yep, that's right. And it's not because I was getting soft, and it's not because the challenge was too much; it's because I decided there's really no reason to keep after gou when there are more important things to do.

Sure, I could've continued with the "madness, the frenzy, the boiling blood and the smoking brow," as Herman Melville framed Ahab's vendetta with Moby Dick, but I don't always get my target fish, and I'm okay with that.[6] Not catching my quarry always assures me that it's still out there to go after if I choose, which is a bonus.

But maybe that's a false objective, and maybe these quests I keep creating are actually harmonicas preventing me from getting at what I'm really chasing. Because maybe what I'm really chasing is a way to find equilibrium so as not to give in to the furious, foaming terror of the times, in which the media keeps repeating a certain word. And the numbers attached to that word keep getting larger.

The first "milestone" was one hundred thousand. The second was two hundred thousand. And the day I cut that buffalo open, the COVID death count hit a quarter million in the United States. And those numbers, those aren't just numbers; those are real people who represent even more real people in grief and economic despair, whose lives have become train wrecks. So now states are closing down again, families are being told not to convene for the holidays, and the vaccines are still in development.

That, though, is only part of the overall picture. Another big thing going on is global warming and all the environmental concerns that come from this abuse. In the past, my research has proposed solutions for a plethora of problems stemming from such threats, including specific fishery issues, how to develop less toxic fuels, and ways to accept personal responsibility.

But this book is different. This one is more intimate because it reflects on the relationship between fish and humans, and between fish and me personally. In this one, I'm trying to hold myself accountable for the actual torture I directly cause to pain-feeling beings. In this one, I'm looking fish in the eye. And what I've discovered is that when you look a fish in the eye, you see yourself staring back, but only if you look close enough.

The truth is, we don't always know what we're fishing for. Fundamentally, we're programmed to try and try to get and get. It's something we have to do, or else we give up. That's why we keep creating gous to get.

Call it a twist, or call it a cop-out, or call it a bunch of baloney, but here's what I'm going to call it: an instance of direct inaction in which I decide to not get a gou in order to give fish a break. How? By breaking the chain of not continuing to evolve in terms of seeing things from any perspective other than an angler's angle. How again? By calling off my manufactured Holy Gou quest, so I can get at what's important.

Because right now, catching a gou is not important. I just don't need to catch a gou, and even if I do, what really matters is getting to the nutmeat of the matter.

So that's what I got cracking on.

## CHAPTER 17

# Toward an Ethics of Angling

A
FTER CATCHING ALL those chunky lunkers in Texas and that delicious psychedelic buffalo in Arkansas, it was easy to lay down my rod and take a break from buffalo. Similarly, after finally catching that snappy gar on a rope fly, I felt no compulsion to run myself ragged getting another via that method. And after horsing in that epic alligator gar, the fever no longer drove me to keep busting my ass for more. But fishing for monster cats in my own backyard, that was something I couldn't go cold turkey on.

During the hell-year of 2020, as most everyone in the world will agree, a number of challenges came up that reset the playing field. COVID chaos swept the globe, violence and protests followed, and the United States saw the maddest, most unprecedented, most disturbing domestic politics since the Civil War. It was a year in which nearly two million people were wiped out by the coronavirus, economies crashed, unemployment skyrocketed, frustrations boiled to the bursting point, and conspiracy-driven disinformation went berserk. Travel was essentially shut down across the board, people were hospitalized en masse, and we all had to learn to live with self-isolation, social distancing, hand sanitizer, face coverings, online learning, Zoom meetings, and a lot less genuine, face-to-face interaction. And because of this, we all had to become a bit more creative with our daily routines so as not to go completely bonkers.

For me, this put an end to traipsing all over the world, which up until 2020 had been my research playground. The idea of monster fishing the world and back had come to me a few years earlier, and I'd been able to get to Mexico and Argentina and various places throughout the US before being forced to focus my monster angling on the regions I was confined to.

Lucky me.

Then again, I've always been lucky, which is something I've always known. Some of this is due to white privilege and growing up in an upper middle-class family in a country where education and opportunity are distributed inequitably. But some of my luck has also been magical, like not getting my brains splattered all over the place when I was a testosteroned teenager wiping out on motorcycles; and having a mother who was an artist, who brought her kids up in a community of artists, and who encouraged her children to double down on their creative visions. I was also fortunate to stumble into the position of writer-in-residence at the infamous bookstore Shakespeare and Company in Paris, where I translated French criminals and misanthropes, which opened doors for me. Another lucky break for me was to run with some extremely influential writers and land a professor job right out of graduate school in a discipline I'm dedicated to, which led to the luxury of tenure. And because of the latter, I managed to land a year-long sabbatical for international research during the most deadly pandemic in a century, which meant I couldn't travel, so got to stay at home.

I've also been fortunate to live on a bountiful lake (my own backyard) with hundred-pound monster cats lurking in the cypress roots. And whether I could prove these supersized cats existed or not, I actually had the time and the tools and the know-how to do it. Yep, I got to paddle out there every day and bait my lines and wrestle in furious flatheads while families fell apart, while children starved, while the threat of a different type of civil war increased in volatility every single day.

Because of the pandemic, it sometimes felt frivolous to over-indulge in fishing. I often wondered if this is what someone who gives a damn about the world should be doing when there's so much pain and despair out there shredding our collective intestines.

Yet that's who I created myself into, I had to remind myself: an environmental fish writer/prof/poet who makes observations and suggests better ways to hold the whole fracking enchilada together against impossible odds. And I didn't do it for shits and giggles. I did it because I was committed to using serious research to send the most vital messages about slowing the environmental degradation we're experiencing right now: like how we need to take responsibility for the $CO_2$ we're adding to the system; like how it's important to search for greener ways to make fuels for the future. And I did this because I wanted to pass on my own inner-naturalist fascinations to evolving imaginations seeking ways to coexist with sea rise, drought, deforestation, messed-up jet streams, mass hurricanes, and misinformation.

But like I wrote before, with this book, I wanted to focus on adventure this time. I wanted it to be like Zane Grey after he made his name, traveling all over the world, catching world-record behemoths no matter the harm he did to them. But as I found out, it wasn't possible to just concentrate on the fishing action. Nope, not at that time. There was just too much at stake to be indulging in selfishly catching novelty fish, ogling them, then throwing them back, injured or not. It seemed to me there had to be a deeper purpose; there had to be a *So what?* to be peeled back and exposed; and, above all, there had to be something which mattered at a much more existential level than going after weird-ass fish. Otherwise, it's all just masturbation.

So I was lucky to be isolated in Arkansas with a side of Texas and the Hudson Valley. In the last year, that's where I existed, apart from a few gas stations and motels in between. But mostly, I stayed in my own backyard, where I discovered a new appreciation for massive cats and buffalo.

These limitations providing the incentive to explore my own turf further also forced me to look inward. That is, rather than going outward by exploring exotic lands and arranging forays into foreign waters, I stayed home more, hung out with myself more, and went deeper into my own mind than I ever would have if I'd had the freedom to keep on globe-trotting.

Sure, I was lucky to sometimes be in lockdown with Lea, and I still found ways to fish with others while practicing social distancing, but I was primarily by myself. And the conversations I had with myself, they really surprised me. I was questioning the consequences of my actions like never before, and because I wanted to see myself become a better steward as well as someone who cares about how my decisions affect others (including fish), I was congratulating myself for easing up on gar and gou.

But you can't always take the fish out of the fisherman. Or, to put it bluntly, knowing that there were extra-mammoth monster cats in my lake, it just wasn't possible for me to ease up on that addiction. And having been raised with the rule that if you kill it, you eat it, I was having trouble resolving the fact that I was slaying bait on a daily basis. If the equation would've worked out to each baitfish equaling one fish eaten, I might've made my peace with that, but sometimes it worked out to twenty baitfish or more for every one I ate. Whatever the case, I used to tell myself that whatever a baitfish felt when I stuck a hook through its back was "noninvasive," because fish don't feel pain like we do. But now, each little sunny I essentially executed to support my identity was eating on me like that gar I killed for art.

Considering this while watching a bobber on Lake Conway, I started thinking of categories. I was fishing from the kayak on a sunny December afternoon, trying to arrive at a rough annual estimate of the fish I'd hurt in 2020 based on a monthly break-down. With a red marker, I scrawled the following on my pants:

*Total amount of baitfish sacrificed for my obsession: 552.*
*Total number of de-eyeballed catfish released back into system: 122.*
*Total sum of miscellaneous fish wounded in ways beyond pierced lip: 42.*
*Total amount of random fish that died from being caught by me: 33.*
*Fish I inflicted pain on, then ate: 24.*
*Grand total: 773.*

Oh man, I was conflicted. Because there I was fishing with a chicken liver, trying to catch an additional monster cat even though I'd already caught a second forty-pounder earlier that month. Then I caught a super-fat largemouth bass, huger than a football. Then I caught another twenty-pound flathead. And the more I kept fishing for my hundred-pounder, the more harmless fish I harmed in the process. And the more fish I harmed in the process, the more I was rewarded with jaw-dropping monsters.

My question, therefore, became how to deal with myself when I was no longer able to summon up the common denial that most anglers find so easy to embrace when doing damage to what they love. Ultimately, I was trying to resolve the fact that after five decades of looking at fishing as something fun enough to pass off as professional research, it had become not only überpersonal, but also unsustainable.

∞ ∞ ∞

I HAD TO know more about whether fish feel pain, and since investigating this was the next logical step to take, I began a new round of research, starting with a 2012 study in the journal *Fish and Fisheries* which had been cited in over 101 contemporary international scientific studies on fish physiology, fish welfare, and fishing ethics. "Can Fish Really Feel Pain?" by J. D. Rose et al. was frank in its findings. The researchers had reviewed the major studies concerning fish and pain, and they found deficiencies in methods used for identifying pain, particularly in distinguishing "unconscious detection of injurious stimuli (nociception) from conscious pain." Their conclusion was that the results of these studies were "frequently misinterpreted and not replicable, so claims that fish feel pain remain unsubstantiated."[1]

This uncertainty about fish feeling pain was also reflected in other credible investigations. For instance, University of Oxford researchers Beth Greenhough and Reuben Message (2019) published similar assessments regarding disagreements in evidence on fish pain and suffering."[2] Likewise, international ichthyologists Robert Arlinghaus, Ian G. Cowx, and Brian Key (2020) found "substantial scientific uncertainty" about whether fish are sentient enough to "feel pain and suffer."[3] Plus, the more I dug into the research on the research, the more I saw the word *controversy* supporting the premise that if the authorities were not united on the question of pain in fish, then fish suffering can't be proven.

This made me feel a little less guilty about releasing compromised fish and burning through large quantities of live bait. But then another question came up, which I can sum up in a memory of a family vacation. It happened a decade ago in Minnesota. My nephew River was six years old, and I had given him a minnow trap, which was tied to the dock in front of our cabin. Every once in a while he'd go out there, pull up the trap, and examine the minnows and crayfish he caught.

One day, I decided to play a trick on him by putting a foot-long bass in that trap. It was way too big to have gotten in there on its own, but River was so young that I figured he wouldn't question this, and he didn't. When he found the bass, he cheered. A split second later, though, his kidface began to pout.

"What are we going to do with him?" he asked.

"Why not throw it in with the other fish?" I suggested, since I was going to fry up a bunch of pike I'd caught.

River scratched his head, looked at the bass, and cocked his head up at me.

"But," he asked, "what if he wants to live?"

It wasn't a question I expected. When I was that age, my objective was to get as much as I could so my mother could make a bouillabaisse. I didn't think of fish as things that had preferences. I thought of them as something akin to squashes or gourds, something you pick off a tree or harvest from a garden, fuel meant to feed the family.

Anyway, it was a simple statement on River's part, but a profound one at that. The question he asked was a question that took me fifty years to ask myself. I can't remember what my response to River was, or if we let that bass go, but River's empathy has been sticking with me.

So now that the question had gone beyond pain, I started thinking more about consciousness. I started thinking more about what fish want, and if wanting to live was something that mass murderers of fish like me should consider more seriously.

The article I was studying by Rose et al. addressed this issue specifically, and not in a way I expected. The researchers had evaluated recent claims for fish consciousness and found those claims to lack evidence. Of course, I'd always suspected what Rose et al. had concluded: that even if fish were conscious, there's no basis to assume they have "a human-like capacity for pain." Similarly, as Prof. Brian Key from the Arlinghaus study stated in his own 2014 article in *Biology and Philosophy*, humans tend to project the sensation of pain onto animals. His conclusion being: fish "do not feel pain."[4]

Meanwhile, because I was studying pain and consciousness at the same time, I began confusing the two. And because I wasn't satisfied with the verdict that fish don't feel pain because the experts don't agree, I knew I had to come up with something more solid to stand on.

I was sitting in a corner of the New York Outpost when I admitted this to myself, piles of fish-pain research stacked up around me. Whenever I made a decision on what my position was, all it took was picking up a new study, and then there'd be a counter-argument sending me back to the drawing board. Still, I kept returning to what leading fish biologists had firmly established in the Rose et al. article, that "fishes are unlikely to experience pain."[5]

*Unlikely.* That word struck a nerve. It showed that these researchers were hesitant to claim there's actual proof that fish feel pain. And eventually, Rose et al.'s "unlikely" conclusion drove me to abandon my panacea that there's no consensus in the scientific community for fish feeling pain. It also drove me to look at what I know from experience: that if you stab a hook through a fish, this causes a visibly uncomfortable electrical jolt to sear through its nervous system. This isn't debatable. Discomfort occurs because of pain. So when I hang a sunfish on a limbline for days, and when its meat starts to deteriorate and inflammation begins to spread, it just seemed *likely* to me that if this fish shows signs of physical discomfort, then what it's feeling is pain.

But if fish don't have a brain-centered mechanism for translating such stimuli into pain, then you gotta wonder if what they feel is really pain. Fortunately, Matthias Michel's 2019 article "Fish and Microchips: On Fish Pain and Multiple Realization" looked at some already established research and reasoned that fish don't have a neocortex, which is a necessity for sensing pain.[6]

Now that the question had to do with the function of the neocortex, I checked with my pal Armadillo Jeff (aka Dr. Jeffrey

Padberg) who's a neuroscientist at my university. He takes arma-dillo brains, slices them into sections, examines the pathways and layers and other organizations in different brain regions, then publishes papers on cortical connections.

"They don't have a 'neocortex,'" he replied, and explained how fish have a simpler cerebrum with groups of neurons arranged in nuclei rather than sheets or areas.

I'd always suspected that fish had a more primitive nervous system than humans (something akin to a DOS operating sys-tem, whereas humans have something more along the lines of Windows 10), but I never suspected fish lacked the specific neu-ral machinery to feel pain like humans do.

The more I plowed through printouts and PDFs, the more I found the ichthyo-authorities in agreement that the neocortex is the prerequisite for fish feeling pain. Agreement within the scientific community being sturdier ground to stand on than disagreement or lack of evidence, it was logical to conclude that because fish do not have a neocortex context for feeling pain, fish do not feel pain.

So there I had it, the answer I'd been looking for, straight from the world's leading fish-brain biologists. But because this wasn't the answer that worked for me, I couldn't accept it because—and here we get to the core of the matter—I wanted to be told that I was causing harm to fish, which would lead me to amend my ways. Instead, science was giving me license to go back to my earlier convictions that what fish feel when their skin is punctured is "noninvasive." Hence, I had to ask myself why this wasn't sinking in, and why I was still resisting.

Hell if I knew. But I did know that now that I was armed with this knowledge, I could stop associating the concept of pain with the collateral damage which happens with recreational fish-ing. This meant I could go on my merry way and continue to be me, albeit an even more confused me.

One thing I couldn't go back on, though, was the no-brainer that all animals want to live. This is why fish fight to get off the line and why wild creatures run from us. This is also why we struggle to survive, and why most of us find slavery and genocide completely abhorrent.

The upshot being, I now had permission from my own neocortex to keep on killing bait and injuring fish like I always had. Yet one thing kept nagging me: the consensus that there is no consensus on fish feeling pain; because if some biologists are still not sure, that's not a consensus. And since lack of evidence is not evidence, the permission I'd granted myself would always be debatable. This meant that even if science was granting me permission to give myself permission to be myself, I'd always default to denial whenever that inexplicable wiggliness told me I was doing wrong.

But maybe that's the way it should be, since we're all conflicted anyway, which is normal, natural, and human: to be confused, to live paradoxically, to search for more clarification—which, at the very least, means we're thinking about what's important.

So like most of us, I decided to accept what I'd convinced myself of, and I moved on from there.

&infin; &infin; &infin;

WHEN I WAS a kid, the question of animal consciousness was always a thing. My father was a sociology professor at the University of Minnesota, where he specialized in cognitive recognition and was one of the earliest practitioners of the mark study (or mirror test) in behavioral studies. He started with human infants by applying a dot of paint to their foreheads, then put them in front of a mirror. He recorded the baby's reaction or lack of reaction with an old-fashioned VHS camera. If the baby made a motion to touch the dot, that said something about the subject's self-recognition.

My father's research soon progressed to other creatures. He tried cats and dogs, but his most interesting subject was a beluga whale at the Minnesota Zoo, where he'd gotten permission to lower a giant mirror into an aquarium. My sister and I accompanied him, and a splotch of paint was applied to the beluga's forehead. When that jovial mammal came swimming over and saw its reflection, it did a double take.

I can't remember what my father's conclusions were, but some subjects he tested were found to be conscious of their identities, whereas others didn't give a hoot. He was making correlations between animals and humans and making connections regarding what stages of development subjects began to visualize themselves as "self-identifying individuals."

This research eventually included primates like Koko the famous "talking gorilla," who my dad finagled access to. Koko knew a vast vocabulary, communicated with sign language, and even had a pet kitten. My father would go off and do research with Koko, then come back with Koko T-shirts for us kids. He also did some work with primates in Washington State.

One summer, my father and sister and I made a stop at the University of Central Washington where my father was working with chimpanzees. My sister and I were looking forward to meeting what we thought were "monkeys," but when we got to the campus, it struck me as odd that the building they were housed in was just as innocuous as all the other ordinary-looking, lackluster structures.

We entered one of those cement rectangles, got on an elevator, went up a few floors, and went into a windowless lab with stainless steel tables and cages. The place looked like a morgue.

"Come on," my dad said, and led us toward the chimps, locked up in the back like that primitive humanoid from the movie *Trog*. When they saw my sister and me rushing up to say hello, they rushed up to greet us. That's what I thought at first, but they weren't leaping forward and grabbing those bars to greet us; they were SCREECHING and YOWLING with flaring canines, spittle flying everywhere. The next thing we knew, they were pelting us with feces.

My sister and I turned and ran, traumatized by their trauma. Even when we got out to the hallway, we could hear them screaming their hatred at us, and it was obvious why: we got to live outside that chromy, cold, clinical room, and they didn't. Nope, they were confined to the life of a lab rat, and they were pissed.

Because here's the thing: they wanted to live. Not only that, they wanted to live the way they were meant to live: in trees, foraging freely, digging up grubs, not poking plastic buttons for chunks of homogenous fruit.

So as far as I'm concerned, all animals have a consciousness, and all life forms want to live. If they didn't, they'd just kill themselves, as some porpoises and eels have been known to do. But as for the amount of consciousness each living thing has, and what that means to a sociology professor or a monster-fish angler or a couple of kids who meet some apes, that's all relative. Yes, you can measure such stuff and collect data and come up with informed opinions. But for me, I've always known what everyone knows: that if something has a desire to live, then it has some degree of consciousness.

ॐ  ॐ  ॐ

CONSCIOUSNESS IS A result of life. All creatures have it to some degree, which is why I had to revisit my conclusions regarding pain. The question to what extent an animal knows itself or others wasn't of interest to me, since the question I was asking was if I was causing fish to suffer. Subsequently, it seemed to me, the issue I should be looking into is whether the results of causing pain could cut an animal's life short.

The renowned ethologist Sir Patrick Bateson had a response to this in his 1991 assessment of pain in animals, entitled "Assessment of Pain in Animals." He wrote that if an animal has sections of its nervous system dedicated to avoiding damage, there's cause to worry that it could feel "something." His suggestion was that this something might be stress or anxiety, which can cause an animal's health to go downhill, thereby leading to an early death.[7]

This is a concern addressed by Bernice Bovenkerk and Franck L. B. Meijboom in their 2020 article "Ethics and the Welfare of Fish." They contend that even if some things can't be measured, the question of fish suffering "is not just an empirical question, but one that also calls for ethical reflection."[8] And my reflection on this, I had to be honest with myself, hadn't been thorough enough.

For one thing, most of the research I'd studied was outdated. The bulk of the articles I'd read were the most popular Google hits, which had popped up because they'd been on the web the longest, and some of them were twenty years old. The more up-to-date research in understanding pain in fish was harder to find because they had fewer hits, but when I went searching, I saw multiple references to advancements in recent years that were taking the pain deniers to task. Also, among the studies I'd read earlier in my research, there were plenty of abstracts and studies of studies I'd dismissed in favor of furthering arguments that advanced my own, and I knew this was bullshit.

To be objective, I had to seriously consider Dr. Lynne U. Sneddon's 2020 article entitled "Can Fish Experience Pain?" Her assertion was that empirical evidence for fish feeling pain has grown considerably in the last twenty years.[9] And since the scientific method informs us that we can't have proof if we don't invite others to disprove our theses, I knew I had to put my convictions to the test.

Dr. Sneddon's research on this subject could be traced back to a 2014 paper, "Defining and Assessing Animal Pain," which contradicted the information I had gathered about fish not feeling pain because they don't have a neocortex. In that paper, Sneddon and her colleagues revealed that fish might not have neocortices, but they do have nociceptive systems similar to those of mammals, and behavioral experiments with pain-relieving drugs demonstrate that "fish respond to pain." These researchers also suggested that if animals possess receptors that detect adverse stimuli caused by injury, and if they have opiate-sensing brain structures which process pain, then they "should be considered capable of pain."[10]

I checked with Armadillo Jeff, and he told me in a text that fish have all those receptors and structures, which Dr. Sneddon said should allow fish to feel pain. "From a neurotheological perspective," he added, "I would expect they *do* feel pain, and that the oral/facial areas and fins are exquisitely sensitive because those are what they use to interact with objects for feeding and breeding. We know nociceptors are present in worms, so I'm sure they're present in fish too. But knowing all this, we get into a bit of a philosophical discussion—can they sense painful stimuli? Heck yeah. Do they suffer? *shrugs*"

A few weeks later, my friend and colleague Dr. Solomon David, one of the world's leading garologists, contacted me. He had just done a podcast entitled "Garology" for a series called *Ologies* and had responded to some of my questions regarding fish pain. When I looked at the web page devoted to that podcast, I saw a number of links under the header "More links you might enjoy." These links included a lot of articles on fish pain, some new studies by Dr. Sneddon, and a 2021 article in *Smithsonian Magazine*. It was originally published in *Hakai Magazine* three years earlier under the title "Fish Feel Pain. Now What?", and it suddenly put all my research into perspective.

"It's Official: Fish Feel Pain" by Ferris Jabr, came straight out and said it: "the balance of evidence says yes." It also stated that sticking a pin into a fish behind its gills causes cascading electrical activity to surge toward areas of the brain that are needed for "conscious sensory perceptions." The article went on to state that the collective evidence for fish feeling pain is now strong enough that "biologists and veterinarians increasingly accept fish pain as a reality."

Another interesting moment I found in that article was when Jabr wrote, "Google 'do fish feel pain' and you plunge yourself into a morass of conflicting messages. They don't, says one headline. They do, says another." That's exactly what I had done, so no wonder I'd received conflicting messages, especially regarding the work of Brian Key, whose research I had relied on. As Jabr noted, thoroughly debunking Key, his article entitled "Why Fish Do Not Feel Pain" provoked forty-plus responses from authorities worldwide, "almost all of whom reject his conclusions."

Jabr also pointed out that the contention of fish brains not being complex enough to experience pain is passé. As he put it, "A mind does not have to be human to suffer."[11]

So with the knowledge that an overwhelming majority of the scientific community was united by the fact that fish feel pain, I was satisfied enough by this disturbing conclusion to return to the question of suffering.

⚭ ⚭ ⚭

DIFFERENT FISH SUFFER in different ways, a dynamic I've seen with my own eyes. For instance, most of the buffalo I met in Texas submitted pretty easily after they were caught. The Buffalo Whisperer laid them in the cradle, Kristina poured water over them, and they only protested with a few minor flaps of their fins. Those fish might've been caught before, and they might've known through experience that they would soon be released; but others didn't seem so passive, like the fish we named Trembly, who shuddered like a dynamo and depleted itself of energy. When we let that fish go, it didn't have enough strength to stay upright so kept listing to one side, letting the waves wash it toward shore. But the Buffalo Whisperer was there to help. He righted the fish, held it, and supported it until its vigor was restored. If that hadn't happened, Trembly would've been buzzard chow.

Catch and release is often depicted as a win-win situation: the angler gets to experience a fish, and the fish gets to live. But the odds are, if you catch a fish, you risk hurting it, either by puncturing it, getting it caught on an underwater snag, or depleting it of the energy it needs to maintain balance. Or you might scuff it up, tear off some scales, break some teeth, or coat it in irritating sand. If it's extra behemoth, removing it from its subsurface buoyancy can do internal damage to its organs. This is why catch and release is not a win-win situation. While an angler definitely gets something from temporarily removing a fish from its environment, a fish cannot gain anything from that experience, except, perhaps, a memory of being handled, which could be useful for lowering its heart rate if caught again. But if caught again, it might not be by someone who practices catch and release.

What I've learned most about fish and stress is that you can usually see it happen. Whenever you catch a gar, for example, blood vessels begin to burst. In minutes, its tail will turn crimson and the fins will follow; this is a physical reaction to terror. To put it simply, something in a fish's chemistry is triggered when it knows it's toast, which is why catfish literally croak when they know their lives are endangered. Of course, the most common reaction of any fish fearing for its life is to thrash around and fight back.

That's what happened when an alligator gar bit monster-fish master Jeremy Wade in self-defense, and I replied, "Score one for the fish." That soundbite made it into the third episode of the Animal Planet TV show *River Monsters*, in which you can see me wrestle that gar into submission. If you've watched this series, you've heard Jeremy repeat this catchphrase throughout the course of its nine-season run. This is because anglers like the idea that fishing is a game with rules respectably agreed upon by players on both sides. But that's not the way it is. With recreational angling, there are no predesigned contracts or even a coin toss to give fish a fair chance before they're forced to compete with us; they're just ripped from their environments. When noodling is involved, which means enticing a fish to chomp onto one's hands or feet in order to haul it up, both male and female catfish are directly removed from dens dug explicitly for reproduction.

The facts show fish react to stress and that humans can lessen the impact of the stress they create for fish. One way of doing this can be seen in US Fish and Wildlife sampling techniques for alligator gar. In Arkansas, the method is to wrap a wet towel around a gar's head so it can't see humans measuring and weighing and attaching tags and transmitters. Likewise, I've been to aquaculture facilities in Mexico where tropical gar are raised in giant tanks for research and food. When humans wade in to handle a gar, they make sure to hold it upside down so that it can only look down, where its buddies are swimming around, and not at its stressors above.

What I'm getting at is that we need to find more ways to send more unified messages about how to handle fish safely and effectively, depending on their specific species-related concerns. For instance, rubbing the protective slime off a trout in an Ozark mountain stream is way more hazardous for that fish's life expectancy than for a hardy gar in the Arkansas River who has excess mucus to spare. And although catfish can survive longer out of water than crappie, we should think a lot harder about how long we keep any creature out of its element for the pictures we send our friends.

These, though, are only half-baked ideas *toward* an ethics

that hasn't been developed yet. I tried to write an all-encompassing manifesto to develop this line of thought further, but it just didn't feel right to suggest solutions when my head was still spinning from questions. But if I would've written that manifesto, I would've called out a completely unsustainable practice currently taking its toll on alligator gar: bowfishing.

Sure, there are plenty of responsible bowfishers out there, like the competition shortnose shooters in Arkansas whom I worked with to design state regulations for gator gar. But I've also seen other members of this culture in action who are not serving the greater good of conservation. Allow me to explain.

One summer on a sandbar, I was fishing with Fishing Support Group at night, and here comes a bowfishing boat with high-powered spotlights lighting up everything in front of it. We had our lines out and those bowfishers could see our headlamps, but that didn't stop them from hooting and hollering as they passed right over them, the roar of their generator drowning our voices out as we yelled at them to back off.

They didn't care what they shot—if it was a carp or a buffalo or a legally protected alligator gar—and they sure as hell didn't care if they couldn't identify it. Those wahooing drunks were just firing away at whatever swam in front of them, then hauling their kills on board and throwing them back into the river. And that's what I've seen in Texas too, where trophy-sized alligator gar are still being dumped at public launches. And that's what I've seen in Louisiana, where annual gar rodeos result in hundreds of gator gar being shot for tournaments. I reported on one in which the ten largest fish a party catches are brought back and weighed for cash awards (you can guess what happens to the eleventh largest gar, and the twelfth largest gar, and so on, caught on each boat). And that's what I've seen everywhere good ol' boys shoot to kill.

As for the most jumbo gar that end up the prey of bowhunters, they aren't just gone forever; their DNA gets replaced by the chromosomes of smaller gar. This leads to less genetically robust populations that are less effective at adapting to problems caused by global warming.

As Dennis L. Scarnecchia and Jason D. Schooley affirm in their recent paper, "Bowfishing in the United States: History, Status, Ecological Impact, and a Need for Management" (2020), bowfishing is now posing some specific challenges for fisheries, including "the impracticality of catch-and-release, non-catch (wounding) mortality, and by-catch mortality of non-targeted native species." They also state that the most mature, egg-producing female alligator gar are targeted by bowhunters more, so are therefore eliminated from populations more, the result being an "evolutionarily disruptive truncation of life histories."[12]

That's what we're dealing with now: *the evolutionarily disruptive truncation of life histories!* So this is what we need to address, like we did in designing new regulations for alligator gar in Arkansas, which yielded positive results. Inviting short-nose shooters to take part in the conversation gave them a role in conserving the state's top aquatic predator, which maintains balance in its systems. It took a while, but the new rules got out through word of mouth, standard media, social media, and signs at boat launches. These messages helped create change, which lessened pressure on gator gar.

Hence, we need more messages like these, and we need to educate some shoot-em-up subcultures more about the damage they're doing. Our ecosystems need this, and they need this now, and it needs to happen from all angles: from the inside, from the outside, from the experts, and in collaboration with everyone who wants to preserve our natural heritage.

ॐ ॐ ॐ

THE MORE I studied physical pain, the more the concept of stress came up. And the more the concept of stress came up, the more I thought about suffering, which basically means pain piled on top of pain to create a timeline of both physical and psychological pain. As Walter Sánchez-Suárez, Becca Franks, and Lauri Torgerson-White state in their 2020 article "From Land to Water: Taking Fish Welfare Seriously," "current behavioral and neurophysiological evidence support the hypothesis that" fish are "capable of suffering from psychological stressors in addition to physiological stressors."[13]

This was the direction to go. Stress causes suffering. There's just no debate. Nor is there any debate that I cause stress, and not just for fish. In fact, it can be scientifically verified that as a professor I traumatize students.

Case in point: For the final project in the Creature Poetics course I taught in the fall of 2020, I had students watch the 2015 documentary *Racing Extinction* and respond to prompts. This movie involved environmental activists who were doing some behind-the-scenes investigative journalism into the illegal harvesting of severely threatened species. My students followed the action as the filmmakers ventured through warehouses packed with tens of thousands of violently removed, black-market shark fins, and they watched graceful, ghosting mantas being harpooned by Indonesian fishermen under the thumb of a wasteful Chinese industry supplying a demand for snake-oil medicine. My students were also forced to witness the vivid scene of a definned shark gasping on the ocean floor as it bled out and died before their eyes.[14]

That was the most disturbing scene in the movie, and I know this because one of the questions I asked my students had to do with what scene resonated most with them. The majority of my students referred directly to this instance. After that, they had to reflect on something from the movie that they kept thinking about, and write a poem based on that.

Then POW! I was slapped in the face by one of those poems. It was written by my student Tory Potter, an African American undergrad from Lonoke, the "baitfish capital of the world." That last bit of information, however, doesn't really matter so much. There's a lot of minnow and goldfish aquaculture that goes on in Lonoke; but more to the point, there's also a lot of middle-income, working-class families in Central Arkansas who send their kids to the most affordable colleges in the area, where I'm frequently amazed by their compassion. When I read that first stanza, I knew I had hit a nerve:

### Swallowing Rocks

*today i swallowed a rock*
*that was so unbearable i became constipated*
*with indigestible stones of truth*
*my way of life cancelled*
*i can only look at what's on my plate*
*and figure out why i contribute to this*

Since dedicated educators spend their careers looking for such flashes of illumination being realized in the next generation, I was psyched to keep on reading:

*I eat to live right?*

*could i choose to live when plenty are dying*
*and what could i even do about that*
*when i am a broke college student*
*awaiting my next meal of slaughter*
*i am miles away from any ocean and*
*every cell in my body aches to be with those*
*creatures that can't help themselves*

Holy Cow! Lea was sitting across from me grading on the couch, and because Tory's poem was coming from the gut, I began reading out loud:

> makes me think of all the things
> i don't do
> who recycles anymore because if you can't
> physically see a sea turtle choking on the water
> bottle you carelessly threw away instead of choosing to reuse
> then why save the ocean
>
> the stones churn in my intestine as I contemplate
> my next meal
> could i really give up cheese and meat
> something i love so much for an entire generation
> of earth's species
> something so small could impact this human world

Lea's eyes were watering up, and mine too. This wasn't just some student trying to BS an A out of me. This was somebody actually trying to swallow something she couldn't fully process, because she was digesting the thought of taking action by giving up something meaningful. And that thought, it made her want to puke.

> i must admit a traumatic experience
> occurred when I watched 10 to 20 thousand
> shark fins sitting there
> just sitting
> waiting to be soaked in someone's bowl
> of conceited soup
>
> is it selfish to want something you like
> is it more selfish to carelessly kill for it

*i am torn*
*i am broken*
*i am at a loss for words*

*I need to sacrifice my selfish wants for something bigger than*
*myself.*

By the end of the poem, Lea was crying, and we could both feel the twisting going on in Tory's gut. So I emailed Tory and told her her poem had blown me away, and that my wife was crying. Tory wrote back that she was crying too and thanked me for boosting her confidence. But if you ask me, she did the heavy lifting, so she did that for herself.

Sure, there were a few recommendations I had for that first draft, but so what?

*So what?* That's what!

This is what I'd been looking for: the whole *So what* of why this monster-fish mish-mash should be of any interest to anyone else! That *So what* being the fact that I now knew what I had to do in order to take symbolic action for myself and for others, and because I can now admit that I'm a stressor.

Yes, I am a stressor to students and fish. But in the case of students, that's okay. That's what I'm supposed to do: provide challenging work that causes intellectual introspection and leads to informed discoveries. But the stress I create for fish, that's something which causes actual agony. I kill bait on a daily basis and mangle half the fish I catch. I can't count the stomach linings I've ripped. All those lost jugs with fish left to die. All those turtles that beat me to my lines. The asphyxiated pickerels rigor mortised in my traps. The gar and bowfin killed for art. All the fish I've ever kept bent in buckets to keep meat fresh.

And in continuing to live this way, I encourage others to do the same.

⚭ ⚭ ⚭

ENTER AN EQUATION proposed by Bovenkerk and Meijboom in "Ethics and the Welfare of Fish." They claim a theory is valid when it achieves coherence between principles, and that their three-pillar model can provide results in discovering "reflective equilibrium," which is a scientific method for "clarifying for ourselves just what we ought to do."

That sounded good to me. If they could consider whether small, round fishbowls are bad for fish, then I could plug my own factors into their formula and figure out what to do.

The first pillar being to use one's "moral intuition" to establish that something is problematic, I filled in the blank quite easily: whether fish feel pain and are conscious or not, stress causes suffering. That's the problem, and my intuition regarding this, which is informed by my sense of morality, is that I have to hold myself accountable for the suffering I cause.

Okay, having done that, I had to test my intuition by squaring it with the facts of the case, which is this whole dang narrative. In essence, these chapters comprise a series of case studies that I've been conducting and documenting. So let's get two things straight:

Number one, the influence from the fish books I write and the direction I provide for hundreds of students and thousands of readers can't be measured. Some might argue that exciting imaginations and offering environmental solutions is more valuable to the world than the few hundred fish I affect per year, but arguments like these are quixotic. They rely on the idealism that harmful acts can be countered by good intentions and that every little bit counts. Still, this doesn't matter to a chubby bubba of a goldfish (as my wife might put it) whose flesh is rotting on my limbline. The fact that I entertain and inform can't help this fish feel less stress, and it certainly doesn't cut down on its pain. And the person responsible for the corrosive, cell-destroying suffering it feels every second it dangles there is me.

Secondly, let's drop this whole monster-fish shtick right here and now. The reason I got into writing on this theme is because I saw a market on TV and the internet, and it was evident that there was a demand for which I could supply a service in the field of eco-lit. Because I've always been obsessed with the concept of monsters as much as fish, and because my lifelong study of monsters and monster fishing had rewarded me for over half a century, this was a perfect fit for me, so I hopped on board.

But now, this whole monster-fish biz is starting to feel a bit sensationalist and a bit insincere because it's not really "monster fish" we care about (yes, I'm including you, since you care enough to have read this far). It's fish, with or without an adjective.

If this declaration bums out any die-hard monster-fish fans, I apologize, but with the world in the shape it's in there's no time be messing around with what kind of drapes to hang in our house when the whole damn thing is ablaze. That's a stance I'm willing to take, even if it undermines what I've been striving to create for the last twenty years: a greater awareness that our forests are burning, our sky is swirling, the seas are churning, all animals are running for cover, and it's only getting worse. Plus, cliché or not, my mother drilled it into me that honesty is the best policy, and honestly, all fish need our help.

Let's return to the next step in Bovenkerk and Meijboom's equation, which is to square the facts of the case with "moral principles." The facts are this: That because I live paradoxically, intentionally hurting what I purport to love, I cause fish to suffer. A basic moral principle of respect for animal welfare being that hurting animals is cruel, we arrive at the point where Bovenkerk and Meijboom indicate these principles can be tested by intuition. And if this testing leads to "counter-intuitive implications" (which they do, because here I am writing a monster-fish book that reconsiders monster fishing), then "we have reason to consider whether it is necessary to refine or change our principles."

Voila! That's what I needed, and that's what I got: a reason to revise my ways! But here's the best part: Bovenkerk and Meijboom allow for this testing to exist as "a temporary judgement."[15]

*Temporary*! Another word I wanted to hear! It's a word that allows me to make a resolution like millions do every New Year's. For example, as noted earlier, I swore off consuming beef and tuna for a year so as not to support the destruction of those industries. After this year is over I'll reconsider, but I expect I'll keep this resolution in place, except in the case of an isolated, environmentally friendly, grass-fed steak or a once-in-a-blue-moon sashimi or two. In the meantime, the Outback Steakhouse won't miss my business (and McDonald's never had it), and I'm appeased by the fact that I'm not directly enabling the overgrazing of cattle and the release of all that methane and carbon dioxide into the atmosphere. On that front, and with tuna, I am at peace with myself.

And temporary being temporary, I can take a similar vow. Like a vow of celibacy, or a vow to exercise more, or a vow to fast. Or like when the Black Beat poet Bob Kaufman took a vow of silence in protest of JFK's assassination and didn't speak until the end of the Vietnam War. He had to do that for himself, which caused others to reflect on his actions. So call it a symbolic gesture, or call it trying not to add to the problem, or call it being self-absorbed, but like my student Tory taught me, "*I need to sacrifice my selfish wants for something bigger than myself.*"

⚭ ⚭ ⚭

As my Creature Poetics students also taught me when I asked them to respond to the message from *Racing Extinction* which had the greatest impact on them, most students referred to the fact that if every American skipped meat and cheese once a week for a year, this works out to taking 7,600,000 cars off the streets. It's a message I totally missed, but they caught. It's a message about how things add up, which relates to how fish add up. And currently, there are hundreds of fish out there swimming around maimed by me, most of them missing an eye. But even worse, there are thousands of fish with unique genes I removed from circulation while causing them to suffer.

Realistically, I couldn't see taking a hiatus from the identity I'd strived to create for myself, from the lifestyle I've been actively engaged in since the age of six, from the pastime I actually dream about. But if I didn't step back, especially after proposing stepping back, I wouldn't just continue being a stressor; I'd be a coward too. And if I didn't attempt to tamp down the stress I create for fish, I wouldn't have learned anything.

So in order to evolve, I need to be who I want to be: someone who slows down and takes time off from causing mass fish to suffer and die from my actions. Otherwise, I'll continue being the me I've always been, who refuses to filter the stressors stressing me, who turns away from hurting fish.

Thus, I need to follow through on a resolution to be a role model for myself. As cockamamie as it sounds to become the counter-intuitive monster-fish fisherman who swears off fishing, this is the only way I can see right now to lead by example. Of course, laying off on this passion won't make much of a dent when three trillion fish are killed every year.[16] But because I could've made a difference for the 773 fish I personally caused to writhe in agony last year, this is what I have to do to get the number down to zero in the coming year.

This might be antithetical to advancing the professional niche I've carved for myself, but so what! This isn't about protecting my literary personality; it's about the bioethics of how I torture hundreds of actual, bleeding, gasping, gurgling, real-ass, pain-feeling beings on an annual basis, and what I'm going to do about this.

And that's the rub: to really pause, to really hold myself accountable by quitting fishing, which might seem easy to anyone who doesn't have that monkey on their back. But for me, it'll be one of the most nerve-wracking challenges I've ever faced: to restrain all those natural impulses screaming at me to be me; to actually stave off all the nervous energy that will accompany a barrage of other withdrawal symptoms, including crankiness, boredom, and depression; to endure all that sitting around and searching for placebos to take my mind off what my chemistry is screeching to do, which is what I live to do. That's what I'm committing to, which is the least I can do on a planet where way more stressors could also call themselves out and lessen the pressures we each create on an annual basis.

So with two million deaths from COVID worldwide, with millions more on the way, with thousands dying every day during what the media keeps calling "the darkest winter in modern history," and with global emissions of greenhouse gasses continuing to rise despite all the lockdowns and slowdowns crippling economies in the last few years we have left to fend off cataclysmic devastation, in which I'm on track to cause as much suffering in the future as I have in the past, then score 773 for the fish.[17]

Or to put it in other terms, score 773 for 773 sentient creatures that will not suffer from my actions in the coming year. Score 773 for 773 fish, who the neuroscience community confirms are not immune to feeling pain. Score 773 for fish, who've historically done more for the growth of all species on this planet than any other species ever has.

As Pablo Neruda wrote in his poem "Ode to the Sea," "in the struggle, / lie the fish, the bread, / the miracle," a metaphor that still holds true.[18] Fish have always been central to the struggle of maintaining life on this planet. They are the bread, the manna, the biological miracle that sustains life as we know it. New land masses and fishing grounds to exploit never could've been discovered if not for salt cod, which made extended excursions in seafaring possible. Human populations are most concentrated along our coasts and near bodies of water because that's where fish exist. Just think of all the sharks and bears and birds and bacteria and myriad other organisms that depend on fish for survival, and how we're tearing through this vital resource at a totally unsustainable pace.

This is something we've known for nearly two decades yet continue to deny. The 2006 *Stanford News* article "*Science* Study Predicts Collapse of All Seafood Fisheries by 2050" places this looming tragedy into perspective. An international team of economists and ecologists found that the worldwide loss of oceanic biodiversity "is profoundly reducing the ocean's ability to produce seafood, resist diseases, filter pollutants and, rebound from stresses, such as climate change and overfishing."[19] Their unequivocal conclusion being just what the title of the article says: all seafood fisheries will collapse by 2050.

Let's think about this for a second: in less than thirty years all wild seafood will be gone! This is serious business because when saltwater fisheries crash, nearly ten billion people will scramble to compete for protein.[20] Freshwater fisheries will then follow and be ravaged unto annihilation.

But there's an even more important reason that fish are more deserving of our compassion than any other species we can fathom, which I keep harking back to: for the countless stories they've inspired in both literature and oral traditions, not to mention song, film, TV, theology, dance, sculpture, architecture, and all narratives in all cultures which keep us dreaming of the mythic Big One. From Jesus, to Hemingway, to all the creation myths, to books like *One Fish, Two Fish, Red Fish, Blue Fish*, which we read to our children, fish have become as inseparable from our imaginations as the cells in our collective plasma.

Consequently, if I suffer in any petty way from not fishing for a year, that's something I can live with. And because humans as a whole are too divided and too distracted to make good on what we owe our evolutionary ancestors, I'll take a time out to reflect on the debt I personally owe to fish for making my life more colorful and meaningful. And foolishly, thankfully, I'll do this with the hope that others will act in comparable ways to help preserve what we have left of this indispensable, irreversible, irreplaceable water world under catastrophic stress.

For fish, who feel pain just like us.

# Notes

Chapter 6: Catching Jack In Mexico

1. Walsh, Bryan. "The Pacific Bluefin Tuna Is Going, Going…," *Time,* January 11, 2013. Accessed October 10, 2021. https://science.time. com/2013/01/11/the-pacific-bluefin-tuna-is-almost-gone/.

2. Leahy, Stephen. "One Million Species at Risk of Extinction, UN Report Warns," *National Geographic,* May 6, 2019. Accessed January 6, 2021. https://www.nationalgeographic.com/environment/ article/ipbes-un-biodiversity-report-warns-one-million-species-at-risk.

Chapter 7: Pike Fever and the Chemistry of Adaptive Fishery Management

1. Scarnecchia, Dennis L. "A Reappraisal of Gars and Bowfins in Fishery Management," *Fisheries,* vol. 17, no. 5 (September 1992: 6–12).

2. Michigan Department of Natural Resources. *Muskellunge: A Michigan Resource*, 2012. Accessed July 6, 2019. https://www.michigan. gov/documents/dnr/Muskellunge_-_A_Michigan_Resource_-_ May_2012_386501_7.pdf.

3. City of Oconomowoc. *Oconomowoc Watershed Protection Program (OWPP)*, 2015. Accessed July 25, 2019. https://www.oconomo-woc-wi.gov/DocumentCenter/View/3752/OWPP-New-Fly-er-20150625?bidId=#:~:text=The%20City%20of%20Oconomo-woc%20is,in%20the%20Oconomowoc%20River%20watershed.

4. Williams, Ted. *Something's Fishy: An Angler's Look at Our Distressed Gamefish and Their Waters—and How We Can Preserve Both* (New York City: Skyhorse Publishing, 2007): 13–14.

5. City of Oconomowoc.

6. Lyons, John, Timothy P. Parks, Kristi L. Minahan, and Aaron S. Ruesch. "Evaluation of Oxythermal Metrics and Benchmarks for the Protection of Cisco (*Coregonus artedi*) Habitat Quality and Quantity in Wisconsin Lakes," *Canadian Journal of Fisheries and Aquatic Sciences* 75, issue 7 (June 12, 2017): 600–608.

CHAPTER 8: AFTER THE GOLDEN DORADO

1. Author's translation, from Arthur Rimbaud, "Le Bateau ivre," *Œuvres de Arthur Rimbaud* (Paris: Mercure de France, 1952), stanza 15, 112. Incidentally, there has been some debate about the exact species Rimbaud was referring to when he wrote, "*J'aurais voulu montrer aux enfants ces dorades / Du flot bleu, ces poissons d'or, ces poisssons chantants,*" in his most celebrated poem, "The Drunken Boat." Some scholars have speculated that he might have been referring to koi or goldfish, or even the saltwater dorado species known as mahi-mahi or dolphinfish (*Coryphaena hippurus*). Still, there's a possibility that Rimbaud was referring to the exotic South American freshwater species *Salminus brasiliensis*, whose redundant English name (golden dorado) literally means "golden fish of gold."

2. Hass, Robert. "On the Coast Near Sausalito," *Field Guide* (New Haven, CT: Yale University Press, 1973): 4.

CHAPTER 9: CHASING CHIMERAS IN THE SALISH SEA

1. Doughton, Sandi. "Rise of the Ratfish in Puget Sound," *The Seattle Times,* August 14, 2010.

2. "Ratfish—An Ancient Fish of a Different Age," *Rosita.* Accessed August 10, 2019. https://www.ratfishoil.org/ratfish-an-ancient-fish-of-a-different-age.

3. *Washington Sport Fishing Rules* (Olympia: Washington Department of Fish and Wildlife, 2019): 115.

4. Grundhauser, Eric. "The Long, Strange Legacy of One of the World's Earliest Fake Mermaids," *Atlas Obscura,* February 9, 2018. Accessed August 10, 2019. https://www.atlasobscura.com/articles/jenny-haniver-history-fake-mermaid.

5. Troll, Ray. "Ratfish Waiting Patiently for Seattle to Go Away," *Ray Troll.* Accessed August 10, 2019. https://www.trollart.com/product/ratfish-waiting-for-seattle-to-go-away-art-poster/.

6. Blaine, Jennifer, Robert Pacunski, and Dayv Lowry. *2019 WDFW Bottom Trawl Survey Cruise Summary* (Olympia: Washington Department of Fish and Wildlife, 2019): 6.

7. Levin, Phil. Qtd. in Doughton.

Chapter 10: Roughing it in Quest of the Trashfish Trinity: Part 1

1. Wagner, Greg. Qtd. in Debbie Elliott. "The Secret to Catching Carp Is All in the Doughball," *All Things Considered,* National Public Radio, July 16, 2006. Accessed May 25, 2020. https://www.npr.org/templates/story/story.php?storyId=5561382.

2. de Kock, Servaas. "Jumping Fish and Swimming Speed," August 1, 2016. Accessed May 25, 2020. https://www.koinet.net/info/docs/SwimmingSpeedofFish.pdf.

3. Grey, Zane. *Tales of Fishing Virgin Seas* (New York City: The Derrydale Press, 1925): 154

Chapter 11: Fly Fishing the Impossible Gar

1. "Fishing for Arkansas Gar—Disrespected, but Formidable, Opponents," *Arkansas Democrat-Gazette,* September 22, 2014. Accessed June 28, 2020. https://www.arkansasonline.com/news/2014/sep/22/fishing-arkansas-gar-disrespected-formidable-oppon/.

2. Sain, Johnny Carrol. "The Gar Hole: Repentance on the Banks of Point Remove Creek," *Hatch Magazine,* October 20, 2017. Accessed June 28, 2020. https://www.hatchmag.com/articles/gar-hole/7714478.

Chapter 12: Monster Fishing Texas

1. Edappazham, Gipson, Saly N. Thomas, and Ashraf Muhamed. "Corrosion Resistance of Fishing Hooks with Different Surface Coatings," *Fishery Technology* 47, no. 2 (July 2010): 123.

2. "Will a Fishing Hook Dissolve in Water?," *Begin to Fish.* Accessed September 24, 2021. https://www.begintofish.com/will-a-fishing-hook-dissolve-in-water/.

3. Lamansky, James A. Jr., Kevin Meyer, Brett Spaulding, and Brian J. Jaques. "Corrosion Rates and Compression Strength of White Sturgeon-Sized Fishing Hooks Exposed to Simulated Stomach

Conditions," *North American Journal of Fisheries Management* 38, no. 4 (May 2018): 896.

4. Grey, 83.

CHAPTER 13: TRANSLATING ARKANSAS' ALLIGATOR GAR MANAGEMENT PLAN INTO AN EPIC FATTY

1. Foster, Melissa. "Support #GARkansas," *Change.org,* 2018. Accessed January 9, 2021. https://www.change.org/p/melissa-foster-support-garkansas.

2. Brinkman, Eric, Brett Timmons, Jimmy Barnett, Aaron Kern, Micah Tindall, and Chad Wicker. *Arkansas Alligator Gar Management Plan, 2nd ed.,* 2017 (Little Rock: Arkansas Game and Fish Commission): 1.

3. Arkansas Game and Fish Commission. "Arkansas Alligator Gar," *YouTube,* September 1, 2015. Accessed January 9, 2021. https://www.youtube.com/watch?v=IBLjyviLW28.

CHAPTER 14: ROUGHING IT IN QUEST OF THE TRASHFISH TRINITY: PART 2

2. Wade, Jeremy. *How to Think Like a Fish and Other Lessons from a Lifetime in Angling* (New York City: Da Capo Press, 2019): 15.

CHAPTER 15: CONSIDER THE LAKE CONWAY MONSTER CAT

1. Wallace, David Foster. "Consider the Lobster," *Consider the Lobster and Other Essays* (Boothbay Harbor, ME: Abacus, 2005): 254.

2. Hass, 4.

3. Spitzer, Mark. "Monster-Cat Apotheosis," *Where in the West Is Mark Spitzer,* August 13, 2018. Accessed January 10, 2021. https://unp-blog.com/2018/08/13/where-in-the-west-is-mark-spitzer-12/.

CHAPTER 16: ROUGHING IT IN QUEST OF THE TRASHFISH TRINITY: PART 3

1. Buffler, Rob, and Tom Dickson. *Fishing for Buffalo: A Guide to the Pursuit, Lore & Cuisine of Buffalo, Carp, Mooneye, Gar and other "Rough" Fish* (Minneapolis: Culepepper Press, 1990): 55.

2. Weiser, Kathy. "White River Monster of Arkansas," *Encyclopedia of Arkansas,* December 2020. Accessed January 1, 2021. https://

www.legendsofamerica.com/white-river-monster-arkansas/.

3. Incidentally, I later found out that what I thought was a nuclear plant was actually a coal-burning power plant with nuclear-looking cooling towers. Another misconception I had that day was that, what I thought was a giant egg, was actually some sort of seed pod dried out by the sun. Such are the misconceptions that occur when we're not in our logical minds because of fear and other factors affecting how we process what we see.

4. Horst, Gerald. "Yes, Buffalo Are Fish," *Louisiana Sportsman,* January 10, 2021. Accessed November 18, 2020. https://www.louisianasportsman.com/fishing/freshwater-fishing/yes-buffalo-are-fish/.

5. Lackman, A. R., Allen H. Andrews, Malcolm G. Butler, Ewelina S. Bielak-Lackmann, and Mark E. Clark. "Bigmouth Buffalo *Ictiobus Cyprinellus* Sets Freshwater Teleost Record as Improved Age Analysis Reveals Centenarian Longevity," *Communications Biology,* 197 (2019): 1.

6. Melville, Herman. *Moby-Dick or, The Whale* (New York City: Penguin, 1992): 591.

CHAPTER 17: TOWARD AN ETHICS OF ANGLING FOR THE GROTESQUE

1. Rose, J. D., Robert Arlinghaus, Steven J. Cooke, B. K. Diggles, W. Sawynok, E. D. Stevens, and Clive Wynne. "Can Fish Really Feel Pain?," *Fish and Fisheries* 15, no. 1 (December 20, 2012): 97.

2. Message, Reuben, and Beth Greenhough. "'But It's Just a Fish': Understanding the Challenges of Applying the 3Rs in Laboratory Aquariums in the UK," *Animals* (December 3, 2019): 1.

3. Arlinghaus, Robert, Ian G. Cowx, and Brian Key. "Pragmatic Animal Welfare Is Independent of Feelings," *Science* 370, issue 6513 (October 9, 2020): 180.

4. Key, Brian. "Fish Do Not Feel Pain and Its Implications for Understanding Phenomenal Consciousness," *Biology and Philosophy* 30, issue 2 (December 16, 2014): 149.

5. Rose, et al., 97.

6. Michel, Matthias. "Fish and Microchips: On Fish Pain and Multiple

Realization," *Philosophical Studies* 176, issue 9 (July 5, 2018): 2411.

7. Bateson, Patrick. "Assessment of Pain in Animals," *Animal Behaviour* 42, no. 5 (1991): 837.

8. Bovenkerk, Bernice, and Franck Meijboom. "Ethics and the Welfare of Fish," *The Welfare of Fish* (New York City: Springer Publishing, 2020): 19.

9. Sneddon, Lynne U. "Can Fish Experience Pain?," *The Welfare of Fish* (New York City: Springer Publishing, 2020): 229.

10. Sneddon, Lynne U., Robert W. Elwood, Shelley A. Adamo, and Matthew C. Leach. "Defining and Assessing Animal Pain," *Animal Behaviour* 97 (2014): 201.

11. Jabr, Ferris. "Fish Feel Pain. Now What?" *Hakai Magazine,* January 22, 2018. Accessed August 16, 2022. hakaimagazine.com/features/fish-feel-pain-now-what.

12. Scarnecchia, Dennis L., and Jason D. Schooley. "Bowfishing in the United States: History, Status, Ecological Impact, and a Need for Management," *Transactions of the Kansas Academy of Science* 123, no. 3–4 (2020): 285.

13. Sánchez-Suárez, Walter, Becca Franks, and Lauri Torgerson-White. "From Land to Water: Taking Fish Welfare Seriously," *Animals* 10, no. 9 (September 2020): 1589.

14. *Racing Extinction,* 2015. Directed by Louie Psihoyos. Produced by Fisher Stevens/Olivia Hanemann.

15. Bovenkerk and Meijboom, 21.

16. According to Jabr, there's "an estimated 10 to 100 billion farmed fish...killed globally every year, and about another one to three trillion fish are caught from the wild." Michel Pellman Rowland notes a similar figure of 2.7 trillion fish harvested per year and includes the estimate "that we could see seafood vanish altogether by 2048" in "Two-Thirds of the World's Seafood Is Over-Fished— Here's How You Can Help," *Forbes,* July 24, 2017. Accessed December 10, 2021. https://www.forbes.com/sites/michaelpellmanrowland/2017/07/24/seafood-sustainability-facts/?sh=7bd043884bbf.

17. Back in 2018, the United Nations' Intergovernmental Panel on Climate Change issued a shocking report warning that there are only twelve years left to avoid devastating, irreversible change from

global warming. This figure has remained consistent throughout the past decade. By the publication of this book, we will only have seven years to avoid the unalterable destruction estimated by 2030. See Watts, Jonathan. "We Have Twelve Years to Limit Climate Change Catastrophe, Warns UN," *The Guardian*, October 28, 2018. Accessed August 20, 2022. https://www.theguardian.com/environment/2018/oct/08/global-warming-must-not-exceed-15c-warns-landmark-un-report.

18. Neruda, Pablo. "Ode to the Sea," trans. George D. Schade. *All the Odes* (New York City: Farrar Straus Giroux, 2013): 598.

19. "*Science* Study Predicts Collapse of All Seafood Fisheries by 2050," *Stanford Report,* November 2, 2006. Accessed January 16, 2021. https://news.stanford.edu/news/2006/november8/ocean-110806.html#:~:text=Based%20on%20current%20global%20trends,of%20the%20species'%20baseline%20abundance.

20. UN Department of Economic and Social Affairs. "Growing at a Slower Pace, World Population Is Expected to Reach 9.7 Billion in 2050 and Could Peak at Nearly 11 Billion Around 2100," *United Nations News,* June 17, 2019. Accessed January 16, 2021. https://www.un.org/development/desa/en/news/population/world-population-prospects-2019.html.

# Acknowledgments

If it wasn't for my wife, poet Lea Graham, who challenged me to reflect on my actions to a depth I'd never delved before, I'd still be inflicting pain on fish on a weekly basis and burning through live bait. Lea accompanied me on fishing adventures from the Amazon to Argentina, where she got mugged with me for daring to help fish out. For that, and for her constant support, I can't thank her enough.

I'm also indebted to a crackerjack cache of editors that few writers in this world are fortunate to learn from. Their wise and discerning eyes didn't just patch up my imperfections; they helped me become a more effective editor who can now pay it back to others much more effectively. Collaborating with Kirsten Johanna Allen, Anne Terashima, Rachel "Gray" Buck-Cockayne, Michelle Wentling, Wendy Natt, Kathleen Metcalf, Scout Invie, Will Neville-Rehbehn, and the rest of the Torrey House staff was one of the luckiest breaks I've ever had, and I appreciate the press for welcoming me so magnanimously to a family whose mission is to publish books that demonstrate the transformative power of wild places, wild creatures, and diversity in all its forms.

I'd also like to thank editors Lacey Thacker, Jeffrey Williams, and Dwain Hebda for publishing early versions of these chapters in *Fish Arkansas* ("The Gar That Wouldn't Die"), *Arkansas Wildlife* ("When the Blood-Gar-Moon Aligns with Earth and Mars"), *Arkansas Wild* ("Secrets for Responsible Alligator Gar Fishing"), and the University of Arkansas Monticello's *Gravel Magazine* ("Getting Myself an Arkansas Alligator Gar"). Other editors to be acknowledged include those at Texas A&M University Press, especially Emily Seyl who supported an earlier version of the manuscript and provided a key reader report from science writer Matthew Miller (thanks, buddy!) which was instrumental in structuring and building tension. As always, I'm grateful for the sage advice of Matt Bokovoy at the University of Nebraska Press, who's been encouraging studies like this for over two decades now.

I'm grateful as well to my fabled Fishing Support Group: Dr. Robert "Turkey Buzzard" Mauldin, Scotty "Goggle Eyes" Lewis (also kick-ass research assistant), and Ben "Minnow Bucket" Damgaard for moral and immoral support. My friend, the wildlife writer Keith "Catfish" Sutton, was also a valuable asset, offering expert insights along the way, as did my pal Dr. Jeffrey Padberg (a.k.a. Armadillo Jeff), from the perspective of a neurobiologist. My friend and neighbor (Big) Larry Betz should also be acknowledged, but not for continually griping that we never catch anything. Thanks as well to my brother-in-law Kraig Rasmussen for almaco-jacking with me and taking me out for northern pike, my nephew River Rasmussen for fun company on the Salish Sea, and fish-print artist Bruce Koike for so gorgeously rendering a sacrificial bowfin and gar.

Fishing guides Kevin Moore, Alejandro Pozzi, Captain Salas, and the Buffalo Whisperer Keith Thompson were masterful in connecting me with monster fish, and I sing their praise. I also appreciate Kristina Thompson, who added to the whole buffalofish bonanza, and Captain Mike Ainsworth for a better understanding of the ever-changing Puget Sound ecosystem. Benjamin Heussner of the Wisconsin Department of Natural Resources, Dr. Dayv Lowry of the Washington Department of Fish and Wildlife, and Lindsey Lewis of the US Fish and Wildlife Service provided information specific to their fisheries, and I thank them for contributing, knowingly or not. Likewise, Dr. Reid Adams, Dr. Henry Bart, Dr. Solomon David, and Dr.

Dennis L. Scarnecchia provided specialized knowledge, and I thank them along with Karen Donahue Robinson and Danny Robinson for making my ratfish dreams come true. A special shout-out goes out as well to my former students Annie Grimes and Tory Potter for their savvy poems included herein, along with the rest of that Creature Poetics class at the University of Central Arkansas during the hellacious fall of 2020, for sticking it out and making me proud. Additional thanks to UCA for a year-long sabbatical to finish research on this project, and Interlibrary Loans at Torreyson Library for expediting articles on fish pain and suffering.

Finally, in thanking all those listed above for what they've helped me realize, and for what they've given to fish, which continually give to us, I'd like to acknowledge my inspiring niece Charlotte Graham (2008–2019), whose passing was a shocking loss for all her communities. I'd also like to remember my stepfather, potter Warren MacKenzie (1924–2018), whose enthusiasm for such ichthyo-investigations always validated years spent in the sweat of revision. In like spirit, this book is dedicated to their unparalleled, optimistic characters.

# About the Author

MARK SPITZER was the author of thirty-plus books, including *In Search of Monster Fish*, *Beautifully Grotesque Fish of the American West*, *Season of the Gar*, and *Return of the Gar*. He appeared on the Animal Planet series *River Monsters* and consulted for *National Geographic*'s *Monster Fish* show. Spitzer was professor of creative writing at both Truman State University and the University of Central Arkansas, with a specialization in poetry and creative nonfiction. He was also editor-in-chief of the avant-garde poetry series Toad Suck Éditions. With his spouse, Lea Graham, he lived part time in New York's Mid-Hudson Valley where he hiked the mountain trails hunting salamanders and wild mushrooms with his dog.

For more info visit www.sptzr.net.

# TORREY HOUSE PRESS

Torrey House Press publishes books at the intersection of the literary arts and environmental advocacy. THP authors explore the diversity of human experiences and relationships with place. THP books create conversations about issues that concern the American West, landscape, literature, and the future of our ever-changing planet, inspiring action toward a more just world.

We believe that lively, contemporary literature is at the cutting edge of social change. We seek to inform, expand, and reshape the dialogue on environmental justice and stewardship for the natural world by elevating literary excellence from diverse voices.

Visit www.torreyhouse.org for reading group discussion guides, author interviews, and more.

As a 501(c)(3) nonprofit publisher, our work is made possible by generous donations from readers like you.

Torrey House Press is supported by Back of Beyond Books, the King's English Bookshop, Maria's Bookshop, the Jeffrey S. & Helen H. Cardon Foundation, the Sam & Diane Stewart Family Foundation, the Literary Arts Emergency Fund, the Mellon Foundation, the Barker Foundation, Diana Allison, Karin Anderson, Klaus Bielefeldt, Joe Breddan, Casady Henry, Laurie Hilyer, Susan Markley, Kitty Swenson, Shelby Tisdale, Kirtly Parker Jones, Katie Pearce, Molly Swonger, Robert Aagard & Camille Bailey Aagard, Kif Augustine Adams & Stirling Adams, Rose Chilcoat & Mark Franklin, Jerome Cooney & Laura Storjohann, Linc Cornell & Lois Cornell, Susan Cushman & Charlie Quimby, Kathleen Metcalf & Peter Metcalf, Betsy Gaines Quammen & David Quammen, the Utah Division of Arts & Museums, Utah Humanities, the National Endowment for the Humanities, the National Endowment for the Arts, the Salt Lake City Arts Council, the Utah Governor's Office of Economic Development, and Salt Lake County Zoo, Arts & Parks. Our thanks to individual donors, members, and the Torrey House Press board of directors for their valued support.

Join the Torrey House Press family and give today at www.torreyhouse.org/give.